Ten Ideologies

Jaipal Reddy's book draws on a lifetime of intellectual engagement in presenting a closely argued analysis of the most influential ideologies of our time. The reading is wide; the canvas, capacious. He links Indian with global developments and the past with the present, drawing our attention to continuities as well as discontinuities. The writing is always clear; the analysis of thinkers, commendably fair-minded. Even those who do not agree with some of its arguments or conclusions will be educated and stimulated by this fine book.

Ramachandra Guha
Eminent historian

For a person who has spent his life in politics, Jaipal Reddy is most unusual, as a man of letters interested in philosophy, history, politics, and economics. This book, on the transition from agrarian to industrial societies, providing glimpses of world history, reveals his talents. Beginning with the Renaissance, the Enlightenment and the Industrial Revolution in Europe, which are seen as turning points, he traces the evolution of ideologies ranging from capitalism and socialism, through nationalism and democracy, to feminism and environmentalism. In doing so, he recognises the limitations of ideologies implicit in their conceptual rigidities, or blind faiths, but emphasises their relevance and necessity as a point of reference in contemporary politics, which is accentuating economic and social divides among people. It is an engaging read that should interest social scientists, public intellectuals, concerned citizens, and aspiring politicians.

Deepak Nayyar
Emeritus Professor of Economics, Jawaharlal Nehru University, New Delhi
Honorary Fellow, Balliol College, Oxford, and former Vice Chancellor, University of Delhi

TEN IDEOLOGIES

The Great Asymmetry between Agrarianism and Industrialism

S. JAIPAL REDDY

Orient BlackSwan

TEN IDEOLOGIES: THE GREAT ASYMMETRY BETWEEN AGRARIANISM AND INDUSTRIALISM

ORIENT BLACKSWAN PRIVATE LIMITED

Registered Office
3-6-752 Himayatnagar, Hyderabad 500 029, Telangana, India
e-mail: centraloffice@orientblackswan.com

Other Offices
Bengaluru, Chennai, Guwahati,
Hyderabad, Kolkata, Mumbai,
New Delhi, Noida, Patna, Visakhapatnam

First published by Orient BlackSwan 2018
Paperback reprint 2019, 2021

ISBN 978-93-5287-551-1

Typeset in
Charis SIL 10.5/12.6
by Le Studio Graphique, Gurgaon 122 001

Printed in India at
Graphica Printers & Binders, Hyderabad 500 013

Published by
Orient Blackswan Private Limited
3-6-752, Himayatnagar, Hyderabad 500 029, Telangana, India
e-mail: info@orientblackswan.com

To

My wife Lakshmi, who has contributed to
my career through her drudgery
for over half a century,
without laying claim to my time or fame

Contents

Foreword

'Ism' is a subtle suffix. So discreet, so vestigial is it as a word-ending that one can miss it altogether; as in alcoholism or altruism, in nudism or nihilism. So totally an appendage of the word to which it is joined, 'ism' curls into itself like the human tail-bone. It is there but we do not see it.

And yet, for all its self-effacing nature, 'ism' is also the strongest of suffixes, as in Buddhism or Jainism, Marxism, Maoism. It turns strong and vital when it stands for an idea or an ideology like communism, socialism or atheism. It becomes a major identity-marker, as in Judaism and Hinduism. The 'ism-ism' in 'ism' then becomes to that thought and belief-system something of a fortress, a stone-girt enclosure at once awesome and, to the uninitiated, somewhat forbidding, until it lets the door open to welcome her/him and withal to become a dwelling place.

Derived from the Latin *ismus* and the Greek *ismos*, the suffix 'ism' is also believed to have journeyed in and through the Tamil *iyam*, as in 'desiyam' (nationalism) or in Gandhiyam, which needs no translation. 'Ism' therefore is, like 'ity' (used in adjectives such as Christianity), a denoter of affiliations, affinities, adherences. It also is, like 'pathy', used to end compound words like empathy, sympathy, telepathy, about feelings, beliefs, and emotions, conditions that have proceeded from an individual experience or an episode or occurrence to become more widely held, professed, human conditions. These have often led in their dramatic forms to what history has described as revolutions, and in less tumultuous but often more abiding modes, as movements.

Scholar-politician S. Jaipal Reddy has excavated these multiple isms born of human experience, philosophic, political, cultural, and aesthetic, and assembled a connected history of human ideas and actions. To describe his work as the product of research would be to put that word—research—to strenuous test. To call his work the gift of insight would be to subject that faculty—insight—to hard labour. It is nothing more and nothing less than the astonishing fruit of what is best described by the Sanskrit word *sadhana*, suggesting the accomplishment of a goal by diligent, even worshipful application.

Reminiscent for its audacious range of Sarvepalli Radhakrishnan's *An Idealist View Of Life* (1932), for its political veracity of Pattabhi Sitaramayya's *History of the Indian National Congress* (1935), for its magisterial overview of Ramdhari Sinha Dinkar's *Sanskrit Ke Char Adhyay* (1956), this work belongs to the genre of the history of ideas. The historian Arthur O. Lovejoy is said to have inaugurated this genre in the 1920s, even as the English Jesuit priest Frederick C. Copleston carried it forward with his *History of Western Philosophy* (1946). In his approach to the study of political philosophy, the author follows the deep investigation tracks laid by the socialist philosopher-statesman Acharya Narendra Deva in his *Rashtriyata Aur Samajvad* (1949) and *Bauddha Dharma Darshan* (1956). This work is, in its essential make-up, a history of the promise and the betrayal of isms and of the ism-isms of isms—taking us from Socrates's down to our cyber times.

There is also in the scheme of his work something of the foldable yet seamless shape of a Chinese screen, recalling the style, including a seam of ironic humour, adopted by Lin Yutang in several of his works. 'Four Great Movements' and 'Ten Ideologies', as he calls the two parts of his book, give us what could be called a silk route to the essentials of the isms that have grown from and sometimes collapsed within these movements and ideologies.

Does the author come to a conclusion?

There is too much of an Indian mystic in him to offer something as insipid as 'a final view' of life's or of humanity's conundrums. But in this book of rare fascination, he enables us to see both the utility and the futility of engaging with humankind's search for a meaning in life's struggles with its mysteries. 'Hast any philosophy in thee, Shepherd?' asks Shakespeare in *As You Like It.* To the universal and ageless Shepherd in all of us, S. Jaipal Reddy presents thoughts, not so much as startling new ideas or as triumphalist recipes, but as intensely engaging questionings and, equally, extensive speculations.

Readers of this book will find in its author a navigator of thought, whose periscope refuses to sink in depression at the fathomlessness of the sea of human suffering. For the reason he sees in the infinity of the night sky stars sparkling, optimistically, on life's great renewals on earth.

Gopalkrishna Gandhi
Chennai, 25 May 2018

Preface

As I began to write the Preface after completing this book, I recalled that I had delivered the XVIIth Convocation Address in 2005 at Kakatiya University, Warangal (now in the state of Telangana). I felt that the topic of the Address, 'The Intellectual Confusions of Our Time', may have some commonalities with the issues discussed in the book. After reading the Address again, I was struck by the similarity between the basic framework of ideas expressed in both the Address and the book. I am therefore reproducing here essential extracts from the Address as part of the Preface.

> Since my twenties, I have been delivering extempore lectures to my contemporaries in colleges, peers in politics, and mavens in the media and academia with unabashed intellectual superciliousness. My good luck has allowed me to get away with my braggadocio for more than four decades. However, the fact of the matter is that I have not been either a polymathic savant or a super-specialist. I have only been a practising politician with enough hunger for such general knowledge as to stand me in good stead either as a parliamentarian or as a political commentator. But Kakatiya University has taken my reputation at its face value and chosen to assign this onerous task to me. On this occasion, I am required to desist from my own wonted impromptu articulation and stick to a written address. It is a tall order, as I am more comfortable with speaking rather than with reading. However, I have no doubt that writing is the best form of exposition. Francis Bacon rightly observed that: 'Reading maketh a full man; conference a ready man and writing an exact man'.
>
> It shall be my endeavour to share with you some of my tentative insights into the 'intellectual confusions of our time' in

the course of this presentation. Both as an activist and an analyst, I have been extraordinarily struck not only by the titanic political collisions, but also by the traumatic philosophical confusions of the time we are passing through. It might be argued that this has been true of every important epoch in history. It is the extreme degree of this feature that clearly distinguishes our era from any other. As G. W. Hegel pointed out, the difference of degree beyond a point would make for a difference in quality as well. Our times are therefore both quantitatively and qualitatively different.

We are living in an age of unprecedented prosperity. What is more, we are torn by apocalyptic conflicts. On top of everything else, we are confronted with bewildering intellectual confusions spawned by extreme divergences in ideologies. There is, therefore, an imperative necessity to rise above the immediate clash of ideological concepts and develop a larger historical perspective in order to make sense of the current chaos and see the way forward.

It is generally admitted that we are living in a modern age. There is, however, no consensus on what elements constitute the modern age, and what factors had led to its birth. The modern age is a product of the vast developments that the two great Revolutions sparked off. The French Revolution, which occurred in the late eighteenth century, destabilised the age-old institutions and ideas and paved the way for new political and social experiments and radical modes of thinking. At about the same time, the Industrial Revolution unleashed new forms of energy, such as the steam-engine, and new technologies such as the telegraph. These two great Revolutions reinforced each other and produced a paradigm shift, both in thought processes and production techniques. Although the radical changes wrought by the two Revolutions were there for the naked eye to see, it is interesting to note that in the nineteenth century, the rulers and diplomats went about their usual way, as though nothing had happened. It is said of the Bourbons, the dynasty at the time of the French Revolution, that 'they learn nothing and forget nothing'. This was not only true of the French rulers indulging in pomp and pageantry, but could also be said to be true of all the advisors to rulers. This only goes to prove that the implications of great changes can be discerned only by perceptive minds, and not by pro-establishment thinkers.

As we are dealing with the two great Revolutions, it might be asked whether they were merely coincidental or the culmination of historical developments. I am among those who believe that the ground for the two Revolutions was prepared through a number of important developments in such varied fields as religion, philosophy, literature, arts, and science. To understand the point, the colossal impact produced by the Reformation and Renaissance, the scientific discoveries of Copernicus, Galileo and Newton, and the new theories produced by John Locke and Hegel, Voltaire and Rousseau need to be recalled. I have briefly referred to the intellectual foundations laid over three centuries for the two great Revolutions. Even a rapid survey of these foundations will provide a vast topic in itself. For reasons of space and time, I am not embarking on that exploration here. I will, therefore, now revert to the consequences of the two Revolutions. Of the two, the impact of the Industrial Revolution is better recognised than that of the French Revolution. Even with respect to the Industrial Revolution, its earth-shattering effects are grossly underestimated. It was a huge deluge that transformed every aspect of human society that had existed thus far.

While there is a recognition of technological effects on our lifestyle, there is no corresponding appreciation of the changes that have taken place in patterns of thought. The modernity of current schools of thought is so obscured as to be considered synonymous with the seamless extension of ancient ideas. The modern age has witnessed not only a vast increase in our economic standards and the destructive potential of weaponry, but also the immense generation of new popular ideologies. Let me allude to ten such schools of thought, that are fundamentally modern and have little or no resemblance to their alleged ancient approximations. They are: (*i*) Nationalism; (*ii*) Democracy; (*iii*) Capitalism; (*iv*) Communism; (*v*) Socialism; (*vi*) Secularism; (*vii*) Humanism; (*viii*) Anarchism; (*ix*) Feminism; and (*x*) Welfare State.

The aforesaid list is comprehensive, although not exhaustive. Contrary to popular perception, nationalism is a notion of recent origin. Before the advent of the nation-state, the primary allegiance of most people was to their immediate locality or religious group or dynastic ruler. In Europe, nationalist sentiments came to be based on language in the context of bloody and protracted confrontation between Protestantism and Roman Catholicism. It also received a fillip through resistance to alien dominations;

for example, it grew with resistance to Napoleon in Germany and with resistance to Austria in Italy. Mao, even while leading the communist revolution, embodied the nationalist sentiment of the Chinese against Japanese imperialism. Mahatma Gandhi not only led the biggest mass movement for national freedom in history, but also inspired anti-colonial struggles all over the world. As Netaji Subhas Chandra Bose knew that nationalism was a new creed, he described Mahatma Gandhi as the Father of the Nation, even while differing from him regarding the techniques of struggle. Nationalism, as a liberating force, is a welcome modern idea. But in order to retain its positive character, nationalism needs to be constantly salvaged from incestuous linkages to language, race, or religion.

Although Westerners would like to believe that democracy had flourished in ancient Greece and Rome, it needs to be emphatically noted that slaves were excluded and the citizenry mostly belonged to small cities. Socrates and Plato, who are among the greatest philosophers of all times, were implacably opposed to democracy, as they thought it had led to the defeat of their beloved city-state, Athens, in the war against Sparta. We also want to believe that democratic regimes prevailed in parts of ancient India, although they were confined only to village panchayats and *janapads*. The House of Commons in Britain is regarded as the mother of all Parliaments. Democracy, even in Britain, does not have a long tradition, as only men with property and rank had suffrage in the nineteenth century. Even when large-scale democratic reforms were introduced in Britain in the last quarter of the nineteenth century, the principle conceded was only that of universal adult male franchise. Women in Britain had to wait for the right to vote until the 1920s. The record of other countries in Western Europe is even worse. It is abundantly clear that the Industrial Revolution and the consequent economic growth facilitated the spread of democracy. In India, the founding fathers had the vision and the courage to let democracy precede development, and indeed, to accelerate development. It is a unique experiment with more than a modest measure of success. As the exciting story of Indian democracy deserves a detailed exposition, I do not intend to deal with it any further.

Capitalism is often confused with mercantilism. In fact, capitalism succeeded mercantilism. The capitalist system could not have sustained itself without the factory system, which itself was a by-product of industrial development. Capitalism could not have survived as a system until our times even with all its modifications, had the snowballing technology not constantly increased surplus to such a degree as to let the fruits of progress be widely diffused. That is the reason why such a vast social security net can be seen in the developed world. Capitalism has managed to survive more through the bountiful blessings of technology rather than through the dynamics of the market. Even Karl Marx looked upon capitalism as a necessary prelude to socialism. Communism was propounded by Marx, in collaboration with Engels, to put an end to the increasing misery of labour and growing monopolies, which were compounded by capitalist exploitation. It advocates the organisation of such a system of communal ownership of the means of production as to secure contributions from each person according to her/his capacity, and to provide to each person according to her/his necessity. Marx was acutely alive to the absolute novelty of his idea. He never confused his post-industrial communism with tribal communitarianism. He, in fact, thought that all socialist thought before his 'Communist Manifesto', which he wrote in 1848, was merely utopian, and that the era of scientific socialism began only in 1848.

Anarchism, like communism, is entirely a product of nineteenth-century philosophy. It holds all forms of government authority to be unnecessary and undesirable, and envisages a society based on voluntary cooperation. P. J. Proudhon, Mikhail Bakunin, and others propounded the anarchist philosophy in their own respective ways, but all of them had raging doctrinal disputes with Marx. Even Marx was not immune to it, as is evident from his prediction that the State would eventually wither away. In our own country, Vinoba Bhave preached a certain variety of philosophical anarchism.

Socialism, be it utopian or Fabian, is a post-capitalist concept. It is aimed at achieving distributive equity in society. It is contradistinct from communism, insofar as it is implacably opposed to proletarian dictatorship, and strongly attached to democracy both as a means and as an end. However, socialism does recognise class as a vital category. In the context of our society, caste is largely synonymous with class.

Secularism as a concept was developed in the historical context of huge confrontation against the medieval papacy. This led to the separation of the state from the church in Europe. This principle has been adopted in all parts of the world, as every religion has a tendency to promote totalitarian belief systems. As the institutions of popular democracy have strengthened, secularism has received an enormous impetus. As a consequence, democracy and secularism have become Siamese twins.

Humanism is animated by an individualistic and critical spirit. It lays emphasis on a human-centred rather than a God-centred universe. It would be absolutely incorrect to equate modern humanism with charity or love in various religious traditions.

Feminism received a great fillip in the twentieth century. Women, after receiving their voting rights and enhancing their educational and economic status, began to assert the right to absolute equality with men. It continues to have great resonance and relevance because even in the twenty-first century, most women are discriminated against. The programme of reservation of one-third of seats in the legislatures of India remains a far cry. Even on the philosophical plane, many intellectuals continue to harbour reservations about the equality of women. The academic controversy, started by none other than the President of Harvard University, Lawrence Summers in 2005, about women being genetically inferior in mathematics and sciences, is a resounding demonstration of the continuing prejudice against women. Such formulations do not take into account the dynamics of the sociology of knowledge. It is difficult to convince even academics that opportunity is a pre-requisite for the growth of talent.

The Welfare State is again a complete product of the twentieth century. For the first time in history, such economic conditions have been created through technology as to let the state provide welfare to all citizens. When John Kenneth Galbraith wrote his groundbreaking work, *The Affluent Society*, in the 1950s, it was a revelation. Amartya Sen developed welfare economics in such a way as to envisage a system of universal entitlements. This is a concept that is still evolving. What is more, it has largely been confined to developed countries. In India, a bold attempt is being made to accelerate economic growth, even while strengthening the system of entitlements. It is to be clarified that all ancient and medieval religious traditions had their systems of welfare, but they were primarily ethical postulates, as at that time there was neither industrial prosperity nor popular democracy to back them up.

While as many as ten popular ideologies have received a brief treatment, no reference has been made at all to such other powerful forces of modern times as imperialism and fascism.

> I am aware of the fact that they have been as powerful as any other. After all, imperialism was the plank behind World War I, while fascism was the cause of World War II. I have not dealt with them as they are pre-modern schools of thought. In fact, they have been receiving impetus from reactions against modern egalitarian forces. The popular ideologies I have dealt with are primarily modern and largely positive. The areas of convergence among these ideologies are much larger than those of divergence.
>
> The paladins of modern ideologies refuse to recognise the many commonalities that bind them together. As a result, they unwittingly end up strengthening feudalism and communalism, which are only indigenous cousins of imperialism and fascism.
>
> Apart from passionate protagonists, who are bothered more about their doctrinal niceties than about the larger picture, the liberal intelligentsia gets confused as the fundamental distinction between the modern and pre-modern philosophies is not clearly made. In the pre-modern phase, the belief systems and production techniques were similar, if not identical, both in the East and in the West. The pre-modern West was as steeped in poverty, superstition and tyranny as the East. The term 'Oriental despotism' is a false Western construct. Who was more despotic in history than Nero, who played the fiddle while Rome was burning, or Louis XIV, who famously said, 'I am the State'?
>
> Our intellectual confusions are primarily the result of our inability to distinguish between the modern and the pre-modern, and propensity to confuse the modern West with the historical West. If these two fundamental intellectual distinctions are driven home, many of our current confusions will be eased. We will then not only be able to partake of all the fruits of the Industrial Revolution, but also enjoy the three great ideals of the French Revolution—liberty, equality, and fraternity. These ideals are more realistic today than they were in the eighteenth century. Let us proceed to fulfil these dreams. This appeal of mine is especially directed towards the young graduates and post-graduates who will receive their degrees today, as they will be more open to new ideas than people of older generations.

It is evident that the paradigm I am presenting in this book is the same as is discernible from the text of the Convocation Address. In fact, I can say that this paradigm, which I developed through wide readings since my younger days, has remained stable. My ideology was reflected in my speeches in the erstwhile Andhra Pradesh Assembly in the 1970s and early 1980s, and in my speeches in Parliament from 1984 to 2014. I may illustrate my point by adverting to a speech I made in 2002 on the Ayodhya imbroglio, appealing to Prime Minister Vajpayee for the removal of L. K. Advani and Murali Manohar Joshi as charge-sheeted ministers of his government. While addressing myself to L. K. Advani in the course of the speech, I said the following, among other things: 'I have long admired Advani for his ability to articulate medieval ideology in a modern idiom. I have also admired him for his gift of presenting his mildewed worldview in a mellowed fashion.' At the risk of complimenting myself, I must say that everybody, including those in the Bharatiya Janata Party (BJP) benches, enjoyed the irony in my praise of Advani. Similarly, in the course of the same speech, I said the following while addressing myself to Murali Manohar Joshi: 'I admire you as a *sui generis* scholar-scientist. But my philosophical problem with you is that you confuse history with mythology, philosophy with theology and astronomy with astrology.' All sides of the House enjoyed the sarcasm in my comment. But while the comments I made on Advani and Joshi were widely (I may say even wildly) enjoyed as being extraordinarily witty, their philosophical significance was lost on most Hon'ble members of almost all parties, as they unconsciously suffer from the same intellectual confusions as Advani and Joshi.

There are many instances in various speeches I made in the Andhra Pradesh Assembly and in Parliament over a period of forty-five years, which testify to my appreciation of the need to distinguish between the worldviews of medieval and modern ages. I am aware that I can be charged with consistency, which has been described by Samuel Johnson as 'the virtue of an ass'. I have never minded this comment, as I think that asses have been more useful than most other animals. As a modern progressive, I place all animals on the same pedestal.

I have been deeply disturbed in recent decades by the fact that ideological debates or intellectual discussions are no longer in fashion. In fact, they are being eclipsed by the obsession with technocratic prescriptions and mathematical formulae. This trend can be strikingly seen in the financial innovations now dominating economic policy. While the new approach of employing mathematical innovations has its merits, it cannot address societal considerations or ethical concerns. I have therefore undertaken this plain presentation of ideologies to contribute my mite to the process of rekindling intellectual interest in political processes. I have confined myself to the discussion of ideologies as I have not found any single compact book dealing with ideologies as such, except as part of larger surveys of political theories.

It is necessary to clarify that social ideologies are inextricably intertwined with arcane areas of philosophy such as metaphysics and epistemology. I have consciously avoided, or at least minimised, these aspects to lessen my task, and simplify all the related issues for my readers. To support my propositions, I have cited eminent authorities (not too frequently, I hope). The purpose here is not to sound pedantic, but bolster my arguments and imbue them with authenticity. Such references that are not obvious at first sight can be easily elucidated through the use of the Internet. No writer, of even the textbook variety, can rise above ideological biases. In my case, I have been a practising politician for half a century, and an ideological partisan at that. I think a disclosure of ideological biases on the part of writers or politicians is more important than the disclosure of assets and liabilities. I must therefore admit to my ideological inclinations towards progressive liberalism or social democracy. Despite this, I have striven to be detached.

Apart from increasing indifference to the philosophy of politics, I have also been worried about the incapacity of the contemporary mindset, still trapped in our agrarian roots and atavistic impulses, to change and evolve the psychological reflexes, cultural patterns and philosophical perspectives that are vital to the understanding of the stresses and strains of industrial society. This problem is afflicting people of both the developing and the developed worlds. I have therefore touched upon this critical asymmetry, which is at the core of all current crises raging in the world, towards the end of the book.

Apart from ten ideologies, I have dealt with four great movements—the Renaissance, the Humanism, the Reformation, and the Scientific Revolution—although not in a detailed way. I am aware that huge academic literature is available on each of the ideologies and each of the movements. Such tomes are meant for scholars. This is not an attempt to duplicate them, and can at best be regarded as their summation. None of the facts or formulations mentioned in the book is new. I have made a sedulous effort to pre-empt, or at least to play down, doctrinal disputations. And yet, some may have crept in, as the issues are interconnected and continue to be inflammable. Within these limitations, I have striven for optimal objectivity.

As my narrative in the book is not India-centric, I owe an explanation. As the subjects are almost entirely global in their origins and implications, their treatment is necessarily country-neutral. It is true that references to the West are disproportionately high. The most compelling reason for this lopsidedness is the historical fact that the Industrial Revolution occurred in the West, although our nation and other ancient nations of the East provided the foundations for this revolution through their agrarian civilisations, mathematics, sciences, and technologies such as the printing press, paper, gunpowder, etc. A global perspective is a *sine qua non* (absolutely essential) for everybody in the world today. We in India need to learn to look at ourselves not only through our national prism, but also as inhabitants of the planet.

I will feel rewarded if this endeavour can lead to the popularisation of the ideological aspects of politics, through which the main aim of maximising welfare and minimising warfare ought to be achieved. As it is not meant for scholars or specialists, I will feel doubly rewarded if political initiates and inquisitive readers are motivated to consult original sources, for everyone needs to discover her/his own philosophy.

S. Jaipal Reddy
June 2018

Introduction

The Industrial Revolution was the biggest break in world history. The transformative momentum of the rapid technological advances and intense socio-economic, cultural, and ideological churning of the eighteenth and nineteenth centuries, which reframed human development, continues to define our world. An explanation of the Industrial Revolution and its impact, therefore, is imperative to our understanding of the present, which should ideally begin with the universally accepted view that we are living in an industrial age.

This rare convergence of perception has come about because of the collective and unalterable impact of the Industrial Revolution. Despite this consensus, however, the size of the change effected by the Revolution has not been consciously comprehended. It was, in effect, a huge deluge that submerged almost every aspect of human society that had existed before its onset.

The Industrial Revolution began with the invention of the humble spinning jenny by James Hargreaves and the more vital invention of the steam-engine by James Watt, almost in the last quarter of the eighteenth century. From that point on, technology advanced relentlessly.

The new science of thermodynamics taught engineers how to build more efficient engines, as a consequence of which the steam-engine began to replace all other forms of power in the field of transport. By the middle of the nineteenth century, a vast network of railways was growing in Europe and North America, and sailing ships began to be replaced by steamers. More snowballing technical changes kept occurring, such as the invention of the telegraph, aircraft, automobile, etc. All such industrial inventions were rightly described as the Second Wave by Alvin Toffler, who applied the same metaphor to the start of the Agrarian Society by calling it 'the First Wave'. They have presently culminated in the invention of the atom bomb and the Internet. The humble mobile phone has now become the most visible symbol of the ongoing Industrial Revolution.

The first great impact of the Industrial Revolution was felt in terms of exponential growth rates. J. K. Galbraith described this new wealth in America as having created *The Affluent Society* (1958). As this effect was first felt in the West, the balance came to be tilted completely against the East. Robert C. Allen, writing in his article in *Cambridge History of Capitalism* (2014), says that before the Industrial Revolution, most of the world's manufacturing production took place in China and India, viz., in AD 1500. He goes on to say that on the eve of the Industrial Revolution, China and India produced 33 per cent and 25 per cent of the world's manufactures, respectively, but their share plummeted so fast after the Industrial Revolution that it came down to just 2 per cent each in the 1950s. Western Europe, through industrialisation, increased its share of manufacturing enormously. North America, particularly the United States, was another success. Allen illustrates his point by stating that North America expanded its industrial output so much after 1800 that, by the 1950s, it was producing almost half of the world's manufactures.

Behind these numerical comparisons lies the fundamental fact that societies all over the world were economically backward in pre-industrial times, and the masses had languished in misery and slavery for thousands of years because of low technology and consequent lack of productivity. A few formidable fortifications (for example, the Great Wall of China) and imposing funeral monuments (for example, the pyramids), and some magnificent mansions and memorials do not imply that the past of any country was golden in any economic or material sense. The techniques of production and construction had remained virtually stagnant from the time of the building of pyramids to that of the Taj Mahal.

The wealth (Gross Development Product [GDP], to put it in the current terminology) had therefore remained severely restricted during three to four millennia, although it may have fluctuated slightly from period to period and from country to country, depending upon seasons, minor technical changes, and quality of regimes.

This ubiquitous poverty of the people had coexisted with extreme concentration of wealth in the hands of the ruling elites (royals, nobles, priestly potentates, military leaders, merchants, moneylenders, etc.), who wallowed in isolated pockets of luxury. These pockets have been historically misrepresented as evidence of ancient affluence. The exclusive attention showered on the lavish lifestyles of the elites, their military adventures, and their amorous affairs, portrayed in literature and art, has dominated the imagination not only of the masses, but also of intellectuals and historians to such a degree as to neglect vital issues like the total wealth of the people, or the conditions of the poor and the level of technology of the community. This emphasis is being laid on the predominance of the ruling classes not to highlight the inordinate inequalities in old societies, but to narrate the causes of the nostalgic attachment of people to their past. With their antecedents thus embellished, every people in the world have mythical notions of their bygone glory, which currently feed romantic revivalisms based on nation, race, religion, etc. As a result, we are witnessing conflicting visions of a non-existent past glory, leading to the current clashes in the world.

The Industrial Revolution, which transmuted society from agrarian to industrial, was not an accident of history. Nor was the end of a 10,000-year agrarian era and the beginning of the industrial age a seamless transition. It was, as the term implies, revolutionary, both in terms of causes and consequences. A series of severe creative jolts in the religious, social, philosophical, and scientific spheres prepared the ground for this total transformation.

Although the Industrial Revolution occurred in the West, it is the culmination of a process of global exchange of ideas and techniques. In those days, the process had necessarily to be slow and took centuries to happen. The inventions of paper and gunpowder, for example, played their part in enabling the West to steal a march over the East. But paper was invented in ancient China when the mortar and pestle method was primarily used. The Muslim world improved upon paper-making with the use of human-animal powered paper mills and trip hammers. In medieval Europe, paper-making was mechanised by the use of water-paper. Gunpowder was invented in the ninth century in China, and the technology thereafter spread from China through the Muslim world to Europe. The origins of the mariner's compass are not being emphasised here, as they date back to antiquity in both the East and the West. On top of everything else, printing technology spread from China, albeit in a relatively primitive form, to the West.

Amartya Sen says, in *Identity and Violence* (2006: 56–57), that:

> Indian Buddhists, who tried to develop printing, in the seventh century, were less successful in this, but they did contribute the material that constituted the first dated printed book in the world, a Buddhist Sanskrit classic (Vajra cchedika prajna paramita) popularly known as the Diamond Sutra, which was translated by a half-Indian, half-Turkish scholar from Sanskrit into Chinese in A.D. 402. When the book was printed in Chinese in A.D. 868, it carried a motivational preface to the effect that it was being printed 'for universal free distribution'.

The credit for the invention of the modern printing press, however, goes to Gutenberg, who was the first to have introduced a method of printing through a movable type in Germany in the fifteenth century. This method constituted such a vital technical improvement that it facilitated a quantum jump in the printing process in Europe. An interesting sidelight here is that this invention came to be recorded through a litigation between the inventor Gutenberg and his financier Johann Fust, and this may well be one of the first venture capitals in history. Gutenberg, it must be noted, is universally regarded now as the most influential inventor of the second millennium (from AD 1000 onwards), as he helped to spread the Renaissance and Humanism imperceptibly and ineradicably, and also enabled the Protestant Reformation to spread like wildfire.

The ground for the conversion of society from Agrarian to Industrial was seeded by four great movements. The first was the Renaissance; the second was Humanism; the third was the Reformation (Protestant); and the fourth was the Scientific Revolution, which commenced with Copernicus and culminated with Newton. Before we look at each of these movements at some length, we must examine some aspects of their immediate historical background.

During the domination of Spain by the Arabs (AD 9–12 century), Arabic philosophical literature was translated into Hebrew and Latin. It contained not only an admixture of Aristotelianism and Neo-Platonism, but also the ideas of influential thinkers such as the Persians, Al-Kindi, Al-Farabi, and Avicenna, as well as the Spaniard Averroes. These translations as well as interpretations of Aristotle influenced medieval Scholasticism and modern philosophy in Europe. In fact, they were taken up by both Jewish and Christian thinkers. At that time, Muslims, Christians, and Jews participated in the Arabic tradition and separated themselves according to philosophic rather than religious doctrines.

Until the fifteenth century, Europe did not seem to be at its height to its own modern historians. H. G. Wells observed in his *The Outline of History* (1921: 140):

> A man of foresight surveying the world in the early sixteenth century might well have concluded that it was only a matter of a few generations before the whole world became Mongolian—and probably Moslem. Just as today most people seem to take it for granted that European rule and ... liberal Christianity are destined to spread over the whole world. Few people seem to realise how recent ... is this European ascendancy. It was only as the fifteenth century drew to its close that any indications of the real vitality of Western Europe became clearly apparent.

H. G. Wells was, of course, a Western progressive intellectual of the early twentieth century. Niall Ferguson, who is considered a neo-Conservative of the twenty-first century, also arrives at the same conclusion in his book, *Civilisation* (2011). He refers to the glory and expanding power of the Ottoman Empire in the sixteenth century under Suleiman, the Magnificent (1520–66), the Safavid Empire under Abbas (1587–1629), and to the mighty Moghul emperor Akbar (1556–1605). In the process, Ferguson does not fail to mention the strength of Ming China. European travellers in the sixteenth century, in addition to being overwhelmed by the might of Eastern empires, were also drawn to the superior quality of Indian textiles and Chinese porcelain. He therefore asserts that it was hardly possible for Europeans in the sixteenth century to imagine that Europe would begin to rise so soon from the mid-seventeenth century.

Another Western author, Jerry Brotton, expressed a similar view in the Preface to his book *The Renaissance Bazaar* (2002), where he argues that

> [M]odern Europe emerged in this period by competing and exchanging ideas and commodities with its eastern (and predominantly Islamic) neighbours. The east-west transactions laid the basis for the great art and culture that we now associate with the Renaissance. They also reveal that Europe emerged in close relation rather than stark opposition to the cultures and communities it has often come to demonise and label as underdeveloped and uncivilised.

It may be recalled that Greek civilisation, which burst upon the history of the world with new energy in the fifth and sixth centuries BC, had itself been deeply influenced by Egyptian and Babylonian civilisations. Bertrand Russell, in his book *Wisdom of the West*, points out thus:

> Among the civilizations of the world, the Greek is a late comer. Those of Egypt and Mesopotamia are older by several millennia. These agricultural societies grew up along the great rivers and were ruled by divine kings, a military aristocracy and a powerful class of priests who presided over the elaborate polytheistic religious systems. The bulk of the population were serfs who worked the land. Both Egypt and Babylonia furnished some knowledge which the Greeks later took over. (1959: 11)

It can thus be seen that the processes of history cannot be explained in terms of race, religion, or civilisation, or even hemisphere, but only in terms of currents and cross-currents across the planet. Western intellectuals would therefore be erroneous in thinking that the Industrial Revolution could be made possible in history only because of their specific religious and philosophical backgrounds. We, in the East, would be similarly wrong in thinking that the Industrial Revolution is a Western product, and that we could therefore do without it. The origin of all the religious and cultural contradictions leading to so many current conflicts in the world lies in our stubborn psychic block, which errs in equating the modern West with the historical West. The historical West, which was composed of the Medieval West and the Hellenic West, needs to be contra-distinguished from the modern West.

The most obvious feature of the modern West is the Industrial Revolution, which was facilitated by an interminable series of technical inventions. But the question is whether these technical inventions materialised as so many miracles out of thin air. The answer is clearly in the negative. There are differences among scholars regarding the causes that led to the inventions. Those who attempt to trace their backgrounds are bound to evolve some consistent approach. The line adopted here derives its sustenance from historical and theoretical perspectives. In history, a specific date can be fixed to such events as conquest, birth, discovery or invention, etc., but philosophical and cultural phenomena defy such a definite temporal determination. In such cases, there is no escape from approximate estimation. A certain historical conjuncture began to take shape in Western Europe in the fifteenth century. We have already seen how the East had made its formative contribution to this process. It is thus evident that what happened in Western Europe was itself a culmination of a series of global events.

We will be discussing the four great movements, (*i*) The Renaissance, (*ii*) The Humanism, (*iii*) The Reformation, and (*iv*) The Scientific Revolution, in Part I of this book. Innumerable scientific discoveries were made possible in the seventeenth century by the first three movements. These movements had themselves received an incalculable impetus from the legacy of China, India, West Asia, etc., as we have noted earlier. At any rate, the Scientific Revolution further led to numerous inventions. In this telescopic process, such an environment came to be created that transmuted the Agrarian Society into the Industrial Society.

In the course of this silent and stupendous shift from one kind of age to another, the entire gamut of thought, covering such varied fields as science, religion, philosophy, culture, political systems, ownership patterns, etc., led to the European Enlightenment (including the French Enlightenment). It also led to the French Revolution. Concurrently, the Industrial Revolution quietly flowed from the Scientific Revolution through technical inventions. While the Industrial Revolution went about its business of creating new infrastructural facilities (in such fields as railways, telegraph, etc.) without being impeded, the European Enlightenment, not to speak of the French Revolution, faced brakes, diversions, and distortions. Even the original sparks of inspiration for scientific rationality, intellectual liberty, etc., which had characterised the European Enlightenment, dimmed. As a consequence, medieval institutions such as the monarchy, papacy, feudalism, etc., which had ruled the roost for more than 1,000 years in Western Europe, returned and swamped the new radical thoughts. This in turn paved the way for reactions against new thoughts, which manifested themselves in such forms as imperialism, narrow nationalism, fascism, and Nazism, which eventually led to World Wars I and II.

All the while, the technological processes of the Industrial Revolution continued to develop at a snowballing pace, producing both unprecedented wealth and weapon-systems. As a result, the world has now come to confront a huge hiatus between the recrudescence of medieval illiberalism and the proliferation of post-industrial armaments. What is worse, illiberalism is no longer the monopoly of non-democratic countries, as even the so-called developed democracies (for example, in Western Europe and America) are being exposed to the tides of nationalism and anti-globalisation, in the guise of nativism and populism. This dangerous reversal of liberalism is also taking place within developing countries such as democratic India and secular Turkey. I therefore feel that the ideological trends that influenced the foundations and features of the Industrial Society need to be restated, however cursorily. To this end, a brief account and analysis of ten modern ideologies will be presented in Part II of the book. The bulk of the pages is devoted to the explication of ideologies that are facing the bleak prospect of getting buried beneath a revival of the divisive identities that had marked pre-industrial times. Each of the ideologies may bear a shallow resemblance to ancient phenomena, but they are essentially new, and have struck far deeper roots than their distant approximations.

The ideologies have a bearing on all social sciences, and their integrated study can therefore help to develop an overall picture. A holistic view is an imperative, as even technocrats, intellectuals, and politicians are confining themselves to their narrow disciplines and tunnel visions. Any interdisciplinary approach leads to the development of ideologies. Ideology, as a phenomenon, is a mixed blessing. It provides a wider frame of reference, which enables people to comprehend social, economic, and political issues in a ready way. The flip side is that it promotes conceptual rigidity. Discerning people, while examining issues through their ideological lenses, understand the limitations of their ideologies, as no ideology can be so comprehensive as to capture all the aspects of issues that emerge dynamically from time to time. They therefore treat ideology as a serious premise, and not as a final inference. People who, for lack of inclination or intelligence, do not go beyond the premise tend to become fanatical. Persons who navigate across the boundaries of various ideologies tend to become intellectual, or philosophically liberal. While these inter-ideological voyages are highly desirable, there is no escape in the first place from a comprehension of ideologies *per se*.

We, however, need to note that the dominant perception today is that ideology has itself become irrelevant, or at least, is in irreversible decline. But humans need ideology or philosophy almost as much as food or water. What is more, ideologies follow them like their shadows, either at the conscious or at the sub-conscious level. The argument that ideologies are mattering less, or that they are not even necessary, does not hold water. In fact, such an argument is often advanced to justify a clandestine return to some defunct ideology. Ideology, in modern times, focuses on social, economic, and political issues. If social ideologies are enervated or extinguished as phenomena, pre-existing cultural identities based on religion or race will resurrect themselves with an elemental fury. Their furies are currently on wild display, in such places as Syria, Iraq, Palestine, etc. Their resurrection not only leads to a strengthening of cultural collisions, but also to a perpetuation of pro-status quo forces. Vested interests play up pre-industrial ethnic divisions to resist the forces of change, freedom, and justice. Dissemination of the knowledge of social ideologies is one of the ways in which intellectual liberalism can be resuscitated. No final truths were discovered either in the Agrarian Society or in the current Industrial Society. In both eras, truths could only be relative. However, in the Agrarian Society, either because of the vaulting ambitions of adventurous individuals or conflicting religious fanaticisms, wars were found to be inevitable. In that period, wars led to considerable destruction; however, wars today can lead to the complete extinction of not only the human race, but of all life-forms. An urgent need to pre-empt all wars (at any rate, all nuclear wars and wars fought with weapons of mass destruction) has consequently arisen for the first time in history. Even as the Damocles' sword of nuclear war continues to hang over the head of humanity, yet another extinction-level threat has arisen in the form of environmental degradation. The solutions to the new, gigantic problems cannot be found in past history, but lie in discovering the essential unity of all humanity based on new scientific findings, or by emphasising the ennobling ethical aspects found in various religious and cultural traditions.

Nobody knows the future shape of Industrial Society, as it is still in its incipient stage. But this society has not yet succeeded in its initial task of creating such a new worldview as to do away with new existential threats. The human mind that has created the Industrial Society therefore needs to be hammered heavily enough to provide solutions to the new problems. Comprehension and contemplation of ideologies can certainly be one of the heavy hammers. The ideologies to be discussed are: (*i*) Nationalism, (*ii*) Democracy, (*iii*) Liberalism, (*iv*) Capitalism, (*v*) Evolutionary Socialism, (*vi*) Revolutionary Socialism, (*vii*) Feminism, (*viii*) Environmentalism, (*ix*) Nuclear Pacifism, and (*x*) Globalism.

Even as we discuss the prevailing ideologies, it is unanimously agreed that a sense of unity and amity among various peoples of the world is the most urgent need of the hour. Unity has hitherto been stressed both on ethical and pragmatic grounds. It will be further helpful to know through science that the primordial address of *homo sapiens* was common, and located in Africa. As Ian Tattersall and De Salle ironically observe in their book *Race?* (2011: 131):

> There are three major genetic observations that have been made about the diversity of people living on the African continent. First, Africa shows more genetic diversity than the other continents. Second, most of the genetic variation outside of Africa is a subset of the variation found within Africa. Finally, genetic diversity decreases with increasing distance from Africa.

The global study based on DNA (Liu, et al. 2015) has also established that the original humans were born in Africa, and migrated to other parts of the world. It says that: 'A first dispersal took place between 130,000–115,000 years ago via northern Africa, but died out or retreated. A second dispersal took place via the so-called Southern Route, which followed the southern coastline of Asia, and colonised Australia by around 50,000 years ago.' According to the study by Tamang, et al. (2012):

> We have demonstrated that the Indian populations are the descendants of the very first modern humans, who ventured the journey of out-of-Africa about 65,000 years ago. The recent gene flow from east and west Eurasia is also evident .... It is well established that a relatively small group of modern humans ventured out-of-Africa through the southern coastal route to

> colonize the Middle East, India, Southeast Asia, Australia and subsequently the other parts of the globe .... This indicates that India served as one of the important corridors for human migration.

Tattersall and De Salle (2011) summed up the entire racial myth with satirical finesse. As Sapp stated, while reviewing their book:

> Few concepts are as emotionally charged as that of race. The word conjures up a mixture of associations—culture, ethnicity, genetics, subjugation, exclusion and persecution. But, is the tragic history of efforts to define groups of people by race really a matter of the misuse of science, the abuse of a valid biological concept? ....
>
> The consensus among Western researchers today is that human races are socio-cultural constructs. Still, the concept of human race as an objective biological reality persists in society. It is high time that policy makers, ... rid themselves of the misconception of race as type or as genetic population. (Sapp 2011: 1)

Almost all modern paleoanthropologists agree that the common ancestry of all *homo sapiens* can be traced back to African aboriginals. Harvard geneticist Richard Lewontin revealed in his seminal paper, 'The Apportionment of Human Diversity' (1972), that human populations are genetically diverse, but that a vast majority of genetic variation was found within these so-called races and not between them.

Further research has supported this conclusion. In 2000, while presenting the first draft of the human genome, Craig Venter (winner of the Nobel Prize) of the Institute of Genetic Research and Francis Collins of the National Institute of Health declared that the concept of race had no genetic basis. On the basis of our ability to understand, all humans are grouped into one species, as *Homo Sapiens*.

It is thus clear that the African aboriginals are the common ancestors of all racial, religious, and linguistic groups. Cultural differences arose among all these groups while settling down in various regions, or while migrating from place to place in history. In other words, people of the same ancient origin are now quarrelling over issues of cultural divergence that arose much later. Even these differences are of relatively recent origin, as they could settle down in various river valleys, such as those of the Nile, Tigris, Euphrates, Ganga (Ganges), Yangtze, etc., no earlier than 11,000 years ago. We are able to mark the period when the Agrarian Society began based on the discovery of the Holocene period, which began about 11,000 years ago. Until that time, for scores of thousands of years, humans, whether in Africa or in the other places to which they migrated, were living as hunters and food gatherers. This aboriginal phase was followed by the Agrarian Society, which in turn prepared the ground for the birth of the Industrial Society. The new industrial incarnation has potentially converted ubiquitous poverty into universal prosperity; accelerated the process of empowering starving masses into emerging as superintending masters through education, agitation, and democracy; banished famines and epidemics; and translated the nightmares of inclement weather into excuses for new scientific amenities (such as air-conditioning and heating), and exotic escapades that former emperors would envy. By the same token, it has prepared the ground for the final destruction of humans through weapons of mass destruction or environmental degradation.

The blessings and curses of the Industrial Revolution are too striking and staggering to be missed by anybody, ranging from philosophers to the populace. However, the ambivalent character of our current existence has not brought about a corresponding degree of change in human philosophy or psychology. A debate on ideologies or on intellectual issues is one of the ways of going about it. Other ways for this purpose can also be explored. If the exploration is open-minded, there is hope for humanity.

Part I

Four Great Movements

1

The Renaissance

As the Renaissance happened to take birth in the West, albeit with massive contributions from the East, there is a need to take a quick glance at the history of the pre-modern West. Coming long after Eastern civilisations, Western civilisation started with Greece, and proceeded to Rome. However, this was interposed by Christianity, which entered from West Asia, when Constantine I was converted to Christianity in the fourth century. The intellectual leaders of Christianity at that point tended to dismiss the Greco-Roman legacy as pagan or heathen, and did not therefore show great respect for it. But the contempt of Roman aristocrats for an Oriental religion like Christianity was even greater. Be that as it may, the eclipse of the Roman Empire by the rise of Christianity was welcomed by pious Christian converts among the people. A number of intellectual and religious adjustments were made by the Church in subsequent centuries to dilute this conflict of visions. The case for the superiority of the Hellenic legacy was resurrected after the Renaissance. For instance, the great English historian, Edward Gibbon (1737–94), believed that the Roman Empire represented a far higher level of civilisation than Christianity, which followed it. Looking back from the vantage point of European Enlightenment in the eighteenth century, he provided a magniloquent expression to this view in his magisterial work, *Decline and Fall of the Roman Empire* (1776–88). He summed up the gist of his work in the following words: ‘I have described the triumph of Barbarism and Religion’ (Toynbee and Somervell 1957: 77). In other words, Gibbon meant to convey that Christianity in the fourth century symbolised nothing better than a mixture of barbarism and religion.

Gibbon's sentiments were also echoed in the first part of the twentieth century by the great British anthropologist James George Frazer (1854–1941), who welcomed the Renaissance in his celebrated book, *The Golden Bough*, and said:

> The revival of Roman Law, of the Aristotlean philosophy, of ancient art and literature at the close of the Middle Ages, marked the return of Europe to native ideals of life and conduct, to saner, manlier views of the world. The long halt in the march of civilization was over. The tide of Oriental invasion had turned at last. It is ebbing still. (Toynbee and Somervell 1957: 78)

It can be seen from Frazer's comment that he saw, even in the twentieth century, after a lapse of 1,500 years, the entry of Christianity into the West in the fourth century as nothing but an 'Oriental invasion'. It is also evident that both Gibbon and Frazer saw an implacable dichotomy between the Hellenic legacy and the Christian tradition. However, another scholar of comparable stature, Arnold Toynbee of the twentieth century, differs from them, as he saw (in his classic *A Study of History* [twelve volumes, 1934–61]) that both the Hellenic and the Christian traditions were mutually complementary, and could therefore be syncretised later. But all three of them (Gibbon, Frazer, and Toynbee) agree on one thing—that the Renaissance began in Italy in the late thirteenth century and spread throughout Europe in the fifteenth century. Western Christendom, after dominating for more than 1,000 years, was inspired by the resurrection of Hellenic tenets of civilisation through 'the Renaissance'. A dominant feature of the Middle Ages in Europe was the overwhelming emphasis on religious faith and philosophy of the Church. When Constantinople fell to the Ottoman Turks in 1453, Greek manuscripts and scholars travelled to the West, leading to a revival of interest in Greek classics and philosophy. To be historically precise, efforts were made in the fourteenth century to learn Greek and acquire the manuscripts of Homer, Plato, Plutarch, etc. But after the fall of Constantinople, what had been a trickle turned into a flood, and the entire treasure trove of Greek legacy became available to European scholars.

As Toynbee says: 'When, at last the Western Christians were ready for Aristotle, they got him, by a roundabout route through Arabic translations' (Toynbee and Somervell 1957: 253). Toynbee continues:

> [S]urely the Italian Renaissance of Hellenic literature in the Late Medieval period, though it may have had its patrons among political grandees such as Lorenzo de Medici, was essentially a spontaneous movement of unorganised scholarship. Perhaps, it was—though the patronage of the 15th century Popes, more particularly Pope Nicholas V (A.D. 1447–55), is not to be underrated. This Pope employed hundreds of classical scholars and copyists of ancient manuscripts, gave 10,000 gulden for a translation of Homer into Latin verse, and assembled a library of 9,000 volumes. (ibid.: 251)

In Italy, the first and foremost bearer of the Renaissance movement was the city of Florence, capital of the Tuscany region, central Italy. Dante (1265–1321), the great epic poet in Italian, had nothing to do with Ranaissance or the Reformation. Yet, he ventured to write *The Devine Comedia* in his native Italian tongue than in Latin (which had been a formidable fashion for centuries until then). On top of this, he took his principled position that the Church should not meddle in politics. Despite his subscription to medieval thought, he can be described as a semi-conscious voice of rising aspirations. Great artists such as Leonardo Da Vinci (1452–1519) and Michelangelo (1475–1564), astronomer Galileo (1564–1642), and political philosopher Machiavelli (1469–1527) were all from the city of Florence, and suffused with the spirit of the Renaissance. Florence can be described as the first modern city that is almost comparable to ancient Athens, in terms of its contribution to the modern West.

Unlike the later period of the Renaissance, which challenged the authority of the Church, the Italian Renaissance, drawing its inspiration from Greco-Roman sources, thrived on Papal patronage. Dubbed by historians as the Renaissance papacy, the period of the Renaissance popes began with

Pope Martin V, who re-established Rome as the centre of Papal power in 1417, after putting an end to the Great Schism. The Renaissance papacy came to an abrupt halt with the sacking of Rome by Emperor Charles V, who ran the largest empire in Europe, in 1527. He was not only emperor of Spain, but also took the titles of Holy Roman Emperor, Emperor of the German Nations.

During this phase in papal history, patronage of the arts had become a part of papal policy. Both Julius II and Leo X patronised Raphael, whose frescoes adorn the Vatican; Raphael also designed Rome's Santa Maria del Popolo Chapel and an area within Saint Peter's newly built basilica. Julius II also commissioned Michelangelo to paint the ceiling of the Sistine Chapel.

Pope Sixtus IV initiated the process of redesigning and rebuilding Rome; he commissioned the widening of its streets and the building of the Sistine Chapel and summoned several artists from other Italian city-states to give shape to his vision. Pope Nicholas V set up the Vatican library, which became a treasure trove of several classical and humanist texts. The arts prospered under the benefaction of the fourteen popes who ruled the Vatican during this period. The papacy, however, did not limit its patronage to the arts. It also employed a number of humanists to work in the Curia (the Papal bureaucracy). Most humanists of this age studied classical texts, which were part of the Papal archives and libraries. As an engine of change, the Italian Renaissance transformed the general outlook of the people in a radical but inoffensive way. The early Renaissance did not set fire to anything, but it did reignite the lamp of Hellenic learning and rediscovery of the mathematics and philosophy of Pythagoras and Plato after nearly 2,000 years.

Of all the great figures of the Italian Renaissance, Leonardo Da Vinci is perhaps the most renowned—an archetypal genius and a quintessential polymath. Da Vinci was a painter, sculptor, draftsman, architect, engineer, and scientist. He is still celebrated for his paintings, the 'Last Supper' (a mural that he painted in the refectory of the Convent of Santa Maria delle Grazie, Milan) and the 'Mona Lisa', which adorns the

Louvre museum in Paris today. His compatriot, Michelangelo, was a sculptor, painter, and architect. He is famous for the fresco depicting the Genesis, which he painted on the ceiling of the Sistine Chapel, and his nude sculpture, 'David'. Both Leonardo Da Vinci and Michelangelo gained great renown for their art, most of which focused on religious themes. They were contemporaries and rivals, and yet their most famous works, 'Mona Lisa' and 'David', share a life-like quality that perhaps remains unmatched till date.

Machiavelli was an original political thinker, now known as the father of modern political science, who wrote of the ruthless and unscrupulous nature of power politics with scientific objectivity, dispensing with moral hypocrisy. His *The Prince* (1532) remains a classic to this day, and is considered a 'handbook for politicians' even now. Unsurprisingly, the then pope, Pope Clement VIII, condemned the book. Machiavelli was an early humanist in that he did not deal with religious issues, but focused instead on political issues.

Another prominent figure of the Italian Renaissance, Galileo, was a mathematician, astronomer, and physicist, who is recognised as both the father of science and the father of modern physics. Galileo introduced us to observational astronomy and was the first to use a telescope to study the skies. He discovered the phases of Venus, observed and analysed sun spots, and came to espouse the Copernican theory of the heliocentric model. Galileo is said to have been exposed to Aristotelian thought as a student, but after experimenting with falling objects, he rejected Aristotle and produced his famous work, *De Motu* ('On Motion'). While he was respected as the most gifted scientist of his time, he had to face the Inquisition for supporting the Copernican system. He was found guilty of heresy, and forced to recant. He spent the rest of his life under house arrest, conducting research even after going blind in 1637.

All the Florentine geniuses grew to their full potential because of the liberal spirit that the Renaissance engendered, thereby reducing the rigours of medieval orthodoxy.

2

The Humanism (Hellenic)

The world of letters, the exposure to Greek thought encouraged the spirit of rationalism, which led to the beginning of the Renaissance Humanism. While it did not have the anti-religious flavour of latter-day humanism, it did sow the seeds for its growth. Humanist scholarship of the time mainly entailed the search for classical texts, and the excision and editing of known classical texts. Early humanism, while continuing the rhetorical and grammatical tradition of medieval scholastics, incorporated Greek moral philosophy and poetry into the mix.

Although the legacy of the Renaissance Humanism is still subject to hot debates among scholars, there is a general consensus that the early humanists were not trying to look forward, but were in fact looking resolutely backwards to the glories of ancient Greece and Rome. However, this very passion for the past ultimately turned into an instrument of change not only in the liberal arts, but also in architecture, politics, social structures, and religion.

The Renaissance and the Humanism were two movements that were inextricably intertwined from their very inception, although each had its distinctive features. Italian writers like Francesco Petrarch (1304–74), the greatest scholar of his age, who wrote in both Italian and Latin on romantic themes like love, and on Roman heritage, stressed the importance of classical culture while upholding the Christian message. The revival of classical literature shifted the emphasis from religious to secular concerns. Petrarch is therefore considered the founder of the Humanism. His influence on

European literature was enormous and lasting, and his deep consciousness of the classical past as a source of literary and philosophical meaning for the present was of great importance in paving the way for the Renaissance. The invention of the printing press had greatly aided in spreading the new spirit of humanism, which is more human-centred than God-centred. The printing press also enabled humanist scholars to bring out editions of the works of ancient masters, both of Greece and Rome. The epics of Homer, the Greek tragedies, sciences, and philosophies of the ancients were being more widely read, generating a new worldview.

Erasmus (1466–1536) of Rotterdam was a Dutch priest and was considered the greatest European scholar of the sixteenth century. He was noted for his editions of the classical authors of Latin, Church Fathers and the New Testament, as well as for his own works. Using the philological studies pioneered by Italian humanists, he helped to lay the groundwork for a historical-critical study of the past. By criticising ecclesiastical abuses, he encouraged the growing urge for reform, which found expression in both the Protestant Reformation and the Catholic Counter-Reformation. Although he saw much to admire in Martin Luther, he took an independent stance, rejecting Luther's doctrine of 'pre-destination' and the powers claimed for the Papacy. His greatest work was a satire, *The Praise of Folly*, in which he heaped much ridicule on the degradation of religious institutions, as well as their ministers, of his time. Being a humanist, his view was that man stands in direct relation to God, and that theology was therefore unnecessary. In his work as a publisher, he aimed at a public wider than scholars.

Thomas More of England (1478–1535) wrote his famous *Utopia*, an ideal State of sorts, which was inspired by Plato's *Republic*. As in Plato's Republic, all things are held in common without any right to private property. Through dialogues, it further propagates that there can be no equality without communism. Besides being a writer, Thomas More was involved in public affairs and was in Parliament, where he earned a high moral reputation by his forthright barring of Henry VII's financial requests. When he rose to the high position of Chancellor, he was opposed to the divorce of King Henry VIII from Catherine of Aragon, as a consequence of which he had to resign his office. When, in 1534, the act of supremacy established the King as the head of the new Church, More refused to take the oath. He was tried for treason for having said that Parliament could not make the King the Head of the Church. He was executed. His literary piece, *Utopia*, which spread an egalitarian message, and his personal life symbolising sacrifice for political principles generated a great impact in favour of the humanism.

The general outlines of those mental attitudes and scholarly interest assembled under the rubric of the humanism were, according to Steven Kreis, forged by the humanist mentality, which stood midway between medieval supernaturalism and the modern scientific critical attitude. 'Perhaps the most we can assume is that the man of the Renaissance lived, as it were, between two worlds ... suspended faith and reason' (Kreis 2000).

Kreis says that as medieval supernaturalism diminished, secular and human interests became dominant. '*Fortuna* (chance) gradually replaced *Providence* as the universal frame of reference' (ibid.). Beauty was believed to afford some glimpse of transcendental existence. This goes far in explaining the humanist cult of beauty and makes plain that the humanism was, above everything else, fundamentally an aesthetic movement.

The dominating element in the finest classical culture was aesthetic rather than supernatural or scientific. In the later Middle Ages, urban intellectuals were well on the road to the recovery of an aesthetic and secular view of life, even before the full impact of classical revival was felt. It was only natural, then, that pagan literature, with its emotional and intellectual affinity to the new world, should accelerate the existing drift towards secularism and stimulate the cult of humanity, and worship of beauty.

Almost everywhere, the humanism began as a rather pious, timid conservative drift away from medieval Christianity and ended in the bold independence of the medieval tradition. Rudolphus Agricola (1443–85) may be regarded as the German Petrarch. In England, John Colet (1467–1519) and Sir Thomas More were early or conservative humanists, and Francis Bacon (1561–1626) represented the later, or agnostic and sceptical humanism. In France, pious classicists like Lefevre d'Etaples (1453–1536) were succeeded by frank, urbane and devout sceptics like Michel Montaigne (1533–92), and bold anti-clerical satirists like Francois Rabelais (1494–1533).

Humanists such as Desiderius Erasmus rejected religious orthodoxy in favour of the study of human nature, and such writers as Petrarch in Italy, Rabelais in France, and William Shakespeare in England produced works that emphasised the intricacies of the human character.

> The leading intellectual trait of the era was the recovery, to a certain degree, of the secular and humane philosophy of Greece and Rome. Another humanist trend which cannot be ignored was the rebirth of individualism, which, developed by Greece and Rome to a remarkable degree, had been suppressed by the rise of a caste system in the later Roman Empire, by the Church and by feudalism in the Middle Ages. (Kreis 2000)

The rise of the humanism gradually paved the way for the Reformation.

3

The Reformation (Protestant)

The material conditions had been developing for a couple of centuries before the Reformation actually broke out. In order to put the Reformation in perspective, we need to start with the initial rise of Christianity. Christianity is based on the teachings of Jesus, who was born in Bethlehem (southwest of Jerusalem). It was originally a reformed movement of Jews who accepted Jesus as the Messiah, but the movement quickly became predominantly gentile at the hands of Saint Paul. Saint Paul, by asserting that non-Jewish disciples of Christ did not have to observe Jewish law, helped to establish Christianity as a separate religion, which had till then been a Jewish sect. Through his theological resilience, Saint Paul aroused hostility among the Jews, leading to the original conflict between Judaism and Christianity. Even as this new hostility (between Judaism and Christianity) began to intensify, the early Church developed great moral appeal for the pagans in Europe. However, the Roman elites did not take kindly to the silent spread of Christianity and consequently took steps to persecute the Christian proselytisers. One of the important officials appointed for the purpose of checkmating this conversion, Pliny the Younger, testified to the high moral character of Christian missionaries. Even Edward Gibbon attributes the spread of early Christianity in the West to the pure and austere morals of the Christians. He further contends that Constantine I was motivated to convert to Christianity with a view to harnessing the strength of 'the union and discipline of the Christian Republic, which gradually formed an independent and increasing State in the heart of the Roman Empire' (Gibbon 1996: 250).

Be that as it may, Christians in the West were persecuted until Constantine I, the Roman emperor in the early part of the fourth century, was converted to Christianity. Constantine I did not stop with his religious conversion, but proceeded to shift his capital from Rome to Byzantium, which he promptly renamed Constantinople. Fareed Zakaria explains the shifting of the capital in his book, *The Future of Freedom* (2003). The emperor, besides being prompted by vanity and the ambition to leave behind a grand legacy of having built a new capital city, was also motivated by the geographical fact that Constantinople would be closer to the great cultural and economic centres of the day, such as Athens, Thessalonika, and Antioch. It was a more strategic point from which to defend the empire against its enemies, mainly Germanic tribes and Persian armies. Like all emperors, Constantine shifted in a heavy way, in that he not only moved his court, but also offered many inducements to senators and nobles to move to the new capital. As Zakaria put it, 'Although he took most of his court, Constantine left behind one person, the Bishop of Rome. This historic separation between the Church and State was to have fateful and beneficial consequences for human kind' (ibid.: 30). Apart from shifting the capital from Rome, he enraged the Romans by refusing to participate in a pagan rite, and never entered Rome again. As Rome thus began to be subjected to the benign neglect of the emperor, reigning from the distance of Constantinople, it began to enjoy a lot of independence, which eventually led to its spiritual leadership of the Christian peoples. To quote Zakaria again: 'It would be more accurate to say that in the west sovereignty was contested; for 1500 years after Constantine's move, European history was marked by continual strife between church and state. From the sparks of those struggles came the first fires of human liberty' (ibid.: 30).

It is not necessary for us to agree with the over-emphasis laid by Zakaria on this single event of shifting of the capital, but its importance, in terms of the unintended consequences that flowed from it, needs to be appreciated. In the aftermath of the self-imposed exile of the emperor from Rome to Byzantine/ Constantinople, the Roman Catholic Church became, in the words of the English philosopher Thomas Hobbes, 'The ghost of the deceased Roman empire sitting crowned upon (its) grave' (Hobbes 2002: 710). The Roman Church soon acquired the grandeur of the Roman Empire, thus slowly losing the original moral appeal of Christianity. The culture of Rome became the culture of Catholicism. To this day, its structure therefore remains hierarchical. While imposing limits on the monarch's rule, it controlled key social institutions such as marriage, and birth and death rites. The Catholic Church thus became the first institution in history that was independent of the emperor. The struggles between Church and state began just over fifty years after Constantine's move.

As the Roman Empire crumbled in the East in due course, the Bishop of Rome's authority and independence grew. He became first among the princes of the Church, called 'II Papa', the Holy Father. Through a number of struggles between the Pope and princes, the Pope emerged as the single greatest authority by the twelfth century.

After the Roman Catholic Church became the highest centre of power, it soon got corrupted to its core, in the fashion of all great centres of power in West Europe. Rome's most scandalous practice was the widespread sale of indulgences, which meant papal certificates absolving the buyer of sins, even those not yet committed. The proceeds of these indulgences were used not only to build and adorn St. Peter's in Rome, but also to enable the Pope and clergymen at various levels to live in such pomp as to make any prince in Europe jealous of them. The Church at one point owned one-third of the land in Europe, and church properties and priests were not even subject to taxation. On top of it all, the Church was also independent of temporal (kingly) authority. Such concentration of power, coupled with corruption, naturally generated a demand for reforms. Reformers such as Jan Huss, John Wycliffe, etc., attacked the abuses in the Roman Catholic Church from the fourteenth century itself, whereas the Reformation is usually dated from 1517, when Martin Luther posted his ninety-five theses on the church door in Wittenberg. John Wycliffe, a British theologian, had preached against church policies earlier, when he argued that the church itself was sinful and should therefore relinquish its huge possessions and return to pristine evangelical poverty. He also represented the Government of England to negotiate for limiting the power of the Church in England. He was the first to involve himself in a translation of the Bible into English, in order to bypass the church and to make the message of God available to all. His followers were known as 'Lollards'. He was known to have inspired the Peasants Revolt (1381). He inspired all reformist thinkers, ranging from Jan Huss to Martin Luther himself. Jan Huss, a Bohemian religious reformer, criticised the corruption in the Roman Catholic Church. He was eventually arrested, tried for heresy, and burned at the stake.

Martin Luther, a German priest, pleaded for the reform of the Roman Catholic Church, protesting the sale of indulgences and other abuses. He was excommunicated by Pope Leo IX. But under the protection of the elector of Saxony, he took refuge in the Wartburg. Luther translated the Bible into German, a work which is even now regarded as a great literary landmark in German literature. The printing press, which had been invented lately, played a huge catalytic role in making German copies of the Bible available to the laymen. Luther's eventual break with Rome led to the founding of the Lutheran church. The German rulers began to take sides, and the Reformation assumed the dimension of political revolt of Germans against the Pope. This was how the Reformation began. One hundred and fifty bloody years later, almost half of Europe was Protestant. The more immediate political impact of Protestantism was to provide kings and princes with an excuse to wrest power away from the Papacy. The first monarch who revolted was Henry VIII of England, as Pope Clement VII refused to accede to the request of the former to annul his marriage to Catherine of Aragon on the ground that she had not produced an heir to the throne. Henry VIII also proclaimed himself the head of the Church of

England. It is evident that the king was not inspired by any principle of Protestantism; however, his revolt accelerated the spread of Protestantism.

The English break was the first and most prominent in a series of religious revolts and wars against the Roman Catholic Church, involving almost every state in Europe and lasting for almost 150 years after the defiance of Luther. Wars resulting from the Reformation came to an end through the peace of Westphalia in 1648. It also ended the Thirty Years' War (a series of wars fought during 1618–48 between various nations in central Europe for several reasons, including religious, dynastic and territorial rivalries) among the Germans. It enabled the princes to choose their state religions, and explicitly permitted religious toleration and migration. Westphalia symbolised an important shift in Western history and finally put an end to the notion that Europe was a great single Christian community presided over by the Pope. Luther's radical message unintentionally helped to generate the 'peasants' revolt'. However, after some initial success, the peasants' revolt under Thomas Muntzer was eventually routed in 1525. Muntzer was thereafter executed. Left historians see in Muntzer the real hero of the Peoples' Reformation. But this revolt was not supported by Luther, as he was only a religious revolutionary, and not a social or political rebel. In fact, Luther was not even a tolerant liberal, but only a puritanical reformer of Christianity. He had more faith, and not less faith, than the Pope in Christianity.

Quite apart from the episode of the peasants' revolt, it was at this point that Luther's teachings struck a favourable chord among various sections. This process of dissemination of Luther's message was also facilitated by the earlier settlement of the doctrine of William Ockham, which stated that Christianity could do well without the supremacy of the Bishop of Rome. The reform movement soon gained the support of John Calvin, Zwingli, etc., in other parts of Europe. John Calvin (1509–64), French Protestant theologian, is the second most important figure of the Reformation. He emphasised salvation by grace, rather than by works. He established Protestantism in Geneva and issued fiats in favour of sexual morality and the abolition of Catholic superstitions. Calvin approved the arrest and conviction of Michael Servetus for heresy. In fact, he succeeded in establishing a theocracy in Geneva. Calvinism emphasised the doctrine of predestination, which deals with the question of the control that God exercises over the world. Calvin sought to purge Christianity of all vices and promoted an intolerant puritanism. Puritanism became a powerful movement in England and in North America. Since it was known for its fanatical zeal, it could not be called liberal or democratic.

The bitter confrontation between Catholicism and Protestantism led to conflicts in various places. For example, in the second half of the sixteenth century, France was torn by the Wars of Religion between the Huguenots (French Protestants from northern France) and the Catholics (1562–98), which included the Massacre of Saint Bartholomew's day, when French Huguenots were massacred in Paris in August 1572. It is instructive to note that the Wars of Religion took place for a period of thirty-six years (between 1562 and 1598) in France alone, and the ghastly incident of the Massacre resulted not only in the mass killing of royal guests, but also in the butchery of about 3,000 Huguenots in Paris itself, and of tens of thousands more in the provinces. This revived the hatred between Roman Catholics and Huguenots and helped provoke a renewal of hostilities. The bloody conflict between Protestants and Catholics unleashed wars for more than a century. The wars in France ended when the heir to the French throne, the Protestant Henry of Navarre, embraced Catholicism and was crowned Henry IV of France. He guaranteed the religious toleration of the Huguenots through the issuing of the Edict of Nantes (1598).

We may recall that the Saviour says in the Gospel that a camel will squeeze through the eye of a needle before a rich man can enter the kingdom of God. We might also recall St Jerome (AD 347–420), who claimed that every rich man is either a thief or the son of a thief. Because of this religious disapproval, moneylending was banned for Christians during the Middle Ages. Above all, the Reformation, despite its self-righteous fanaticism, paved the way for the intellectual freedom of individuals when it called upon each one of them to read the Bible and interpret it according to their conscience, and not to be guided by the interpretation of the Church. It is perhaps from this point that the word 'Conscience' came to be used in the modern sense, and became the foundation of the intellectual liberty of the individual.

Meanwhile, Catholicism, confronted by the vertical split in Western Christendom, did not keep idle and launched its own initiatives to meet the challenge. Paul III was the first Pope to respond by convening the Council of Trent, which reacted to the Protestants' criticisms. The Roman Inquisition was established in 1542 to control heresy within Catholic territories. The Jesuits, under Saint Ignatius of Loyola, embarked on educational and missionary work aimed at conversion or reconversion. Emperors Charles V and Phillip II took military steps against the growth of Protestants. All these developments have come to be known as the Counter-Reformation or Catholic Reformation, which bore fruit in not only achieving its original aims, but also provided new dimensions of service to Christianity in the fields of health and education. This constructive step on the part of Catholicism prompted the Protestants to also render their services. This new characteristic of social service, incidentally, helped Christianity to spread in colonised countries.

4

The Scientific Revolution

When the great humanists of Italy revived Greek learning, the influence of Pythagoras, Plato, etc., came to be resurrected. It needs to be observed that during the last phases of medieval scholasticism, Aristotle's thought predominated for a variety of historical and philosophical reasons, including the support lent by the greatest scholastic, Thomas Aquinas. This does not mean that the scholastics had adopted Aristotle's philosophy as a whole. It only implies that they had used the authority of Aristotle by emphasising certain parts of his thought for their own theological ends, in the process of which the role of mathematics happened to be neglected. With the Renaissance, the mathematics of Pythagoras and Plato came back into play. The numerical structure of the world was once again emphasised. This was an important development that led to the great revival of scientific enquiry in the sixteenth and seventeenth centuries. Bertrand Russell contends that the Renaissance was responsible for the birth of modern science.

Copernicus (1473–1543), a Polish cleric who came under the influence of the mathematics of Pythagoras, propounded the heliocentric (regarding the Sun as centre) theory in the first half of the sixteenth century. This apart, Copernicus himself had got a hint of this theory from the notes of Aristarchus (310–230 BC), who was the first to have discovered that the Earth revolves around the Sun in the third century BC. We should digress a little by referring to Indian conceptions about the Sun. S. Radhakrishnan, a prominent Indian philosopher of the twentieth century, says the following in his scholarly work, *Indian Philosophy*:

> We may quote a passage which is certainly not less than 2,000 years before the birth of Copernicus, from the Aitaraya Brahmana: 'The Sun never sets nor rises. When people think to themselves the sun is setting, he only changes about after reaching the end of the day, and makes night below and day to what is on the other side. Then when people think he rises in the morning, he only shifts himself about after reaching the end of the night, and makes day below and night to what is on the other side. In fact, he never does set at all.' (Radhakrishnan 2008: 8n4)

The similarities between the theory of Aristarchus and the passage cited by Radhakrishnan are significant. It is difficult to say whether it was the Indian astronomer or Aristarchus who deserves to be given credit for the discovery. At any rate, in the context of the modern West, the fact is that the theory (whether discovered or rediscovered by Copernicus) itself revolutionised modern science, and this revolution triggered all later astronomical discoveries. When Galileo adopted this theory, he was faced with the hostility of the entire Christendom. Copernicus had earlier escaped the censure of the Church by wisely dedicating his theories to the Pope. We need to note that both the Catholics and the Protestants were united as one in opposing the theory of Copernicus and Galileo. Until that time, the Church had adopted the principle of Ptolemy's astronomy, according to which the Sun revolves round the Earth. Ptolemy worked in Alexandria in the second century AD and based his theory on the authority of Aristotle. It needs to be said that although Aristotle was wrong on the count of the Earth being the centre of the solar system, this shortcoming does not detract from his paramountcy in philosophy. It is not Aristotle's fault that his scientific testimony that the Earth is flat was treated as inviolably sacrosanct. This was only a sad reflection on the credulity of the medieval Church. In any case, the medieval Church adopted Ptolemy's theory and treated it as an article of faith. It therefore opposed Copernicus' theory even after it was supported by Galileo. Galileo, the greatest scientist of the modern age before Newton, was tried for heresy and kept under house arrest for the rest of his life. While Galileo's life was spared because of his stature as a scientist,

Giordano Bruno (1548–1600), an Italian astronomer who also propagated the heliocentric theory in the same period, was burned at the stake by the Spanish Inquisition. Bruno has since remained an evocative symbol of free thinking, both in the natural and the social sciences.

The Spanish Inquisition took recourse to indiscriminate methods of suppression of freedom in the wake of its visceral reaction against the onslaught of Protestant Reformation. This is not being mentioned by way of defending such a record, but merely to put it in its historical context.

The findings of Galileo, coupled with those of Kepler, enabled Newton to come out with his masterly vision of the 'Laws of Motion'. Newton also worked out the fundamentals of Calculus, although this work went unpublished for more than thirty years. This delay in publication led to a historic dispute with G. W. Leibniz, German mathematician, regarding the original authorship of Calculus. It is instructive to note that this dispute between the two mathematical giants lasted for twenty-five years. It largely received impetus from the geopolitics of the seventeenth century; Europe supported Leibniz, while England stood by Newton as one man. It can thus be seen that the division was inspired more by geopolitical sentiments than by mathematical merits or historical facts. In the end, it was proved that both had discovered Calculus independently, and that Newton discovered it first. At any rate, Newton emerged as the supreme scientific authority of the time. The mathematics and sciences of the ancient world, be they of the East or the West, may have been very advanced in themselves, but the astrophysics of Newton was absolutely new, ushering in a new era in world history. Voltaire rapturously described Newton's science as 'Newton's religion'. The English poet Alexander Pope sang of Newton's impact thus:

> Nature and Nature's Laws lay hid in night.
> God said 'let Newton be' and all was light. (*Concise Oxford Dictionary of Quotations* 1964: 164)

Apart from the discoveries of Copernicus, Kepler, Galileo, and Newton, many other discoveries took place from about the middle of the sixteenth century to the end of the eighteenth century. We can do no better than to refer to a list of just the most important twenty-nine breakthroughs of the period, from 1530–1789 (Ferguson 2011: 65):

1530 Paracelsus pioneers the application of chemistry to physiology and pathology.

1543 Nicolaus Copernicus' *De revolutionibus orbium coelestium* states the heliocentric theory of the solar system.
Andreas Vesalius' *De humani corporis fabrica* supplants Galen's anatomical textbook.

1546 Agricola's *De natura fossilium* classifies minerals and introduces the term 'fossil'.

1572 Tycho Brahe records the first European observation of a supernova.

1589 Galileo's tests of falling bodies (published in *De motu*) revolutionise the experimental method.

1600 William Gilbert's *De Magnete, Magnestisque Corporibus* describes the magnetic properties of the earth and electricity.

1604 Galileo discovers that a free-falling body increases its distance as the square of time.

1608 Hans Lippershey and Zacharias Jansen independently invent the telescope.

1609 Galileo conducts the first telescopic observations of the night sky.

1610 Galileo discovers four of Jupiter's moons and infers that Earth is not at the centre of the universe.

1614 John Napier's *Mirifici Logarithmorum Canonis Descriptio* introduces logarithms.

1628 William Harvey writes *Exercitatio Anatomica de Motu Cordis et Sanguinis in Animalibus*, accurately describing the circulation of blood.

1637 Rene Descartes' *'La Geometrie'*, an appendix to his *Discours de la methode*, founds analytic geometry.

1638 Galileo's *Discorsi e dimonstrazioni matematiche* founds modern mechanics.

1640 Pierre de Fermat founds number theory.

1654 Fermat and Blaise Pascal found probability theory.
1661 Robert Boyle's *Skeptical Chymist* defines elements and chemical analysis.
1662 Boyle states Boyle's Law—that the volume occupied by a fixed mass of gas in a container is inversely proportional to the pressure it exerts.
1669 Issac Newton's *De analysi per aequationes numero terminorum infinitas* presents the first systematic account of the calculus, independently developed by Gottfried Leibniz.
1676 Antoni van Leeuwenbock discovers micro-organisms.
1687 Newton's *Philosophiae Naturalis Principia Mathematica* states the law of universal gravitation and the laws of motion.
1735 Carolus Linnaeus' *Systema naturae* introduces the systematic classification of genera and species of organisms.
1738 Daniel Bernoulli's *Hydrodynamica* states Bernoulli's Principle and founds the mathematical study of fluid flow and the kinetic theory of gases.
1746 Jean-Etienne Guettard prepares the first true geological maps.
1755 Joseph Black identifies carbon dioxide.
1775 Antoine Lavoisier accurately describes combustion.
1785 James Hutton's 'Concerning the System of the Earth' states the uniformitarian view of the earth's development.
1789 Lavoisier's *Traite Elementaire de Chimie* states the law of conservation of matter.

Keeping in view this deluge of discoveries, John Dryden, the neo-classical English poet, said of the seventeenth century:

> In these last hundred years, almost a new nature has been revealed to us. More errors ... have been detected, more useful experiments have been made, more noble secrets in optics, medicine, anatomy, and astronomy have been discovered than in all those doting and credulous ages from Aristotle to us. (Dryden 1668)

Dryden's observations have been substantiated by Edward Gibbon's description of the dismal nature of the medieval ages in his epic history, *Decline and Fall of the Roman Empire* (1996).

The triumphs of science are silently subversive, unlike those in the political, religious, and military spheres. As the mathematician Jacob Bronowski observes: 'Like other creative activities which grew from the Renaissance, science has humanised our values' (Ferris 2010: 5).

Francis Bacon is often called the prophet of the scientific revolution. Bacon wrote that 'nature cannot be commanded except by being obeyed'. He said, without any element of modesty, 'I have taken all knowledge to be my province'. He further said: 'I have only taken upon me to ring a bell to call other wits together' (Ferris 2010: 51). The miracles of modern science wrought since the seventeenth century have ushered in the Industrial Age.

The four historic phenomena that have so far been dealt with relate to (*i*) the Renaissance, (*ii*) the Humanism, (*iii*) the Reformation, and (*iv*) the Scientific Revolution, which together produced such a synergistic effect as to bring about the modern age, the Industrial Revolution, and various socio-economic ideologies. These ideologies will now be considered.

Part II

Ten Ideologies

5

Nationalism

The concept of a nation, in its current connotation, is of modern origin. However, people all over the world have had notions of their nations in cultural, religious, linguistic, ethnic, or geographical or imperial senses since ancient times. There is, therefore, an imperative need to distinguish the old cultural notions from the current political ideas.

Nations are situated in specific historical moments and are constructed by shifting nationalist discourses promoted by different groupings competing for hegemony. The concept of the 'nation-state' assumes a complete overlap between the boundaries of the nation and the boundaries of those who live in a specific state.

The commonly accepted definitions for the terms 'nation' and 'nation-state' are:

> A Nation is where the great majority are conscious of a common identity and share the same culture (Yuval-Davis 1997: 10).
>
> The nation-state is an area where the cultural boundaries match up with the political boundaries. The ideal of {a} 'nation-state' is that the state incorporates people of a single ethnic stock and cultural traditions (Kazancigil and Dogan 1994: 188).

Francis Fukuyama, in *The Origins of Political Order* (2012), argues that the first nation-state was formed in China. He says:

> [D]uring the Eastern Zhou dynasty (770–256 BC), genuine states began to coalesce in China. They established standing armies that were capable of enforcing rules throughout a defined territory; they created bureaucracies to collect taxes and administer laws; they mandated uniform weights and measures; and they created public infrastructure in the form of roads, canals and irrigation

> systems. One state in particular, the kingdom of Qin, embarked on a remarkable modernizing project whose direct target was the kinship-based, patrimonial social order of the early Zhou .... Compared to the militaristic societies, China under the Zhou was remarkably violent. (ibid.: 110)

The estimates of the forces mobilised in terms of the percentage of population of each State of the ancient world (both East and West) confirmed the fact that China did far more than any other State. The same is true of the number of casualties in the wars of the period. Although the estimates are far from exact, the capacity of China for any militaristic activity was admittedly far higher than that of its Western counterparts.

In ancient China, huge and long-lasting dynasties were the order of the day, although they fulfilled most of the criteria of the nation-state. But China became a republic and a modern nation only in 1911 under the leadership of Sun Yat-sen. Chiang Kai-shek succeeded Sun Yat-sen, but his rule was disturbed for a long period by civil war with the Communists led by Mao. Mao, who led the revolution, founded the current People's Republic of China. Chinese history has been mostly influenced by a cultural and ethnic feeling of oneness, but this feeling was used for the consolidation of the dynasties. In the twentieth century, nationalism in China grew by way of resistance to Japanese imperialism. Mao, in addition to being a Communist revolutionary, catered to the nationalist feelings of the Chinese, and in fact embodied nationalist fervour more than Chiang Kai-shek's regime during the Chinese Revolution. Mao's intense nationalism manifested itself even after the Revolution through his regime's extended claims on land and sea, which are even today threatening the peace in Asia.

While dealing with India soon after China, Fukuyama observed:

> The evolution of Indian politics diverged from the Chinese pattern in dramatic ways right around the time of the emergence of the first real states on the Indo-Gangetic plain .... The Indian states fought with each other and with the gana-Sanghas throughout the following centuries, but never to the bitter degree of mutual extinction .... It is very revealing that the more

> primitive gana-sangha form of organisation survived in India up to the middle of the 1st millennium AD without being absorbed by more powerful states. (Fukuyama 2012: 160)

Ancient Indian society did not experience prolonged warfare. Instead of concentrating authority in a single emperor, it was split between a well-differentiated class of priests and a class of warriors who depended upon each other. Fukuyama observes that India's persistent inability to concentrate political power like China was rooted in the Indian religious system. He further remarks that India created the beginning of a rule of law with limits on the power of the State.

Regardless of the nature of the nation-state that ancient India developed, the peculiarity of the geography of India played a critical part. The Indian peninsula is divided from the rest of the world by the seas on three sides, and the Himalayas in the north. This insular geographical character has always inspired philosophers and poets from ancient times to lend India a dimension of cultural unity. From the Vedic era to the epoch of the freedom struggle, India was imagined as one entity in legends and ballads, in scriptures and stories composed in varied tongues, such as Sanskrit, Prakrit, Pali, Tamil, Hindi, Urdu, and English, with or without any connection to ground realities. In ancient India, innumerable kingdoms of varying sizes ruled, until the Maurya dynasty was established by Chandragupta in the fourth century BC. The Mauryan empire rose to its greatest height under the reign of Asoka, when it nearly occupied the whole of the Indian peninsula. No Indian empire ever grew as big again until the emergence of Emperor Akbar. In the period before the emergence of Akbar, India witnessed many empires, such as the Delhi Sultanate, Deccan Sultanate, Gupta Empire, Harsha Empire, Chalukya Empire, Kushan Empire, Vijayanagar Empire, etc., in various parts of the country. The unification of India under the Moghuls was weakened after their dynasty declined. Even as the Moghul dynasty was getting weakened, many empires, such as those of the Marathas, Sikhs, the Deccan Sultanates, Mysore, and Kakatiya flourished, with some of them aiming at an 'all-India empire'.

In the meantime, British imperialists supervened in the process and re-established an all-India empire, building on the foundations of Moghul rule. The British regime not only reunified India through the central administration, but also generated such nationalist reactions throughout the Indian subcontinent as to lead to a huge movement for independence, beginning with the First War of Independence in 1857 and proceeding to the establishment of the Indian National Congress Party in 1884. There were also violent revolts in various parts of the country, culminating in the martyrdom of (among others) Sardar Bhagat Singh, and the formation of the Indian National Army under the leadership of Subhas Chandra Bose during World War II. The freedom movement, which came to be led by Gandhiji in its last three decades through his unique technique of non-violent mobilisation of the masses, wove silken bonds of unity among the Indian people, which went beyond the barriers of religion, region, race, caste, and language and produced a new Indian nation.

Although modern India meets all the requirements of the nation-state, such as external sovereignty, internal control of all parts of the country, etc., it is different in a positive way from all others by being the most multilingual, multi-racial, and multi-religious nation in the world. Gandhiji's India thus gave a new definition and a new dimension to the modern concept of nationalism. This multicultural phenomenon of the Indian State provides a paradigmatic example for other nations which are suffering internal conflicts among their cultural entities. It needs to be noted that there is no nation today, big or small, without cultural minorities. The notion of the cultural compactness of a nation needs to be consequently modulated. India is therefore both a prodigious experiment and a positive example. The vision of and leadership provided by Nehru, Patel, Ambedkar, etc., in the post-independence phase paved the way for the emergence of India as a unique nation-state.

Nationalism in Vietnam was bred through reactions against French imperialism under the revolutionary leadership of Ho Chi Minh (1890–1969). It also had to contend with a great war with the USA under the political leadership of Ho Chi Minh and the military leadership of General Vo Nguyen Giap for the unification of Vietnam. Even after this unification, they pursued nationalist objectives to the point of fighting a war with China after the Vietnamese Revolution.

Similarly, Indonesia's nationalism triumphed when Sukarno (1901–70), the first President of Indonesia, liberated his country from Dutch imperialism.

In ancient Greece, which marked the commencement of Western civilisation, city-republics prevailed. All these city-republics were united only to repel the invasion by the Persian Empire in the fifth century BC. This first war between an Eastern empire and a Western region was graphically depicted by Herodotus, the world's first historian. But after the successful war with the Persian Empire, the city-republics of ancient Greece did not proceed to become a nation, but instead retained their original independent status. What was more, the city-republics soon began to fight among themselves. The most memorable of these fights was the Peloponnesian war between Athens, led by Pericles, and Sparta. Although Sparta won in the end, its victory was pyrrhic in that the war itself brought the glory of Greece to an end, leading to its incorporation into Alexander's empire and eventual absorption into the Roman Empire. Thus, the Greek city-republics, which shone for a short period as nascent nations, lost their independence and failed to become examples of nationhood in the ancient world. Even Athens, which achieved its pinnacle with Pericles as its supreme leader, and Socrates, Plato, and Aristotle as founding philosophers of the West, was only a small city-republic. It soared like a rocket of nationalist fire, but fell like a comet.

The fall of Athens and Greece was followed by the conquests of 'Alexander the Great' and the emergence of the Roman Empire. The Roman Empire continued to expand at a frenetic pace, incorporating new races and geographical areas. Its vast area and populations were not characterised by any feeling of nationality for want of cultural homogeneity, but were united only by effective central administration through one common law. Roman Catholicism, which succeeded the Roman Empire after the conversion of Constantine I, governed through its religious law. During the regimes of both the Roman Empire and Roman Catholicism, the concept of nation did not figure at all. The idea of a nation based on language had to wait for more than 1,000 years in the West, and it acquired a practical shape only after the Reformation.

Ancient times in West Asia and parts of Africa were characterised by absolute dynasties, although marked by their respective civilisations such as the Sumerian, Babylonian, Mesopotamian, Egyptian, etc. The regimes of Islam, which succeeded these civilisations, were dominated by the religious concepts of the Caliphate, and not by notions of a nation. Most countries in West Asia happened to be formed by accidents of history or by the designs of erstwhile colonialists. The ideas of a modern nation-state are yet to prevail there, although the Arabic people share the commonality of race (Arab), language (Arabic), religion (Islam), and even sect (Sunni). The ongoing and never-ending crises of the region substantially owe their origin to the non-emergence of nationalism, which shows that nationalism is a necessary phase that every people have to go through as part of modernisation, nay, of globalisation.

Nationalism began with the decline of the medieval system, which had been influenced by the Roman Papacy for 1,000 years in Western Europe. In every country, the trigger was provided by the reaction to foreign domination, or perceived threat from domination. For example, it began in France with the young peasant girl Joan of Arc's resistance to the English (during the Hundred Years' War) in the 1420s. The unexpected victory of Joan of Arc, nicknamed 'The Maid of Orleans', provided the first impulse to the patriotic pride of the French. Although she was tried for witchcraft and heresy and burned at the stake in 1431, at the age of nineteen, she was later canonised in 1920 and hailed as a martyr. St. Joan can therefore be regarded as the first martyr to the cause of nationalism. Although nationalist sentiment was thus generated in France, republican sentiment took three more centuries to break out. In the meantime, the Bourbon dynasty ruled in a despotic manner and the French developed vast colonies throughout the world, with wanton disregard for the national sentiment of local people in their colonies. Napoleon Bonaparte (1769–1821), the greatest modern conqueror, set out to conquer Europe and other parts of the world by appealing to the nationalist spirit of the French, while inspiring others with the promise of the progressive ideals of the French Revolution. Although Napoleon was eventually defeated, the patriotic pride of the French has forever remained. Charles De Gaulle (1890–1970) represented that spirit in the twentieth century in the same way, and almost to the same degree as Napoleon. Regardless of France's fluctuating fortunes, and the pioneering role that it played in forming and developing a supra-nationalist entity like the European Union, any call for the glory of France generates the same kind of resonance even today as it did in the past.

Nationalism, which began in England during the reign of the House of Tudor (1485–1603), acquired fervour with resistance to the Spanish Armada in the 1580s. Spain embarked on this invasion with two objectives. The first was to dethrone the Queen of England, Elizabeth I, and the second was to overthrow the Tudor establishment of Protestantism. By the time the Spanish Armada took place, national conflicts had begun to acquire a sectarian colour, as the Spanish had become champions of Catholicism while the English championed Protestantism. Poets, notably William Shakespeare (1564–1616), gave literary expression to the patriotic sentiments of the English at the time. While English nationalism was becoming increasingly liberal at home, Englishmen set out to establish their intercontinental empire in every part of the globe. Triumphant nationalism, whether liberal or otherwise, has this tendency to acquire imperial dimensions abroad. The British were not willing to grant independence to their siblings in America, because of which the Americans had to wage and win a war under the leadership of George Washington (1732–99), the first President of the United States, in the last quarter of the eighteenth century.

The Conservative Party under the leadership of Prime Minister Winston Churchill (1874–1965) was not prepared to grant independence to India even after World War II. The victory of the Labour Party under the leadership of Clement Attlee (1883–1967) in 1945 played its part in granting independence to India. It is another matter that modern Indians are more impressed by the bombastic oratory of Winston Churchill than by the anti-colonial progressivism of Attlee. The role played by the UK and France in the Suez Crisis showed that they were not prepared to respect the nationalist sentiments of Egyptians even in the late 1950s. Regardless of the imperialist record of the UK, the historical fact is that nationalism in the modern world started with England in the early sixteenth century.

Although the city of Florence unleashed a tide of patriotic pride amongst Italians by throwing up their literary giant, Dante Alighieri (or simply Dante, 1265–1321), in the fourteenth century, and ushering in the Renaissance in the fifteenth and sixteenth centuries, which witnessed such preeminent artists as Leonardo Da Vinci and Michelangelo and a pioneering political thinker such as Machiavelli, it took three more centuries for Italians to be unified into a nation. This inordinate delay was caused by the fact that its provinces were plunged in internecine conflicts. It was imperialist threat from Austria that lit the last spark of Italian nationalism. Italian politician and journalist Giuseppe Mazzini (1805–72) initiated the movement in Italy in the nineteenth century. It amounted to challenging the agreement reached at the Congress of Vienna in 1814, which, under the guidance of Metternich, redrew the map of Europe. The task was therefore huge and had to be pursued by Garibaldi and others right into the early twentieth century.

Mazzini was a prophet not only of Italian nationalism, but also of nationalism in the world. He said, 'Nationality is sacred to me, because I see in it the influence of labour for the good and progress of all men' (Russell 1934: 351). In fact, he assigned a certain function to each nation in Europe. To summarise Mazzini's vision in the words of Bertrand Russell, 'Mazzini thought that England should look after industry and colonies; Russia should handle the task of civilising Asia; Poland was to take care of Slavs; Germany was to think and

France was to act; and Italy was to unite thought with action' (ibid.). It is another matter that even Mazzini envisioned a divine role for his country, Italy, and a special role for Europe. Despite the limitations of his vision, he provided inspiration to nationalists all over the world during their anti-colonial struggles in the twentieth century.

Even before Mazzini, Lord George Gordon Byron (1788–1824), the romantic English poet who died a martyr in the early nineteenth century to the cause of the freedom of Greece from the Turks, espoused the freedom of all nations. Byron's sacrifice was unique in that he had fought for the freedom of a country he did not belong to. He was an archetypal product of romantic fascination with the historical glory of ancient Greece.

German nationalism was aroused through resistance to Napoleon. Johann Gottlieb Fichte (1762–1814), through his addresses to the nation in the early nineteenth century, directly appealed to all German people to unite, despite being under different regimes. Fichte believed in the superiority of the German race and the purity of the German language. After Napoleon's defeat at the Battle of Waterloo in 1815 and the Congress of Vienna, nationalism as such was disfavoured under the influence of Metternich, and Fichte's addresses were proscribed. However, the emotional and intellectual impact of Fichte survived all such political fluctuations. Otto von Bismarck (1815–1898) used the German sentiment during the three wars he won for Prussia—against Denmark in 1864; the Seven Weeks' War (1866), and the Franco-Prussian war (1870–71)—to unify most of the Germans under the Prussian king. Apart from Bismarck's epic achievement, the powerful ideas of philosophers like Fichte and Friedrich Nietzsche (1844–1900) helped Adolf Hitler (1889–1945) to develop both the Nazi philosophy and chauvinist Germany. Hitler's example shows that beyond a point, nationalism leads to militaristic jingoism. Hitlerism is not a one-off phenomenon or a thing of the past, but an eternal reminder of such demons lurking in the corner of every nation's mind. Brexit and the phenomenon of Donald Trump are euphemistically portrayed as nativism, but who can guarantee that they are not disturbing symptoms of the atavistic nationalism of both Britain and the USA?

It was not easy for the United States of America to become a proper nation even after Independence. It took the American Civil War of 1861–65 and the exceptional genius of Abraham Lincoln (1809–65) to cement its unity. Countries in Latin America witnessed decolonisation movements in the early nineteenth century, but soon fell into the hands of dictators, a situation that persisted right into the twentieth century. This apart, their national independence has been subjected to the Monroe doctrine imposed by the US right from the early nineteenth century. At any rate, the state of nationalism in the region has been differing from country to country.

Anthony D. Smith, in *Nationalism and Modernism* (1998), points out that nationalism emerged fitfully in the sixteenth and seventeenth centuries in England and Holland, but emerged clearly in late eighteenth-century France and America. It then made its way in many guises in Central and Latin America; Southern, Central, and Northern Europe; and Russia, India, and the Far East. It then further marched into the Middle East, Africa, and Australasia. Although the forms of nationalism in these countries assumed different shapes, there was a central thread that bound and divided the people of the modern world. Whatever be its various shapes and sizes, Smith asserts that nationalism is a modern movement. He also argues that while it reached its apogee in the two World Wars, it has now begun to decline with global forces transcending the boundaries of nation-states. Despite such relatively recent assertions by scholars, we now see clearly that the global forces have begun to recede. This reassertion of nationalism has been provoked by economic globalisation, as well as by ethnic reactions to immigrations.

Historians may differ over the exact moment of nationalism's birth, but social scientists are clear: nationalism is a modern movement.

> In chapter 7 of Nations and Nationalism, 'Thoughts and Change', Gellner develops his key arguments by focussing on the 'break in human history'—the transition of society from pre-industrial

> (agrarian) to industrial—to explain this transition, which radically changed the human condition, but was sufficiently specific to be understood, especially as it was accompanied by the emergence of reason and science which provides us with the requisite intellectual tools .... (Breuilly 2006: xxii)

Supporting Gellner's reflections, E. J. Hobsbawm (1990) says,

> ... along with Gellner, I would stress the element of artefact, invention and social engineering which enters into the making of nations. Nations as a natural, God-given way of classifying men as an inherent ... political destiny is a myth; nationalism which sometimes takes pre-existing cultures and turns them into nations, sometimes invents them and often obliterates pre-existing cultures; that is a reality. (cited in Gellner 1983: 48–49)

Aside from the continuing debate on the nature of nationalism, a rapid survey of vast areas of the globe has been offered so far to demonstrate that the ancient history of no part of the world witnessed any significant nationalist periods, and that it is the modern age that has thrown up nationalism as a new phenomenon. The most positive achievement of nationalism in the twentieth century was decolonisation and the consequent freedom of a large number of states in Asia, Africa, and South America. The most negative consequences of nationalism can be seen from World Wars I and II. World War II, through the deployment of atom bombs, reduced all previous wars in history to a child's game. Atom bombs have since become a thousand times more powerful. This atomic race has been further compounded by other kinds of weapons of mass destruction. The United Nations (UN), which was formed in the wake of World War II to eliminate global tensions, has proved ineffective. The major global powers like the United States, the Russian Federation, and China are now further engaged in refining their weapons and delivery systems. The Cold War at least wore the pleasing disguise of an ideological race. The current race is nakedly nationalistic, and has all the storm-signals of a global apocalypse. Apart from larger global conflicts, the problem of ethnic minorities in each nation-state is getting more tense by the day. At the risk of sounding trite, one can only say that global humanism needs to be revived and strengthened to douse the conflicts among nations, and ethnic conflicts within nations. A point has now been reached where one has to wonder: Has nationalism returned with a bang as the most serious menace to international peace?

Nationalism, which was once a positive force, seems to have turned into a Frankenstein's monster. As far back as 1919, playwright George Bernard Shaw (1856–1950) had the foresight to say: 'You will never have a quiet world till you knock the patriotism out of human race'.[1] Albert Einstein also said, 'Nationalism is an infantile sickness. It is the measles of the human race.'[2] Rabindranath Tagore (1861–1941), the first Asian to receive the Nobel Prize for Literature, had spoken about the negative aspects of nationalism even before Shaw and Einstein, in 1917, and said the following:

> The ... spirit of conflict and conquest is at the origin and ... centre of the western nationals .... It has evolved a perfect organisation of power, but not spiritual idealism .... In fact, these nations are fighting among themselves for the extension of their victims and their reserve forests .... Western Nation acts like a dam to check the free flow of the Western civilization .... Because this civilization is the civilization of power, therefore it is exclusive, ... naturally unwilling to open its sources ... to those whom it has selected for its purposes of exploitation. (Tagore 2012a: 19)

While delivering his lecture in Japan in the same year (1917), Tagore observed:

> What is dangerous for Japan is, not the imitation of the outer features of the West, but the acceptance of the motive force of the Western nationalism as her own. Her social ideals are already showing signs of defeat at the hands of politics .... Nations, who sedulously cultivate moral blindness as the cult of patriotism, will end their existence in a sudden and violent death. (Tagore 2012b: 69–70)

---

[1] *Bernard Shaw O' Flaherty V.C.* (1919), 178. Taken from *Oxford Dictionary of Modern Quotations* (1991: 273).

[2] Albert Einstein, *The Human Side* (1979), 38. Taken from *Oxford Dictionary of Modern Quotations* (1991: 99).

Tagore's prescience can be seen in the poem, 'The Sunset of the Century', which he wrote in Bengali (and which he personally translated into English) on the last day of the nineteenth century (31 December 1899), long before World Wars I and II:

> THE LAST SUN of the century sets amidst the blood-red clouds of the West and the whirlwind of hatred.
> The naked passion of self-love of Nations, in its drunken delirium of greed, is dancing to the clash of steel and the howling verses of vengeance.
> The hungry self of the Nation shall burst in a violence of fury from its own shameless feeding.
> For it has made the world its food,
> And licking it, crunching it, and swallowing it in big morsels,
> It swells and swells
> Till in the midst of its unholy feast descends the sudden heaven piercing its heart of grossness.
> The crimson glow of light on the horizon is not the light of thy dawn of peace, my Motherland.
> It is the glimmer of the funeral pyre burning to ashes the vast flesh, the self-love of the Nation, dead under its own excess.
> Thy morning waits behind the patient dark of the East, Meek and silent.
> Keep watch, India.
> Bring your offerings of worship for that sacred sunrise.
> Let the first hymn of its welcome sound in your voice, and sing.
> Come, Peace, thou daughter of God's own great suffering.
> Come with thy treasure of contentment, the sword of fortitude,
> And meekness crowning thy forehead.
> Be not ashamed, my brothers, to stand before the proud and the powerful,
> With your white robe of simpleness.
> Let your crown be of humility, your freedom the freedom of the soul,
> Build God's throne daily upon the ample bareness of your poverty.
> And know that what is huge is not great and pride is not everlasting.[3] (Tagore 2012c: 117–19)

[3] Written in Bengali and translated into English by Tagore himself.

As we have seen so far, not only through the events of history but also through the visions of poets, philosophers, and scientists, nationalism has both positive and negative aspects. Its results depend on the uses it is put to. It is emancipating when used to bestow freedom on a group of suppressed people, but enslaving when used to conquer other groups of alienated people.

6

DEMOCRACY

Small tribal societies, which marked the beginning of political history, were necessarily democratic in that they could take decisions only in assemblies of all people where everybody's voice counted equally. In due course, some of them developed democratic procedures and became republics in their own way. This was the case in ancient India, too, with *ganatantra* republics and *janapadhs*. The same was true with ancient Greece and ancient Rome as well.

Even in political thought and practice, systems in ancient India were on the same level as in the city-states of Greece, except the city-state of Athens. Only Athens witnessed a more advanced form of democratic institutions under the leadership of Pericles. However, this phenomenon was not sustained, and was in fact of short duration. Athens was a small city-republic with a population of 400,000, out of which 150,000 were slaves without voting rights. For the rest (except women), who were equal and free citizens, it was a direct democracy, with everybody enjoying voting rights and participating in public debates. Pericles was not only a charismatic leader for thirty years, but also an outstanding general. He could mobilise the masses, as he was clearly for the poor and against the rich. His critics from the patrician class assailed him as a demagogue. He could be elected endlessly, as the poor favoured him as their champion. He can therefore be regarded as the original social democrat (even radical democrat) of the world. What was more, he preferred the commonsense of the people to the skill of specialists. He was also a great builder, as can be seen from the Parthenon on the Acropolis at Athens even now.

Athens, Sparta, and other city-states of Greece were all united in fighting the Persian invasion, but came to be divided amongst themselves after their great victory. There was rivalry between Athens and Sparta. As Sparta frankly represented a military autocracy, this rivalry also assumed a serious ideological dimension, with Athens representing and pleading for democracy. These tensions eventually led to a long fratricidal war between Athens and Sparta, known as the Peloponnesian War (431–404 BC). Athens was hit by a huge plague amidst the war, in which Pericles died. According to the celebrated historian Thucydides, Athens, which lost the war in the end, could have won if Pericles had survived the plague and led the Athenian forces until the end. The war was not seen as merely a conflict between the two city-republics, but was proclaimed as a war between democratic Athens and despotic Sparta. The great funeral oration delivered by Pericles in the memory of martyred soldiers in the midst of battle, at the end of the first year of the Peloponnesian War, as part of the annual public funeral for the war dead, describes the incandescent ideological character of the war, and the democratic fervour of Pericles. In order to savour the flavour of the oration, some parts of it are reproduced hereunder:

> We are lovers of beauty without extravagance, and lovers of wisdom without unmanliness. Wealth to us is not mere material for vainglory but an opportunity for achievement; and poverty we think it no disgrace to acknowledge but a real degradation to make no effort to overcome ... Let us draw strength, not merely from twice-told arguments—how fair and noble a thing it is ... to show courage in battle—but from the busy spectacle of our great city's life as we have it before us day by day, falling in love with her as we see her, and remembering that all this greatness she owes to men with the fighter's daring, the wise man's understanding of his duty, and the good man's self-discipline in its performance ... to men who, if they failed in any ordeal, disdained to deprive the city of their services, but ... sacrificed their lives as the best offerings on her behalf. So they gave their bodies to the commonwealth and received, each for his own memory, ... praise that will never die, and with it the grandest of all sepulchres, not that in which their mortal bones

> are laid, but ... a home in the minds of men, where their glory remains fresh to stir to speech or action as the occasion comes by .... For the whole earth is a sepulchre of famous men, and their story is not graven only on stone over their native earth, but lives on far away, without visible symbols, woven into the stuff of other men's lives. For you now it remains to rival what they have done and, knowing the secret of happiness to be freedom and the secret of freedom a brave heart, ... not idly to stand aside from the enemy's onset. (Thucydides, 'Pericles' Funeral Oration')

Pericles believed in the democratic mission of Athens. In the words of George H. Sabine from his classic *A History of Political Theory*: 'This is the meaning of Pericles's proud boast that Athens is the school of Hellas' (1973: 33).

Despite the democratic glory of Athens, this war eventually led to the fall of both Athens and Sparta, and Greece as a whole. Greece, in due course, ended up as a small colony of Alexander's empire, and later of the Roman Empire. Even as Athens fell, it produced great philosophers like Socrates and Plato, who not only produced stratospheric metaphysics, but also pioneered a soaring political philosophy.

Socrates (d. 399 BC) became pre-eminent as a thinker and discourser after Athens had lost the war. He was legendary for his austere life characterised by complete self-denial, which reduced the personal family of Socrates to the level of subsistence and drove his wife, Zanthippe, to despair. Even so, the ruling elites of Athens were despairing of his dialectical logic, which relentlessly exposed the hollowness of democracy after the death of Pericles and the defeat of Athens in the Peloponnesian War. In the process, Socrates discovered and perfected the method of seeking definitions for each word used in a debate. This semantic logic came to establish him as the founder of Western philosophy. While his life of self-sacrifice and his eventual martyrdom lifted the morality of politics to unimaginable heights, his philosophy, though profound and original, was not above controversy. Socrates did not believe in polytheism, which, in other words, meant that he did not believe in the divinity of many gods worshipped by the

Greeks of his day. He, however, believed in the immortality of the soul. He therefore refused to be rescued from the death sentence, pleading that it would only kill his body and not his soul. Socrates blamed the democracy of his day for the defeat of his beloved Athens. He was also impressed by the military prowess of Sparta, so much so that he pleaded for a despotic system.

Plato, the gifted disciple of Socrates, immortalised the latter's metaphysics and politics in his treasured treatises. The burning torch of Athenian democracy, which had been reduced to a flickering flame by its defeat in the Peloponnesian War, was further doused by the cold water poured on it by Socrates and Plato. The portrait of the inspiring personality and philosophy of Socrates drawn in Plato's works is the principal source of knowledge about Socrates. The Platonic Socrates and Plato feared that democracy would inevitably degenerate into mobocracy. Their elitist view was not shared by the Athenian people of their time, despite the defeat of Athens against Sparta. This shows that the glorious experience of Periclean democracy was still animating the people. It is often forgotten that even after the death of Socrates, democracy, such as it existed in Athens then, had the eloquent support of Democritus, a redoubtable rival of Socrates in philosophy; Demosthenes, the greatest orator of ancient Greece; Thucydides, the first professional historian of the world; and many other eminent Athenians. Nevertheless, the execution of Socrates betrayed the limitations of Athenian democracy. Democracy without liberalism is a contradiction in terms. The idea of mixed systems of governance had not yet emerged, and had to wait for the Roman legal system.

Socrates through his life, and Plato through his literature, have since become inexhaustible founts of moral idealism, which by its very nature cannot be controversial. But their metaphysical idealism, though not above controversy in philosophical terms, has provided direction and inspiration to Western philosophy. The other part of their philosophy is political, which is far more controversial, as it makes the State all-powerful. As a result, the ideal State that has been portrayed in Plato's Republic, the greatest utopia ever envisioned, leaves no room for democracy. Plato actually stated that democracy is the second worst form of government, next only to tyranny. For Plato, competence of governance, which can be ensured only through the benevolent dictatorship of his Republic's guardians, was the only consideration. In the world of his imagination, such a thing as liberty did not matter. Plato's conception of the ideal state would be no better than George Orwell's *Animal Farm* (1945). In fact, Plato pleaded that strong women could be chosen to produce capable rulers. Political scientists therefore say that Plato would have been the reddest of reds, had he been alive now. The guardians of Plato's utopia would be chosen on merit and made permanent rulers. Plato had no answer to the question of who and what would regulate the conduct of his guardians. He came up with a half-hearted answer to this quintessential question with his two works, viz., *Statesman* and *Laws*, in his old age. The latter works were less splendid in style, but more realistic in substance.

Aristotle, the great disciple of Plato himself, tried to repair the damage caused to democracy by Socrates and Plato through his great book, *Politics*. No great enthusiasm could, however, be generated about popular participation through democracy for more than 2,000 years for historical reasons. Aristotle built up his philosophy on the basis of the second phase of political thought of his master, Plato. Aristotle's ideal State is constitutional and not utopian. Although he did not plead for democracy as such, he provided for democratic elements in his system. Aristotle did not attach too much importance to the institution of the state, but provided for a proper role for the family and other social institutions. After examining the constitutions of about 120 countries, he concluded that the best form of government is one with a mixed form of constitution, in which elements are drawn judiciously from oligarchy and democracy. He was firmly opposed to the concentration of political power in the hands of individuals or classes. He thus presaged the theory of separation of powers, developed by John Locke and Montesquieu in the modern age.

Ancient Athens failed to see that the days of city-republics were already numbered, and that the era of empires was round the corner. They also failed to see that the solution to the problems posed by the system of direct democracy could lie in representative forms of democratic government.

Rome had had a representative form of government for about five centuries before Julius Caesar (100–44 BC). In the pre-Caesar system, power was broadly divided between the Consuls and the Senators, with an unstable equation between the two. The equations among different tribes were also unstable and managed in various ways. There was also a class element in Roman society, evidenced by the tensions between the patricians (the rich) and the plebeians (the poor). Despite such differences, however, the system had its democratic elements. When Caesar became popular as a military conqueror, some Senators felt that the balance of power was being tilted against the Senate and that the Senate itself was being packed with his loyal supporters. It was against this background that dissenting Senators feared that Caesar was planning to bring back the empire originally present in Rome, and have himself enthroned. These conspirators, led by Marcus Brutus (85–42 BC) and Gaius Cassius (87–42 BC), assassinated Caesar with a view to continuing and strengthening their democracy. But Caesar's murder inevitably led to military conflicts, resulting in the defeat of Brutus and the emergence of Augustus Caesar as the first Roman emperor.

Although Augustus Caesar turned out to be a relatively conscientious ruler, the imperial character of the Roman system was strengthened even during his regime. Yet, the Senate as an institution survived, although in an emaciated form. One of the redeeming features of the Roman Empire was the development of legal systems. As Fareed Zakaria points out:

> [T]he gaping hole in Roman Law, however, was that as a practical matter, it did not apply to the ruling class, particularly as the republic degenerated into monarchy by the first century. Emperors such as Nero, Vitellius, and Galba routinely sentenced

> people to death without trial, pillaged private homes and temples and raped and murdered their subjects. Caligula famously had his horse appointed senator .... (Zakaria 2003: 33)

The lesson from Rome's republican years is that strong institutions, rather than good intentions, are required to protect democracy. The Papacy, which succeeded the Roman Empire, acquired the authoritarian character of the empire more than the piety of early Christianity. As a result of all these developments, the medieval age in Europe witnessed the wholesale erosion of democratic institutions. England proved an exception to the European pattern when its monarchy signed the Magna Carta in the early thirteenth century to concede certain rights for a free church, reform of law and justice, and for the regulation of the behaviour of royal officials. Although the Magna Carta was only a compact between the monarchy and nobles, it led to the weakening of the former. In the seventeenth century, the monarchy had to give way to the Parliament in the English Civil Wars of 1642–51, a series of armed conflicts between Parliamentarians and Royalists over the manner of England's government. Oliver Cromwell (1599–1658) led the parliamentary side, and the first war was settled with Cromwell's victory for Parliamentary forces at the 1645 Battle of Naseby. King Charles I was brought to trial, found guilty of high treason, and executed in January 1649.

As Lord Protector of the Commonwealth of England, Scotland, and Ireland, Cromwell pursued democracy and permitted personal liberty, from which the right of judgement emerged. The idea of individual conscience arose powerfully in the wake of the Protestant Reformation led by Martin Luther, who asserted every Christian's right to read the Bible for himself/herself without the intermediation of the Church. This, in turn, paved the way for a popular assertion of personal freedoms. John Milton, in his memorable tract 'Areopagitica' (1644), pleading for unlicensed printing, said the following:

> And though all the winds of doctrine were let loose to play upon the earth, so Truth be in the field, we do injuriously by licensing and prohibiting to misdoubt her strength. Let her and Falsehood

> grapple; who ever knew Truth put to the worse, in a free and open encounter .... For who knows not that truth is strong next to the Almighty, she needs no policies, nor stratagems, not licensings to make her victorious, those are the shifts and defences that error uses against her power.

Milton was not afraid of the prospect of the multiplication of sects and parties as experiments in the quest for new truth and new freedom. Even he had a blind spot when it came to the toleration of Catholicism. Apart from this exception, Milton is second to none in history in propagating the right to free expression, which is the foundation of democracy.

Although the English monarchy returned after the death of Cromwell, it was soon de-fanged through the Glorious Revolution of 1688, when James II was overthrown by the joint monarchy of his Protestant daughter Mary and her Dutch husband, William of Orange. The new co-monarchy accepted more constraints from Parliament, and the new constitution created the expectation that future monarchs would also remain similarly constrained. After the Revolution, Parliament exercised complete control in matters of legislation and finance. In due course, Parliament also extended its authority into the field of executive action. By the middle of the eighteenth century, the monarchy had become completely constitutional, and the supremacy of Parliament was established. Above all, this revolution of 1688 led to both the American and French Revolutions. The low-profile philosopher of the 'Glorious Revolution' of 1688, John Locke (1632–1704), propounded the theory that the right to life, to liberty, and to estate is natural and inviolable for every individual. He further argued that this natural right of man is created by an original social contract, which precedes the establishment of government. He also argued that violation of the terms of this contract confers the right on society to depose and replace the rulers. In order to ensure that violation does not occur, he prescribed the separation of the powers of government and legislation. This remedy was further reinforced when, in the eighteenth century, the French thinker Montesquieu (Charles-Louis de Secondat, Baron de La Brède et de *Montesquieu;* 1689–1755) added that the powers of the judiciary should also be made independent.

It needs to be clarified that while Locke was generous in granting the right to life and liberty, he was cautious about defining estate or property, even as he conceded its right. Locke's democratic theories proved to be the foundation for democracy, not just in England, France, and America, but all over the world. More than three centuries later, they continue to resonate, albeit with the complaint that his right to property has come to be massively misused by corporates. George Sabine says that Locke's

> right to property arises because by labour a man extends, so to speak, his own personality into the objects produced. By expending his internal energy upon them he makes them a part of himself. In general, their utility depends upon the labour expended upon them, and thus Locke's theory led to the later labour theories of value in classical and socialist economics. (Sabine 1973: 487)

It is evident, according to Sabine, that it was Locke who provided the labour theories to the influential British classical economist, David Ricardo (1772–1823). There is therefore a need to understand that endowing multinational corporates with the rights of actual persons was farthest from Locke's thoughts. Locke, as the most non-doctrinaire philosopher in history, would not have minded any improvement on his thought. Lockeans should therefore not be hobbled by doctrinal nostrums.

The English example of constitutional monarchy played a major role in the evolution of modern constitutional democracy. However, the English Parliament itself was not very democratic in character, except that the balance of power had shifted from the King to Parliament. The English Parliament was oligarchic, as the landed gentry was the overwhelming force in the hereditary 'House of Lords'. What was more, the 'House of Commons' was also dominated by this class because of limited franchise, and marked inequalities of representation. The struggle for change in the character of British Parliament yielded the first successful result in the form of the Reform Bill of 1832. Although the aims of the Reform Bill were radical, the actual implications were moderate in that the number of voters went up from about 500,000 to 813,000. Due to this limited increase in the number of voters, political power still rested in the hands of wealthier classes. Yet, it made a significant class difference in that control shifted from the agricultural and commercial aristocracy that had monopolised it since 1689 to the newer industrial aristocracy and the upper bourgeoisie.

Parliamentary institutions in Britain did not make much progress because of their feudal character for more than a century. The push for further reforms came from the Chartist movement, a British working-class movement for parliamentary reform that existed from 1838 to 1857. Their People's Charter made six demands: manhood suffrage; annual parliaments; vote by secret ballot; no property qualification; payment of members; and equal electoral districts. The Chartist movement was suppressed and many of its leaders imprisoned. The aims of this movement were partially achieved only when British statesman John Bright (1811–89), himself a middle-class cotton manufacturer, took interest in the franchise for urban working men. Benjamin Disraeli (1804–81), being a shrewd politician, seized the occasion and got the bill passed in 1867. In the 1867 Bill, franchise was conferred on urban working men, while excluding rural labourers. The latter got their franchise at the initiative of Gladstone in 1885. Despite these reforms, recognition of the right of all adult males to vote did not come until 1918. Full women's suffrage had to wait until 1928. It can now be seen that it took a century for the extension of the franchise in Great Britain, the country which had started the parliamentary system.

The theories of the English philosopher John Locke (1632–1704) were enormously popularised during the French Enlightenment under the leadership of Voltaire (or François-Marie Arouet, 1694–1778). John Locke influenced not only the French Revolution, but also the basic scheme of the Constitution developed in America. While Voltaire and other French Encyclopaedists (the Encyclopaedists were members of a French writer's society, who contributed to the development of the Encyclopaedia from June 1751 to December 1765, under editors Denis Diderot and Jean le Rond d'Alembert) were content with Locke's theory, Voltaire's ideological rival, Jean-Jacques Rousseau (1712–78), insisted that no democratic law would be legitimate except as an expression of the general will, a consensus of the whole community. In his book *The Social Contract* (1762), Rousseau favoured direct democracy of the kind prevalent in ancient Greece, although it was no longer practicable. Even though he was not a polymath, his radical approach and romantic appeal to the poets and thinkers were enormously influential.

The American Revolution, though motivated mainly by the desire for independence, witnessed the first major experiment in constitutional democracy. The American Declaration of Independence (drafted by Thomas Jefferson [1743–1826], the third President of the United States [1801–09], in 1776) was directly inspired by the ideas of John Locke. Among other things, it stated:

> We hold these truths to be self-evident: that all men are created equal; that they are endowed by their Creator with certain inalienable rights; that among these are life, liberty, and the pursuit of happiness; that to secure these rights governments are instituted among men, deriving their just powers from the consent of the governed; that whenever any form of government becomes destructive of these ends, it is the right of the people to alter or abolish it. (Russell 1934: 232)

The real significance of the American Revolution lies in the fact that the government it threw up was both constitutional and democratic. Franchise was generally broadened, although property qualifications were retained for a long period. The democratic principle was recognised in that the state and national legislators, Governors and the President, were to be chosen by the people, but the power of popular majorities and governments was stringently regulated by an elaborate system of checks and counter-checks. This system of separation of powers amongst the three organs, viz., the President, the Congress, and the Judiciary, was the direct result of the impact of the theories of John Locke and Montesquieu. Thomas Jefferson was hugely important in shaping American democracy. His doctrine had two aspects: (*i*) it should be democratic; and (*ii*) there should be as little government as possible. With regard to joint action, Jefferson also asserted that the will of the majority should prevail, but without treading on certain inalienable natural rights. Bertrand Russell, in *Freedom Versus Organisation* (1934), comments thus:

> Jefferson deserves to be regarded as the founder of American democracy for three reasons; first, he wrote the Declaration of Independence; second, he led and largely created the Republican Party, by which the Federalists, who were anti-democratic, were overthrown; third, he was the first President who believed in democracy and sought to establish it. (ibid.: 229)

Jefferson, while retiring as the third President of America in 1809, said that Americans were the

> sole depositories of the remains of human liberty, our duty to ourselves, to posterity, and to mankind, call upon us by every motive which is sacred or honourable, to watch over the safety of our beloved country, during the troubles which agitate and convulse the residue of the world. (Russell 1934: 226)

Fifty-four years later, the same exalted feeling informed Abraham Lincoln's Gettysburg address. Lincoln said:

> Four score and seven years ago, our fathers brought forth on this continent, a new nation, conceived in liberty, and dedicated to the proposition that all men are created equal. Now we are engaged in a great civil war, testing whether that nation, or any nation so conceived and so dedicated, can long endure .... This nation, under God, shall have a new birth of freedom—and the government of the people, by the people, for the people, shall not perish from the earth. (Lincoln 1967: 51)

Two things need to be noted from the above quotation. The first is that Lincoln was concerned about equality among citizens of all nations; and the second is that he provided the best definition of democracy by asserting that the government of the people and by the people should also be for the people. The common feeling among Americans that Great Britain, after being the first modern democratic nation, had later halted somewhat in advancing the cause of democracy was reflected in the poem by the national poet of America, Walt Whitman (1819–92):

> Have the elder races halted?
> Do they droop and end their lesson, wearied over there beyond the seas?
> We take up the task eternal, and the burden and the lesson, Pioneers,
> O pioneers! (Whitman 2004)

By the middle of the nineteenth century, constitutional democracy in America had attained maturity with the adoption of adult male suffrage. However, two broad limitations, viz., the denial of suffrage to women and Blacks, were still operative. But by the standards of the time, democracy in America was the most advanced in the world, even more advanced than in Britain. This quiet revolution was celebrated by Alexis de Tocqueville, French diplomat, political scientist, and historian (1805–59), in his *Democracy in America* (1835).

The next great landmark in the history of modern democracy was the French Revolution. Inspiration for this Revolution was derived from the intellectual tsunami of the Enlightenment, led by Voltaire and the Encyclopaedists. Rousseau, who sharply differed from the tone and tenor of the Encyclopaedists, provided his own fiery fillip. Voltaire, who had derived his inspiration from the science of Isaac Newton and the philosophy of Locke during his forced sojourn in London, set France on fire upon his return through his histories and satires. He pilloried nobles and clergymen in such a devastating manner that the French laughed at them to their hearts' content. As French poet, journalist, and novelist Anatole France (1844–1924) said, 'In Voltaire's fingers, the pen runs and laughs' (Durant 1991: 227). Voltaire provided leadership to intellectual giants like Diderot (1713–84), D'Alembert (1717–83), and the others who produced the great Encyclopaedia volumes from 1752–72. As Thomas Paine (1737–1809) put it, this inaugurated the age of reason. As Sabine rightly points out, Voltaire's ideas of religion and toleration were not new in themselves, as they were derived from John Locke. But they assumed a radical tone as the environment in France, be it of the government or of the Church, was so conservative as to make even moderately liberal ideas subversive.

The French Enlightenment emancipated Europe from its medieval mindset and inspired it to go beyond its Hellenic heritage. What is more, it continues to inspire the world with its message of freedom, justice, and reason.

The influence exerted by Rousseau was different from that of Voltaire, Diderot, D'Alembert, Claude Adrien Helvetius (1715–71), Baron d'Holbach (1723–89), Anne Robert Jacques Turgot (1727–81), and Marquis de Condorcet (1743–94), both in ideological and emotional terms. While Rousseau, through his *Social Contract* and his elemental appeal to the nobility of human instincts, was romantic in his impact, Voltaire and the others were deeply rational and analytical in their approach. With all their differences, they inspired the French Revolution to an incalculable extent. Without their impetus, the Revolution would not have been possible. When the Revolution actually broke out, it was not only France, but also the whole of the Western world that experienced deep and long tremors. Never has a single public event in history convulsed the people so much and for so long as the French Revolution. William Wordsworth rhapsodised his privilege to have witnessed it[1]:

> Bliss was it in the dawn to be alive,
> But to be young was very heaven.

It also aroused elemental fears amongst the kings and nobles of the time. Irish statesman Edmund Burke (1729–97), a champion of freedom himself, reacted against the killing of the Emperor and Empress of France, and wrote a fierce declamation. It can thus be seen that the Revolution left behind a mixed legacy. Despite its mixed character, the Revolution itself unleashed the forces of freedom on an unprecedented

[1] William Wordsworth, taken from *The Concise Dictionary of Oxford Quotations*, 246.

scale at the global level, thereby giving a radical push to the progress of democracy. Above all, it immortalised the ideal of a society based on liberty, fraternity, and equality. It was embodied in a series of legal reforms, from the Declaration of the Rights of Man to the Napoleonic Code.

In other European countries, the main impetus towards democratic movement came from the ideas of the French Revolution. When Louis XVIII returned to France, he was obliged to issue a constitution, which practically converted France into a constitutional monarchy, based formally on the British pattern. The example of France, which imitated the British system in letter without following it in spirit, was extended to other European countries. Even this limited imitation is surprising, because the Congress of Vienna, held in 1814, had redrawn the map of Europe to facilitate the return of the monarchies to their respective kingdoms. Despite the discomfiture of the French Revolution and the defeat of Napoleon, the residual momentum of the French Revolution throughout Europe was such that this obeisance had to be paid to democratic forms. However, this obeisance gained no substance for a century, as much of nineteenth-century Europe was dominated by powerful dynasties.

Germans, for example, had not only been divided, but also ruled by numerous feudal princes for nearly 200 years without any trace of democracy. They were united by Bismarck in the 1860s into a powerful Prussian empire which lasted up to 1918, but experienced no democratic freedoms. Democracy in Germany came to be established in 1918, but shortly gave place to Hitler's Nazi regime. It was only after World War II and the division of Germany that West Germany came to enjoy democracy. Democracy was extended to the erstwhile East Germany in the early 1990s with the unification of Germany. Germany has since been enjoying unity, democracy, prosperity, and welfare. For all the dizzying heights that Germans rose to in various phases of their history, their democratic experience has not been long. Germany's democratic character is once again being threatened by the resurgence of ultra-nationalist elements.

France has a history of centuries of monarchy, which culminated in the absolute rule by Louis XIV in the last quarter of the seventeenth century. This rule lasted a century, and was terminated by the French Revolution in 1789. While the Revolution unleashed both democratic and radical forces that affected not only France, but also the entire world, it failed to develop democratic institutions on the soil of France. On the contrary, it exposed the French to the tumult of the Revolution as well as to the wars of Napoleon. After the defeat of Napoleon, monarchy was restored, and lasted from 1814 to 1871. After the fall of the Second Empire and the suppression of the Paris Commune, the New Constitutional Laws were adopted in 1875, establishing a regime based on parliamentary supremacy. This regime, which came to be known as the Third Republic, lasted till 1940. It was in this period that France experienced democracy and industrialisation. But the third Republic came to an end when Germany occupied France between 1940 and 1945. Democracy could be restored in France only in 1945 after the defeat of Germany in World War II, and has since been prevailing. Even while going through several traumas—the despotism of the Bourbons, the Reign of Terror, the tragedy of Napoleon, the experience of the Paris Commune, and the humiliation of German occupation—it never relinquished its colonial conquests and pursuits.

Greece, as we noted earlier in this chapter, provided not only the ancient cradle of philosophy, science, literature, and culture, but also the democratic legacy of Pericles for the entire West. Despite the glory of its hoary heritage, Greece had to endure the conquest of Alexander, the rule of the Roman Empire, the Byzantine Empire, and the Ottoman Empire for more than 2,000 years, before gaining independence in 1832. Even independence led not to democracy, but to monarchy. It then had to experience the humiliating occupation by Nazi Germany during World War II. Even after the German troops left, the Greeks could not enjoy democracy for long, but allowed themselves to be ruled by the military junta from 1967–74. It is only since 1974 that Greece has had democratic governments.

Ancient Italy inherited the mantle of Greek legacy with Rome becoming the capital of the Roman Empire. Unlike Greece, however, Italy witnessed its glory for a much longer period. The Republic of Rome was founded in 509 BC, but it was replaced by the Empire that came to be established in 27 BC. Both during the Roman Republic and the Roman Empire, it witnessed the efflorescence of legal philosophies and systems based on the principle of mixed governments. Despite its promising beginnings, democracy came to be eviscerated during both the Roman Republic and the Roman Empire, and was buried formally during the Roman Papacy. Although the Italian city of Florence was the first to experience the Renaissance in the fifteenth century, Italy did not experience unity, much less democracy, for three more centuries. It was through the nationalist efforts of politician and activist Giuseppe Mazzini and General Giuseppe Garibaldi (1807–82) that the unification of peninsular Italy was completed by 1870. But Italy experienced social unrest in the 1920s, which brought to power Benito Mussolini (1883–1945), leader of the National Fascist Party. Italy became a democracy only after the defeat of Mussolini in World War II, and has since remained one.

A small country like Portugal managed to spread and establish colonies in Brazil, Goa (India), East Timor, Angola, Mozambique, and Macao. But it did not become a democracy until Antonio de Oliveira Salazar (1889–1970), Prime Minister of Portugal from 1932–68, was removed from office in 1968.

Notwithstanding changes in dynasties, Spain remained under monarchy from the Middle Ages until 1931. The Spanish did not experience democratic freedoms during these long centuries; on the contrary, Spain came to be known for the Spanish Inquisition, established in 1478 by Catholic monarchs Ferdinand II of Aragon and Isabella I of Castile as a court for the detection of heretics. The Inquisition gained notoriety for burning the scientist Giordano Bruno at the stake, and for imprisoning the celebrated astronomer Galileo for supporting the heliocentric theory. The monarchy also came to be marked for sponsoring the navigation of Christopher

Columbus (d. 1506), who discovered the Americas in the fifteenth century, leading to the establishment of Spanish colonies in the Americas. Spain, after losing all its colonies, became a republic in 1931. However, this republic did not last long. In the Spanish Civil War (1936–39), the victory of the nationalists under General Francisco Franco (1892–1975) led to his dictatorship until his death in 1975. Spain, therefore, became a constitutional monarchy as well as democracy. In other words, France had to wait for the death of its dictator Franco to become a democracy.

It is evident from the foregoing account that substantial regions of even Western Europe had to wait till almost the last quarter of the twentieth century for a taste of democracy.

It should be noted that beyond the so-called developed world, democratic institutions have less depth. The causes are primarily historical. With regard to non-Western Christian nations, which primarily cover Russia, the Balkans, and Ukraine, there is a need to go back to the 'Schism' of AD 1054. This division led to a formal break, which further led to the establishment of the Orthodox Catholic Church in Constantinople. While the countries under the Roman Catholic Church were exposed to the breeze of the Renaissance and the storm of the Reformation, those under the Orthodox Church were far removed from them. The Orthodox Church thus escaped both the experiences of the Renaissance and Reformation, and their transformative benedictions. As a consequence, the modern democratic winds did not blow in countries under the Orthodox Church, and democratic institutions have not taken root, even in the twenty-first century.

This is true not only of countries of the Eastern Orthodoxy, but also of much of the rest of the world. It is important to recognise that a huge intellectual ferment is a necessary condition for liberation from a medieval mindset. Without the spirit of a modern mindset, it is difficult to build or stabilise democratic institutions. Due to this lack of anti-medieval ferment and the consequent inability to develop a modern temper, the countries in Asia or Africa or Latin America are facing difficulties in either introducing or stabilising democratic regimes. Most countries, in the immediate aftermath of decolonisation, went in for democratic systems, but could not sustain them. Despite recurrent failures, the spirit of modernity is so powerful at the global level that democracy is beckoning everybody with increasing illumination.

In China, the case is very different. Maoist communism has surreptitiously given way to State-guided capitalism, but is not prepared to pay even symbolic obeisance to democratic transparency. North Korea has moved back in time and plunged into medieval darkness. With its nuclear weapon status, it portends the worst. Russia, in its post-soviet phase, is still in transition and cannot claim to be a responsive democracy yet, despite the periodic conduct of elections. As for regimes in ex-Soviet Asian Republics, they seem to be moving towards imperial dictatorships, notwithstanding their oil wealth—or perhaps because of their oil wealth. Ex-Soviet regimes in Eastern Europe seem to be trying to catch up with their West European counterparts, and also recover from the stasis of the Orthodox Church. Latin American countries, while experiencing turmoil, seem to be advancing towards democracy. The same is true of countries in Africa, although to a lesser degree. South Africa is a democratic exception, with all its limitations.

India is a gigantic, glowing exception in the developing world. Intellectuals in the developed world are now scratching their heads, wondering how they had missed the positive democratic signals in the Indian story. Indian exceptionalism is multi-dimensional. The first dimension relates to the bewildering cultural diversity that characterises the Indian nation-state. India recognises twenty-three official languages, while Indians speak in numerous languages and dialects. All India Radio broadcasts news in more than 150 languages on a daily basis. There is no country in the world that recognises more than two or three official languages. Even China, the only country bigger than India, effectively projects 'Han Chinese' as the only official language. It is to be noted that nations in Western Europe were formed on the basis of language in the wake of the Reformation. That is why Winston Churchill had mockingly remarked that even the equator could be a nation if India became one. It is against this background that almost all political scientists in the West were loudly pessimistic about India remaining united upon attaining independence. India has proved the intellectual Cassandras of the West wrong, thereby setting a new healthy multicultural precedent for the future.

The same lesson has to be learnt with regard to the multi-religious character of the Indian polity. India, the country with the second largest concentration of Muslims in the world, suffers far less than Pakistan and most other Muslim countries from international terrorism. Both linguistic and religious divides have been conjured away by the magic wand of democracy. It is not often noted that a liberal democracy provides a huge shock-absorber. It is in a democratic crucible that antagonistic elements are dissolved. India is an exemplar of this virtue of democracy.

The question is therefore raised: How can democracy succeed in a developing country? Answers to this question seek to provide the keys to Indian democratic exceptionalism. The relative enlightenment of British colonialism is an answer that is often given. This is far from adequate, considering that it did not help Pakistan or many other former British colonies. The second answer refers to the pagan, polytheistic, and syncretic character of the Hindu religion. This is also inadequate, considering the chronic problems of Nepalese democracy. Without dismissing the positive elements of the various answers, it can be stated that the unique nature of Indian polity derives from the fact that its freedom struggle was noted for its ethically uplifting technique of non-violence. History has never known a struggle in which millions courted imprisonment over decades in a peaceful way. In this supreme mass struggle animated by sublime moral ideas under the stewardship of Gandhiji, an overarching chord of unison was struck. This elevating spirit forged the foundations of the Indian nation. It also generated the climate of tolerance and temperance so essential for the smooth functioning of democracy. Political democracy and national unity have now become Siamese twins in India. The future of democracy in India bids fair, so long as its multi-religious or multi-lingual character is not threatened. A majoritarian hubris or minoritarian nemesis can spell danger even now to Indian democracy, as either could jeopardise the consensus of Gandhian nationalism.

It is seen time and again that democracy is not a sapling that can be transplanted on an ill-prepared soil; however, democratic struggles at the popular level can prepare the soil itself. Even though historical conditions helped the countries in Western Europe and Northern America, we have seen earlier how democracy, even in these countries, took centuries to acquire a mature shape. Be that as it may, its eventual success did not spur popular struggles elsewhere in the world. As has been rightly emphasised, eternal vigilance is the price of liberty. Democracy, as a form of government, cannot be taken for granted, as internal imbalances can always threaten it. It is important to note that major areas of the world have been unable to realise the dream of democracy, even as all of them continue to sing its verbal praises. These paeans to democracy have often forced elections in many countries, although they have not been sustained. Egypt, for example, held an election after 7,000 years. But those elected were thrown out through a military coup, nipping the Arab Spring in the bud.

Despite repeated and continual setbacks in various parts of the world, democracy continues to have an undiminished appeal for people. Its popularity compels all sorts of rulers to promise electoral democracy. It is true that elections, when held, are often rigged, and people are swayed through diversionary ethnic slogans. But democracy, as a political system, is universally acknowledged. There was a time, not long ago, when religious fanatics challenged it on the ground that democracy was not consistent with their religious traditions. Even the Communists, before the demise of the Soviet Union, challenged democracy, referring to it as yet another bourgeois gimmick. But now, even the obeisance paid to democracy, however disingenuously, will generate its own dynamism. Besides, economic change and mass literacy, despite their slow and uneven growth rates, are bound to engender pressure for democracy. All these factors, coupled with an increase in global connectivity, will make democracy irresistible. This conjuncture of circumstances gives a feel of inevitability and wipes out the last vestiges of doubt about the future of democracy.

7

Liberalism

Liberalism, as a word, has lent itself to multiple definitions. While it has become robust with a burgeoning democracy and industrial economy in the modern age, it had its patches of a glorious past. As for the past, it had a lot more to do with the philosophy of tolerance and the coexistence of diversity. In the dim distant past of India, liberalism was engendered by intellectual curiosity, which was also attended by philosophical scepticism. To begin with the Rigveda, the oldest extant book available in ancient India: the Creation Hymn (Rigveda, 10.129) raises the following questions not only about the birth of the universe, but also about the possibility of ever coming to grips with its mystery:

> Then even nothingness was not, nor existence.
> There was no air then, nor the heavens beyond it.
> Who covered it? Where was it? In whose keeping?
> Was there then cosmic water, in depths unfathomed?
> But, after all, who knows, and who can say,
> Whence it all came, and how creation happened?
> The gods themselves are later than creation,
> So who knows truly whence it has arisen? (Thapar 2002: 131)

In the Hymn, the burning curiosity about the primordium of the universe and ultimate queries about hypothetical possibilities are evident. Such open-minded queries are proof of the philosophical liberalism in ancient India. The materialism of ancient India (Lokyatha, as propounded by Charvaka), prevailing during Vedic times, shows that antagonistic philosophical visions coexisted through debate, and without the forcible intervention of either rulers or priests.

The same was true of Jainism, which is said to have existed almost during Vedic times. It believes in a philosophy called 'Syadvada', which, according to S. Radhakrishnan, holds:

> all knowledge to be only probable. Every proposition gives us only a perhaps, a maybe or a syad. We cannot affirm or deny anything absolutely of any object. There is nothing certain on account of the endless complexity of things. It emphasises the extremely complex nature of reality and its indefiniteness. It does not deny the possibility of predication, though it disallows absolute or categorical predication. The dynamic character of reality can consist only with relative or conditional predication. Every proposition is true, but only under certain conditions, i.e., hypothetically. (Radhakrishnan 2008: 250)

Even David Hume, who is rightly regarded as the ultimate sceptic of the modern age, could not go beyond the 'Syadvada' of Jainism. The Buddha himself, after attaining Enlightenment, preached his new message with the emphatic clarification that each intellectual enquirer should examine his message with their own hands. The Buddha's offer of intellectual liberty to his disciples is the epic example of liberalism. This intellectual liberalism was perhaps possible because there was no powerful emperor or powerful clergy in ancient India at that time. Emperor Asoka, after being converted to Buddhism, was tolerant of other religions during his reign—such as the Vedic tradition, Jainism, etc.—in true Buddhist spirit. This climate of liberalism also obtained in ancient Greece, evident from the fact that their tradition of thought started with the natural philosophers, beginning with Thales, long before Socrates. Socrates was perhaps the first victim of governmental persecution. Aristotle said, '[O]f all the varieties of virtues, liberalism is the most beloved.' He further amplified that 'it is the mark of an educated mind to be able to entertain a thought without accepting it' (Aristotle 2004: 82). Even in the twenty-first century, it is impossible to improve on this definition of intellectual liberalism.

In ancient India and in ancient Greece, this intellectual liberalism was accompanied by polytheism, that is, the simultaneous belief in many gods. It is not unreasonable to hypothesise that the simultaneous veneration of multiple deities naturally created a climate of cultural and religious tolerance. In ancient Greece, as in ancient India, no powerful king or single powerful religion had yet emerged on the scene. The great conquerors like Alexander or Genghis Khan were purely motivated by their hunger for power, and were not prompted by a desire to spread any particular religion. In fact, neither of them believed in any particular religion, even as they conquered the world. They were in fact so supremely self-assured about their military prowess that they did not need any religion, either as a provocation or as a vindication. Less self-confident rulers, more often than not, tended to use religious appeal to attain their aggressive political goals. Emperor Asoka was an exception to this phenomenon, as he embraced Buddhism after winning the bloody Kalinga war, and became deeply remorseful about the repulsive nature of wars. Asoka's repentance was so deep and lasting that he never engaged in another war after becoming a Buddhist. His conversion was so profoundly personal that he never used the power of his monarchy to convert others, including adherents of the Vedic religion or the Jain religion, to Buddhism.

The ancient period was succeeded by medieval times, which did not witness any major philosophical or technological breakthroughs. One of the notable phenomena relates to the Crusades, which were military expeditions beginning in the eleventh century AD, organised by Western Christians in response to Islamic wars.

The Crusading declined rapidly during the sixteenth century with the advent of Protestant Reformation. As a consequence of the bitter experiences of the Crusades, religious tolerance grew, and became one of the defining features of the Modern Age. While the great movements like the Renaissance, Reformation, Humanism, and Scientific Revolution blurred the defining borders of various religions and sects, philosophy played its unobtrusive and ubiquitous part in the dissemination of the spirit of tolerance. Sir Francis Bacon (1561–1626) was the first modern philosopher who insisted upon the supreme importance of the observation of nature and the experimental method in science. Sir Francis asserted that 'our only hope is in genuine induction'—the building up, from observations and experiments, through progressive stages of certainty to larger conclusions. He had the temerity to say that 'the reverence for antiquity, and the authority of men who have been esteemed great in philosophy, and general unanimity, have retarded men from advancing in science' (Bacon 2015). Although Aristotle had emphasised the significance of the induction method, Bacon did not spare even him, and wanted people to go much beyond him. Bacon was thus distrustful of not only the authority of religion, but also the authority of philosophers. The continual scrutiny of propositions through observation and experimentation was the only way for Bacon. He thus debunked the sanctity of both religious revelations and philosophical premises.

Thus, in the modern age, philosophy began with Bacon on an iconoclastic note. His junior rival in philosophy, French philosopher Rene Descartes (1596–1650), who believed in the deductive method, also argued that knowledge could be gained through rigorous reasoning without having to rely on divine revelations. Although Sir Francis Bacon and Descartes believed in antagonistic philosophical methodologies, they both contributed to the discounting of the sanctity of religious scriptures, albeit in different degrees. This philosophical degradation of the authority of religious sources led to the broadening of human horizons, and thus to liberalism. John Locke is credited with founding liberalism in several senses of the term. First, he founded the philosophy of empiricism, which argues that sense experience is the only source of knowledge. Empiricism attacks the validity of religious revelation or testimony or intuition, thereby liberating the human mind from the trammels of tradition of all kinds. In political science, he perfected the idea of democracy, coupled with the theory of separating the powers of government from parliament. As mentioned in Chapter 6, he is celebrated for advocating the right to life, liberty, and estate (property), although his right to property came to be subjected to both misuse and misinterpretation.

Having rapidly considered liberalism from the perspective of philosophy, we need to go back briefly to the other source of its origin, that is, ancient international commerce. Even in pre-historic times, businessmen travelled from country to country on land or by sea through their slow-moving modes of transport—horses or primitive boats—to buy and sell goods such as spices, silk, etc. They stayed in different climes for long periods, thereby exposing themselves to different traditions and cultures. This extended exposure enabled them to appreciate the comparative merits and demerits of different systems, and developed a spirit of wider understanding. That was how they developed cultural and intellectual catholicism. But in the modern age, liberalism has also acquired the dimension of economic ideology. The trouble with its economic dimension is that it is understood in different ways in different nations. No two nations in the world can be more organically interconnected than the UK and the USA, in terms of race, religion, philosophy, political development, and industrial growth. Yet, strangely, the word 'liberalism' is used in these two nations in two different senses. In the UK, it is associated with classical liberalism, which entails a commitment to limited government and *laissez-faire* economic policies. In the USA, since the time of President Franklin Roosevelt (1882–1945; he was the thirty-second President of the US) and his New Deal programme, it has been associated with welfare liberalism.

Both senses of liberalism were derived from John Locke's right to estate (property). While the application of the term 'liberalism, right to property' propounded by Locke has been invoked by conservative liberals, Locke's definition of property has been used by welfare liberals. These two senses of the word are still used widely, which is responsible for its dual use. In Europe, the classic left still refers to conservative liberalism as neo-liberalism. Harold J. Laski of the London School of Economics used the word 'liberalism' in the sense of conservative liberalism. In the USA, left-of-centre economists like Joseph Stiglitz and Paul Krugman (both Nobel Prize winners for economics) are known as liberals. Even while the semantic ambivalence about the economic implications of the word 'liberalism' continues, there is a need to explore some of its historical roots.

British philosopher and political economist John Stuart Mill (1806–73) set an absolute value on the freedom of judgement in his epic essay on 'liberty', evident from his statement that 'all mankind has no right to silence one dissenter'. But Mill, who struggled painfully to liberate himself from his stern father's utilitarian influence, did not succeed notably, as he could not convince himself of the merits of the positive intervention of the State in the larger public interest. As George Sabine points out, '[W]hat Mill's theory of liberty required was a thoroughgoing consideration of the dependence of personal liberty on social and legal rights and obligations. It was this which T.H. Green (1836–82) tried to add to liberalism' (Sabine 1973: 644). British philosopher and political theorist Bernard Bosanquet (1848–1923), while supporting Thomas Hill Green's liberalism, argued that there is no happiness at all except when it is experienced by each and every person on the ground that there is no common self submerging the soul of men. In other words, Bosanquet means to say that there is nothing like a collective self, and everyone has his own or her own self, requiring its separate happiness. According to Sabine, Green did away with the distinction between economics and politics, by which older liberals tried to prevent the state from regulating the market. Green asserted that even a free market was a social institution rather than a natural condition. He therefore looked upon the State as a positive agency for necessary legislation to contribute to 'positive freedom'.

The principles of Green's liberalism did not differ sharply from those of the Fabian Society (founded in 1984). The Fabians also defended their programme as nothing more than an extension of new liberalism. Sidney Webb, in *Fabian Essays in Socialism* (1889), asserted that the economic aspect of democracy was the same as socialism. Sydney Olivier added that socialism was nothing more than individualism rationalised. It is, however, important to note that the Fabians went beyond even the new liberals, and pleaded for the nationalisation of basic industries on pragmatic grounds, and not on dialectical lines as the Marxists did.

William Ewart Gladstone (1809–98) embodied positive liberalism more eloquently than any other politician of his time. Gladstone, who is widely regarded as the most dominating British statesman of the nineteenth century, represents the evolution of the political climate of the nineteenth century in a striking way. He evolved ideologically from a position of conservatism to that of liberalism, albeit in a phased manner. Gladstone's personality dominated liberalism so much during 1865–95 that liberalism almost became Gladstoniasm. In a famous speech at West Calder (1878), he expressed anti-imperialist views. He also expressed his sympathy with the Irish cause, to such an extent that it led to a serious split in his own party's ranks. In the end, he went much beyond liberalism and became a champion of the masses. In a speech made in 1886, he declared that 'all the world over, I will back the masses against the classes' (Radcliffe 2011: 82). It can therefore be said that Gladstone represented three schools of British ideology in the nineteenth century, viz., conservatism, liberalism, and the initial phase of socialist sentiment. Together, Green's theory and Gladstone's politics provided a strong social dimension to liberalism at the turn of the twentieth century in Britain.

The New Liberals, which included intellectuals like L. T. Hobhouse and John A. Hobson, argued that conditions of poverty and illiteracy could be addressed only through a strong welfare-oriented and interventionist state. Hobhouse (1963) asserted that 'Liberty without equality is a name of noble sound and squalid meaning'. The People's Budget of 1909, championed by David Lloyd George and fellow liberal Winston Churchill, introduced heavy taxes on the wealthy in Britain and added radical social programmes to the country's policies. It was Britain's first budget with the explicit intent of redistributing wealth among the public. It is interesting (without being irrelevant) to note that Winston Churchill moved from liberalism to conservatism and imperialism in the twentieth century, in sharp contrast to Gladstone's ideological odyssey from conservatism to progressive liberalism and anti-imperialism.

Liberalism began to gain momentum in the beginning of the twentieth century in other European countries. However, this was a passing phase. World War I created conditions that led to the triumph of communism in Russia and the emergence of Mussolini in Italy in 1922. These liberal reverses in Europe were further accelerated by the 'Great Depression' of the 1930s. This apart, in Britain itself, the influence of the Labour Party, which represented a bold blend of political liberalism and economic socialism, grew in the meantime, thereby making the Liberal Party less relevant. This period (between the Great Depression and World War II) witnessed the rise of Hitler in Germany and that of dictatorship in Spain after the Spanish Civil War. Even Japan, which was generally liberal in the 1920s, turned illiberal in the 1930s under pressure from the military.

In the UK, however, the Great Depression extorted a progressive liberal response from the economist John Maynard Keynes (1883–1946). Brought up as a classical liberal, he was drawn to progressive liberalism. His major work, *The General Theory of Employment, Interest and Money* (2007 [1936]), provided theoretical justifications for interventionist policies. He argued that in the event of market failure, the government should stimulate the economy until private funds could start flowing again. The influence of Keynes motivated President Roosevelt of the United States to launch his New Deal programme, which successfully rescued the American economy from the Great Depression. Since the Labour Party largely replaced the Liberal Party, it also inherited the legacy of the latter. In the USA, the Democratic Party led by Roosevelt not only embodied the liberal programme, but also came to absorb the spirit of the Labour Party. After World War II, most West European countries adopted the policies of welfare liberalism or social democracy. In the meantime, economic growth experienced a quantum jump owing to the superior technology in the Western world. Even in the Third

World countries, significant growth rates were witnessed through the adoption of industrial technology. However, in the Third World, liberalism as a political philosophy did not flourish much. India became an island of liberalism, albeit a vast island. During the Cold War period, the conflict between the North Atlantic Treaty Organization (NATO) countries and Soviet Union dominated international diplomacy, so much so that even countries that claimed to stand for liberty were more interested in Machiavellian strategy than in liberalism. It is difficult to say that the American Central Intelligence Agency (CIA) was more scrupulous than the Russian KGB. The American foreign policy, developed by diplomat John Foster Dulles (1888–1959) and adopted by his successors, did not come out smelling of liberal roses.

After the demise of the Soviet Union, the tensions of the Cold War subsided, but new conflicts arose. These new conflicts have posed more urgent threats than the problems during the Cold War. The Cold War was at least being waged by well-organised states like the United States and the Soviet Union, with a Hot-Link between the heads of the states to avoid an emergency or accidents. The new threats that are now tormenting the world cannot be either quantified or predicted. Most of them are being precipitated by non-state actors with whom a meaningful conversation is not feasible. It is, of course, instructive to realise that these Frankenstein forces were unleashed by the myopia of Western countries. The Western countries, in the aftermath of the collapse of the Soviet Union, adopted a triumphalist approach and sought to dominate the world. Be that as it may, neither Cold War diplomacy nor the current guerrilla warfare has helped the dissemination of liberal forces. On the contrary, old medieval conflicts have been revived with new weapons of untold destructive potential. There is therefore an imperative need to address the new problems for the causes of both peace and freedom. It is a monumental challenge to liberalism at the global level.

In the West, it was believed during the Cold War period that the mutually antagonistic demands of individual liberty, social justice, and economic growth had been resolved satisfactorily. There appeared to have evolved a new intellectual consensus, with the State intervening positively to regulate the capitalist economy, strengthen the welfare system, and levy high taxes on the rich. This consensus was so overwhelmingly bi-partisan that President Nixon said in the early 1970s that 'we are all Keynesians now' (Fox 2008: 60). But this seemed to have broken down imperceptibly by the early 1980s. As a result, the tax burden on the rich was reduced, leading not only to a reduction in welfare benefits for the poor, but also to a disturbing increase in wealth and income inequalities between the rich and the poor. The consensus that had prevailed in the third quarter of the twentieth century in Western countries is also under a cloud. The old debate between socialism and capitalism has been resurrected with new vigour. This is evident from the fact that the Labour Party in Britain has been stormed by internal revolt, led by one of its old leaders, Jeremy Corbyn, and the Democratic Party establishment in the USA has been subjected to considerable insurgency through the rise of Bernie Sanders. These internal storms are not confined to liberal parties; conservative parties are also under threat, as can be seen from the vote in favour of Brexit and the resignation of David Cameron as Prime Minister. This is even more strikingly noticeable in the triumph of Donald Trump, and the marginalisation of mainstream leadership within the Republican Party. The surprising victory of Donald Trump as President demonstrates that even the conservative liberal forces in America have taken a beating. Feelings based on identity are much stronger than the forces of even conservative ideology.

This new trend seems to be spreading from the UK and USA to other parts of Europe, and is the latest and most insidious threat to liberalism as a political philosophy. It should be recalled that the rise of fascism in Italy and Nazism in Germany was facilitated by the Great Depression. Although the marginalisation of the poor and middle classes in Europe and America is leading to deep unrest, this situation is once again being used by nativist forces to promote their reactionary illiberalism and xenophobia. It is to be noted that the poor and middle classes were drawn to Bernie Sanders as the Democratic presidential candidate in the US presidential elections of 2016, as he was offering to assist their children and families with quality access to education and health. He proposed to raise the requisite money through an increase in the taxes on the rich, and by reducing the influence of corporates on American polity. When Bernie Sanders failed to become the Democratic candidate, these sections allowed themselves to be enticed by Donald Trump, who offered to provide the deprived classes with jobs through the targeting of ethnic minorities. Hitler had proved in the second quarter of the twentieth century that the targeting of minorities would be an easy diversionary tactic from real social and economic problems. This unacknowledged imitation of Hitler's tactics in the most enlightened parts of the globe, such as the US and Europe, poses a serious threat to liberalism, which embraces ethnic diversity.

American philosopher John Rawls (1921–2002) wrote primarily on ethics and political philosophy. In his groundbreaking work, *A Theory of Justice* (1971), he offered an alternative to 'Utilitarianism' that led to very different conclusions on justice. While dealing with distributive justice, he attempted to reconcile the competing claims of the values of freedom and equality. Rawls tried to show that the notions of freedom and equality could be integrated into a seamless unity he called 'Justice as Fairness'. *A Theory of Justice* includes a thought experiment he termed 'the original position'. His original position is reminiscent of the constructs of such social contractarians as Thomas Hobbes, John Locke, and Rousseau. The 'original position' is Rawls' hypothetical scenario in which a group of persons is given the task of reaching an agreement about the kind of political and economic structure they want for society. Each individual, however, deliberates behind a 'Veil of Ignorance': each remains ignorant of her/his gender, race, age, intelligence, wealth, skills, education, and religion. Rawls asserted that the people choosing principles of justice in such conditions would not seek to maximise the overall utility, but would instead both protect liberty and safeguard themselves against the worst possible outcome. They would thus sanction only those inequalities (for example, in wealth) that will benefit the worst-off, even while permitting such inequalities that are necessary to incentives that benefit all. Since Rawls emphasised the need for individual liberty without diluting the claims of equity, he is regarded as a 'liberal socialist'.

Through his further work, he developed another theory, 'reflective equilibrium'. Rawls held that there will inevitably be 'give and take' between a person's first-order about justice and the higher-order commitments that take the form of principles of justice. In other words, he settles down to the relative priority of principles and a commonsense method of reasoning about morality. Through this position, he rejected the theory of absolute priority of principles. In other words, it is nothing but a description of our commonsense method of reasoning about morality. In *Political Liberalism* (1993), he pleads for multiculturalism, intellectual tolerance, etc. At the core of 'political liberalism' lies its plea to the liberal state to maintain commitment to the ideal of public reason. Political reasoning, according to him, should proceed purely in terms of public reason. In view of his original contributions, he is widely regarded as the greatest political philosopher of the twentieth century.

Robert Nozick (1938–2002), like Rawls, was a professor at Harvard University, and is celebrated for his book *Anarchy, State and Utopia* (1974), known as the libertarian answer to Rawls' *A Theory of Justice*. Libertarianism is a political philosophy that argues that the role of the State ought to be very limited and confined to police protection, national defence, and administration of the courts of law. His position is similar to that of classical economists such as Adam Smith and David Ricardo; however, he goes further and takes an *a priori* position concerning respect for individual rights. He followed the position of Immanuel Kant—that a human being has an inherent dignity and cannot therefore be treated as a mere 'thing' or used against his will as a means, in the way an inanimate object can. He described individual human beings as 'self-owners'. Almost on the lines of John Locke, he argued that individuals, as self-owners, have certain rights, in particular, the right to life, liberty, and the fruits of labour.

While John Locke had formulated his limited right to property with a view to protecting the rights of nobles and others against the threat of expropriation by kings, Nozick provided a metaphysical foundation to the unfettered right to property. He also rejected the concept of inalienable rights as propounded by Locke. None of the original capitalist thinkers had gone so far as Nozick with respect to his concept of 'minimal state'. He had in fact opposed income tax even for providing a minimum welfare state, not to speak of any redistributive scheme. Nozick is best known for this work on political philosophy, although he later did some notable work in such esoteric spheres as epistemology. American conservatives coined the term 'Libertarian' by confining liberty to the economic enterprises of individuals.

8

Capitalism

Contrary to general impression, capitalism is a modern system. During the agrarian phase of human civilisation, which followed the development of agriculture in major river-valley systems like those of the Nile or the Ganga (Ganges), business was necessary and was seen everywhere. This business related to agricultural products or hand-made products of cotton or leather, spices or metals, etc. It used to take place either within societies or across kingdoms, either over land or across the seas. However, a fortuitous conjuncture of historical circumstances helped agrarian societies in Western Europe to develop into the modern form of capitalism. As the economist J. Schumpeter observed, the Crusades provided a major opportunity for the formation of considerable capital, notably the legendary one of the Templars. Commerce, banking, and finance flourished first in the Italian Republics of the thirteenth and fourteenth centuries, and then in Holland and England. He further points out:

> With the invention of the printing press, progress in Metallurgy, employment of the water power and use of carts in the mines, the second half of the 15th century was distinguished by clear advance in the production of metals and textiles. During this time, the first canons and other fire arms began to be produced, while improvements in the construction of caravels and navigation techniques allowed for the opening up of new routes. (Beaud 2004: 14)

Against this background, in 1487, Bartholomeu Dias (1450–1500) of Portugal rounded the Cape of Good Hope; in 1492, Christopher Columbus discovered America; in 1498,

Portuguese explorer Vasco da Gama (d. 1524), having skirted Africa, arrived in India. This is one of the points at which the West overtook the East, and a great colonisation by European countries began. Columbus hit the imperialist nail on the head through his observation that '[O]ne who has gold does as he wills in the world, and it even sends souls to Paradise' (Beaud 2004: 15).

All expeditions of the Spaniards were prompted by the same motive. They, however, justified this process to themselves and others by arguing that they were serving a pious purpose by converting the inhabitants of colonised countries to Christianity. Hernan Cortes (1485–1547), conqueror of Mexico, confessed: 'We Spanish suffer from a sickness of the heart for which gold is the only cure' (ibid.). According to official figures, 18,000 tonnes of silver and 200 tonnes of gold were transferred from America to Spain between 1521 and 1660. Other estimates have doubled this quantity. The costs of this pillage were colossal, not only in metals, but also in lives.

As Michel Beaud points out:

> In a little more than a century, the Indian population was reduced by 90 per cent in Mexico ... and by 95 per cent in Peru. Las Casas estimated that between 1495 and 1503, more than 3 million people disappeared from the islands of the New World. They were slain in war, sent to Castile as slaves, or consumed in the mines and other labours. Who of those born in future generations will believe this? (2004: 15)

We will now turn from hapless sufferers to bountiful beneficiaries. The wealth from new metals not only enriched the bankrupt king of Spain, but also the adventurers, nobles, and the merchants. They also purchased metals from the markets of Italy, France, Holland, and England. These precious metals were dispersed in increasingly wider waves. The possession of precious metals became the measure of the wealth of kingdoms. Beaud observed:

> The prescription for doing this was simple: 'prevent precious metals from leaving, by prohibiting their departure and limiting imports; make the entry of precious metals easy by encouraging the export of what was not necessary to the kingdom.' Both of

> these measures encouraged national production .... The way was opened to the idea that the wealth of the kingdom depended on the wealth of the merchants and manufacturers. (2004: 18)

Beaud further stated, 'With the flow of precious metals from America and the development of production, commerce improved in Europe; with forced labour in America ... and the lowering of real wages linked to European inflation, an additional surplus was released; .... The merchant and banking bourgeoisies gathered strength' (ibid.: 19).

Besides, the wealth of the prince had to be guaranteed not only for himself, but also to finance the wars. Such traditional business acquired a new dimension from the sixteenth to the eighteenth centuries in Europe, which Adam Smith termed 'mercantilism'. It called for government regulation of a nation's economy in order to increase its power at the expense of rival nations. Mercantilism's emphasis on the importance of gold and silver holdings led to policies designed to obtain favourable trade balances for nations. Colonial countries were serving as markets for exports and as suppliers of raw materials to colonial powers, thereby fuelling resentment in the former. Mercantilism provided a congenial climate for the early development of capitalism, but advocates of *laissez-faire* capitalism later opposed government controls as being contrary to free trade theories. They further argued that all trade was beneficial, and that government controls were counter-productive.

Capitalism gained in dominance after the break-up of feudalism. In fact, feudalism's decline was accelerated when long-distance trade between capitalist centres resulted in the development of commercial and industrial towns. Flanders (which is now partly in Belgium) in the thirteenth century and Florence in the fourteenth century were the two capitalist pockets; but violent conflict between urban workers and cloth magnats led to the destruction of the cloth and woollen industry. This industry was soon revived, however, because of the domestic availability of raw wool and the innovation of simple mechanical fulling mills. The English cloth industry learnt its lessons from the bad experiences of Flanders and

Florence, and avoided the class strife. After overcoming other problems, the English cloth industry continued to grow at a rapid pace during the sixteenth, seventeenth, and eighteenth centuries. Hence, it was the woollen industry that spearheaded capitalism and rooted it for the first time in English soil. Instead of building pyramids and cathedrals, the social surplus of the cloth industry was used to invest in ships, warehouses, raw materials, and finished goods. Surplus was thus converted to enhance productive capacity for the first time in history. Certain historical circumstances favoured this process. One of them was the sanction of the Protestant religion for hard work and frugality, which was completely different from the economic ethics taught by medieval Catholicism. Interest could not be charged through moneylending in medieval times. It may be noted that interest cannot be charged even today by banks in Islamic countries, which shows how the Protestant movement made a difference to the Western economy. It also shows how Islam, without its own radical version of the Reformation, remains out of tune with the modern world. Without stating that Protestantism was the main cause of modern capitalism, it can be safely said that the Protestant ethic provided a bracing stimulant to the emerging economic order. Calvin, the most important Protestant leader after Martin Luther, justified commerce and lending at interest, and went on 'to make of commercial success a sign of divine election' (Beaud 2004: 14).

Aside from the change in the religious ethic, the second circumstance that favoured capitalism was the impact of precious metals from the new world on the relative shares of income going towards wages, profits, and rents. The third circumstance was the role played by nation-states in helping to provide the necessary conditions and circumstances: the creation of a domestic market, free from tolls and other barriers, to trade within the nation's borders; a uniform monetary system; a legal code appropriate to capitalistic progress; a skilled and disciplined labour force; safeguards against internal violence; national defence against attacks; sufficient literacy and education among the business classes, enabling them to use credit instruments, contracts, and other documents required for commercial civilisation; and basic facilities for communication and transportation, and harbour installations.

The *Encyclopaedia Britannica* (1967: Vol. 4, 820) states:

> [T]reasure from the new world had a profound impact on European capitalism .... Gold and silver from ... Mexico, Peru and Bolivia increased Europe's supply of precious metals sevenfold and raised prices two or threefold .... Landlords ... suffered because ... money rents failed to rise as rapidly as the cost of living .... In England the enclosure movement ... encouraged sheep raising to supply wool to the expanding woollen industry. Among labourers, money wages failed to keep pace with the cost of living, causing real wages to fall .... The chief beneficiaries ... were capitalists, ... merchants, manufacturers and ... employers.

It is evident that wealth could be accumulated at the cost of workers. At any rate, that wealth could be used as capital for utilising new inventions such as the steam engine to generate industrial capital. Aggressive entrepreneurs like Richard Arkwright found the capital to finance factory-type organisations for the utilisation of new machines.

Adam Smith (1723–90), Scottish social philosopher and political economist, was a multi-splendored genius and a friend of all leading intellectuals of the day, including the philosopher David Hume (1711–76) and French physiocrat Francois Quesnay (1694–1774), who founded the physiocracy, the first scientific school of economics. While he looked up to Hume for beneficial interaction, he differed from his French friend Quesnay, who felt that land was the only source of wealth (as capitalism was yet to commence in France). He opposed mercantilism, which called for government regulation of a nation's economy, but supported *laissez-faire* (a policy dictating minimum governmental interference in the economic affairs of individuals and society). While Smith supported *laissez-faire*, he argued that labour is the source of 'value'. He had discovered the importance of labour, as Great Britain had begun to experience problems of labour in the developing phase of its capitalist process. Apart from the special conditions in Britain, Smith knew about the importance that John Locke had attached to the labour of every individual, as the foundation for developing his 'right to property (estate)' in the seventeenth century. In any case, Adam Smith's stress on labour led to political economist David Ricardo's (1772–1823) theory of labour value, which became the fertile source of the philosophy of Karl Marx (1818–83) in the nineteenth century.

Adam Smith spoke in favour of an economic system spurred by self-interest. This would operate as an 'invisible hand'. By 'invisible hand', Smith was not referring to God, but to the mechanism of the market: '[I]t is not from the benevolence of the butcher, the brewer, or the baker that we expect our dinner, but from their regard to their self-interest. We address ourselves not to the humanity, but to their self-love, and never talk to them of our necessities, but of their advantages' (Smith 2003: Ch. 2). The advantages of the market, according to him, include the way prices are kept ranging arbitrarily away from the actual cost of producing a good; producers of commodities are induced by society to provide it with what it wants; and high prices turn out to be a self-curing disease as they cause production in those lines to increase.

It is evident that Smith believed the market is self-regulating. To a large extent, it was so in the days of Adam Smith. Even in his time, there were factors that acted as restraints against the free operation of the market system. At any rate, the world of Adam Smith has rightly been called a world of atomistic competition, a world in which no agent of the productive mechanism, on the side of either labour or capital, was powerful enough to interfere with and resist the pressures of competition. But the nature of the market has changed vastly since the eighteenth century. The market mechanism later came to be characterised by such new elements as the huge size of its participants, viz., giant corporations and strong labour unions. Each of these elements could withstand the competition and disregard price signals, at least in the short run. Adam Smith was percipient enough to see the tremendous gain from the minute division and specialisation of labour; he was impressed enough with a small factory of ten people to write about it in *The Wealth of Nations* (2003). Its advantage lies in its capacity to increase what Smith called 'that universal opulence which extends itself to the lowest ranks of the people' (ibid.: 16). There was actually not much opulence in Smith's time by modern standards, but it was still better than had been the case ever before; in pre-industrial times, the masses and farm workers never had any chance to escape from grinding poverty.

For all Smith's fabled farsightedness, he did not foresee the rise of industrial capitalism, although it had begun to take shape in his time. Contrary to general perception, Smith was neither anti-labour nor anti-capital. If he had any bias, it was in favour of the consumer. He actually said that 'consumption is the sole end and purpose of all production' (2003: 13). His entire philosophy sprang from his implicit faith in the vitality of the market. He did not believe that the market would deliver all the goods for society, and therefore said that the State should perform at least three tasks. First, it should protect society against the violence and invasion of other States. Second, it should provide an 'exact administration of justice' for all citizens. Third, the government has the duty of 'erecting and maintaining those public institutions and those public works' which 'may be in the highest degree advantageous to a great society', but which 'are, however, of such a nature that the profit could never repay the expense to any individual or small number of individuals' (ibid.). To put it in today's context, he explicitly recognised the need for public investment in such things as roads and education. He was not innocent of the monopolistic tendencies of his time. He, in fact, said that 'people of the same trade seldom meet together, even for merriment and diversion, but the conversation ends in a conspiracy against the public, or in some diversion to raise prices' (ibid.). He further admitted that they 'generally have an interest to deceive and even to oppress the public'. He also observed that 'with the greater part of rich people, the chief enjoyment of riches consists in the parade of riches, which in their eye, is never so complete as when they appear to possess those decisive marks of opulence which nobody can possess but themselves' (ibid.). But his solution to these negative tendencies of businessmen was nothing more than putting his rational faith in the proposition that the market would set them right.

The market had existed in history from the beginning, albeit in primitive forms. But Smith was prophetic in that he could see some great merit in the modern mechanism of the market. This mechanism is such that it leads to sharp competition among manufacturers to minimise the cost of production, which in turn would benefit the consumers. If Smith's discovery of the market's special virtues marked his unique genius, his faith in the total sufficiency of the market was his limitation. However, Adam Smith has turned out to be the prophet of capitalism, which has survived for over two centuries, despite business cycles, depressions and recessions, labour revolts, and revolutionary tempests. The unlikely survival of capitalism has been made possible by quantum jumps in technology, enlargement of labour rights, and generous welfare systems. The market still remains an irreplaceable mechanism, which is today supported by everybody, including socialists. Adam Smith also did not neglect the ethical implications of market operations. Amartya Sen, who has done pioneering work on this aspect of Smith's work, asserts that the complex attitude of Smith towards motivation and markets has been so misinterpreted as to lead to the distancing of economics from ethics. Sen further observes:

> Smith did, in fact, make pioneering contributions in analysing the nature of mutually advantageous exchanges, and the value of division of labour, and since these contributions are perfectly consistent with human behaviour sans bonhomie and ethics, references to these parts of Smith's work have been profuse and exuberant. Other parts of Smith's writings on economics and society, dealing with observations of misery, the need for sympathy, and the role of ethical considerations in human behaviour, particularly the use of behaviour norms, have become relatively neglected as these considerations have themselves become unfashionable in economics. (Sen 1987: 27–28)

Sen also argues that the narrowing of the Smithian view of human beings is one of the major deficiencies of current economic theory. This philosophical impoverishment of Smith's theory is closely related not only to the distancing of economics from ethics, but also to the weakening of welfare economics.

Adam Smith was an integrated economic philosopher who needs to be studied from a variety of angles. David Ricardo, who emerged as the foremost exponent of Adam Smith, interpreted him in his own way. Without neglecting Ricardo, other aspects of Adam Smith need to be exhumed.

British economist David Ricardo, who arrived on the scene just three decades after Adam Smith, witnessed the economic scene being altered by new industrial technology. For example, the spinning jenny, the steam engine, and the puddling of iron were perceived as new avenues for economic growth. Ricardo looked upon the capitalist who made efforts and took risks to set up new industrial factories with sympathy, while he viewed the landlord as a passive beneficiary of rent. He therefore fought against the Corn Laws (tariffs and restrictions on imported food and grain), enforced in Great Britain between 1815 and 1846. They were designed to keep grain prices high to favour domestic producers and highlighted the advantages of free trade in bringing cheap grain into Britain. The power of landlords can be seen from the fact that it took many decades for the British Parliament to abolish the Corn Laws. Ricardo also examined the movement of wages and the determination of value, asserting that the domestic values of commodities were largely determined by the labour required for their production. Karl Marx derived his theory of 'surplus value' from Ricardo, and developed his communist theory. Ricardo propounded the 'Iron Law of Wages' and stated that attempts to improve the real income of workers were futile, and that wages tended to stabilise at a subsistence level. While Ricardo built his theory on the work of Adam Smith, he defined the scope of economics more narrowly than Smith did. Ricardo also restricted the scope of economics as a discipline by refraining from focusing on the allied aspects of social philosophy. His theories of surplus value were later exploited by both the Utilitarians and the Marxists to advance their respective ideological positions.

Thomas Robert Malthus (1763–1834), British economist and demographer, in his work *An Essay on the Principle of Population* (1798), argued that population will always tend to outrun the food supply—that increase in population will take place, if unchecked, in a geometrical progression, while the means of subsistence will increase only in an arithmetical progression. He also believed that population would expand to the limits of subsistence and would be held there by famine, war, and ill-health. He further argued that relief measures for the poor should be strictly limited, since they tended to encourage the growth of excess population. He spread such pessimism that he gave a bad name to economics, so much so that Scottish philosopher Thomas Carlyle (1795–1881) called economics a 'dismal science'. Although his pessimistic theories turned out to be erroneous because of augmented industrial technology, improved agricultural productivity, and the subsequent invention of measures of birth control, the discipline of economics has not recovered from the sobriquet of dismal science. Malthus's influence went beyond economics and was extended to biology. It was Malthus who first set English naturalists and biologists Charles Darwin (1809–82) and A. R. Wallace (1823–1913) on the train of reasoning that led to the principle of natural selection. At any rate, Malthus's pessimism has returned in our own time as the limits to growth are viewed from the angle of the environment.

Jeremy Bentham (1748–1832), British social and political theorist, was a fervent atheist. It may be mentioned in passing that Adam Smith and David Ricardo were not ardent theists either. Bentham was a supporter of the new *laissez-faire* economics of Smith and Ricardo. As a founder of Utilitarianism, he promoted the theory of the greatest happiness for the greatest number, and advocated utility as a measure of goodness. He therefore opposed the notions of social contract and natural law, considering them superfluous. He believed that society could advance through the calculation of pleasure and pain. 'The greatest happiness principle' is the most important formula of the Benthamite school. According to this principle, actions are good when they promote the greatest happiness of the greatest number, and bad when they do not. Bentham took intense interest in legislation. In fact, he became a leading theorist in the Anglo-American philosophy of law. He was a philosophical radical who supported economic freedom, separation of the state and church, freedom of expression, equal rights for women, the right to divorce, and de-criminalising homosexual acts. He called for the abolition of slavery and the death penalty. Above all, he supported democracy and universal compulsory education. His views on education were so influential at the time that a Bill was introduced in Parliament in 1807 to provide elementary school education throughout England. It is, however, important to note that this advanced bill was defeated in the House of Lords at the instance of the Archbishop of Canterbury. It is also important to note that the Bill was opposed by the President of the Royal Society, which had been set up purely for the promotion of modern science.

After noting so many positive aspects of Benthamism, it is important to examine one great difficulty. While its support for *laissez-faire* is understandable, it became a dogma and was carried to extremes. Bentham was lucky to have friends like James Mill, who popularised Benthamism like a cult. Mill was so over-enthusiastic about Benthamism that he even rigidly indoctrinated his gifted son, John Stuart Mill.

Nineteenth-century Britain witnessed the rise of free trade. The manufacturers worked for the abolition of customs duty on corn (the Corn Laws, as discussed earlier), as corn was being produced at a cheaper price in other countries, while the landlords were likely to be affected by a decline in the corn price in the case of internationalisation of the corn trade. Traders rose through their own efforts and were enthused by the philosophy of the Utilitarians, which projected competition as the motive force of progress. Landlords, in their defence, criticised the evils of child labour and long hours in factories, even as industrialists complained of the high costs of bread. In the end, Lord Shaftesbury (Anthony Ashley-Cooper, seventh Earl of Shaftesbury; 1801–85) succeeded in getting the Factory Acts passed, to the relief of labour, while Richard Cobden (1804–65) had the corn trade liberalised for the benefit of manufacturers.

Richard Cobden, British politician and cotton manufacturer, was not only a champion of free trade, but also argued that free trade would help the world and the cause of world peace. Because of the prestige that he acquired through the success of the Anti-Corn Law agitation, his influence extended beyond Britain to the rest of Europe. His own liberalism led him to want nations to pursue wealth without too much regard for such things as glory and territory. He advocated against war on the ground that they were wasteful investments, and that belligerent nationalism would diminish the wealth of humanity. Apart from his pro-trade convictions, he had a kind heart and a good deal of humanitarian sentiment. Being true to his utilitarian philosophy, he was not for improving the conditions of labour; however, he refused to support the 'Iron Law of Wages' propounded by Ricardo. He maintained that free trade would improve the position of both the employer and labour, and the limited experience of the time showed that he was right. Cobden was an ideologically committed politician, and actually lost his seat for opposing the Crimean War (October 1853–February 1856). When, in 1859, Cobden was offered the Cabinet office by Palmerston (Henry John Temple, third Viscount Palmerston [1784–1865], who served twice as Prime Minister), Cobden refused because of his disagreement with Palmerston's aggressive foreign policy.

Unlike his political contemporaries, Cobden regarded industry, rather than armaments, as the source of national power. He therefore regarded America as more important than Russia way back in 1835. His wisdom shines in contrast to that of Kaiser Wilhelm II (the last German Emperor and King of Prussia from 1888–1918), who expected Spain to win the Spanish-American war as late as 1898. Cobden's anti-imperialistic convictions led him to support India in India's First War of Independence in 1857. It is instructive to note what he said on the subject at the height of fury against India in Britain. He publicly stated that he did not believe that England could reform India through the Company (East India), or through the rule of the Crown under the control of Parliament. In his own words:

> If the House of Commons were to renounce all responsibility for domestic legislation, and give itself exclusively to the task of governing one hundred millions of Asiatics, it would fail. Hindustan must be ruled by those who live on that side of the globe. Its people will prefer to be ruled badly—according to our notions—by its own colour, kith and kin, than to submit to the humiliation of being better governed by a succession of transient intruders from the Antipodes. (Russell 1934: 135–36)

In his advanced anti-imperialist position, Cobden was being true to Benthamism.

Cobden's prestige was greater in Europe than in England. He made a triumphal tour of Europe in 1846. In Spain, he was likened to Christopher Columbus. His reception in Italy and Germany was also overwhelming. The Pope was extremely deferential and heaped high praise on him. Cobden's commercial cosmopolitanism did not succeed to a great degree, as emotional nationalism gained on the ground. One of his great political contributions was through his personal impact on Gladstone, the most pioneering statesman of nineteenth-century Britain.

In 1879, Henry George (1839–97), US land reformer and economist, published *Progress and Poverty*, in which he proposed that the State should tax the income from the use of bare land, but not from improvements. He consequently pleaded for the abolition of all other taxes. He envisaged the government's annual income from the single tax to be so large that there would be a surplus for the expansion of public works. His book made him tremendously popular and controversial. Although he was reviled by academic economists, he exerted his influence on men like American President Woodrow Wilson (1856–1924), American philosopher John Dewey (1859–1952), etc.

Henry George's theory was not subscribed to either in America or in Britain. However, in practice, the imperialists-cum-merchants went about occupying more and more land in foreign countries. As Robert L. Heilbroner, in *The Worldly Philosophers* (1999: 190–91), points out:

> The map-makers of the West were changing the colours that denoted the ownership of the darker continents. Between 1870 and 1898, Britain added 4 million sq. miles and 88 million people to its empire; France gained nearly the same area of territory, with 40 million souls attached; Germany won a million miles and 16 million colonials; Belgium took 900,000 miles and 30 million people; even Portugal joined the race, with 800,000 miles and 9 million inhabitants.

In the late eighteenth and much of the nineteenth century, professional economists ranging from Adam Smith, Jeremy Bentham, James Mill, to Richard Cobden did not have much love lost for the colonies. Politicians, who did not dare to differ from the logic of the founders of capitalism, actually proceeded to conquer colonies. Archibald Primrose, fifth Earl of Rosebery (1847–1929), who served as Prime Minister from March 1894–June 1895, epitomised the sentiment of the day when he called the British Empire the 'greatest secular agency' for good the world has ever seen. Mark Twain, in his characteristically sarcastic manner, observed that 'the English are mentioned in the Scripture—Blessed are the meek, for they shall inherit the earth' (Heilbroner 1999: 191). In France, poet, novelist, and dramatist Victor Hugo (1802–85) declared that France was needed by humanity. All Western colonial powers were sending their surplus products abroad, which sparked a race to partition the world. Thus, Africa became a huge market (and a source of cheap raw materials) to be split among the capitalists of England, Germany, Italy, and Belgium; and Asia became a rich pie to be carved up among the Japanese, Russians, and the Dutch. India became a dumping ground for British industry, and China became an India for Japan. It was this kind of imperialism that led to World War I. The imperialist ambitions were whetted by new technology, which had the singular capacity for replacing outmoded methods of production in the non-capitalist colonies.

Alfred Marshall (1842–1924), British economist, improved on the ideas of Adam Smith and Ricardo. He assailed the ideas of Henry George as being too simplistic. In his best-known work, *Principles of Economics* (1890), he introduced several influential economic concepts, including the elasticity of demand, consumer's surplus, quasi-rent, and the representative firm. His writings on the theory of value proposed time as a factor in analysis and reconciled the classical cost-of-production principle with the theory of 'marginal utility'. He did much to rescue economics from dogmatism by insisting that economic reasoning and laws were not themselves a body of complete truth, but an engine for the discovery of truth. Marshall was interested in the self-adjusting, self-correcting nature of the economic world. Keynes, his most brilliant pupil, said that Marshall created 'a whole Copernican system, in which all the elements of the economic universe are kept in their places by mutual counterpoise and interaction' (Heilbroner 1999: 207). He is today regarded as the founder of neo-classical economics. It was Marshall who took economics to a more mathematically rigorous level, but he did not want mathematics to overshadow economics, and thus make it inscrutable to the layman.

Capitalism grew more through technology than through theory. The new technology gave it a tremendous spurt. Railways, for example, had revolutionary effects on the economy. While in Britain, industry was strengthened through the private initiative of businessmen and through technological advancements with governments playing an enabling role, the governments in Germany and Japan themselves took huge initiatives to develop business and industry. In Japan, under the leadership of Emperor Meiji (1868–1912), a programme of modernisation and industrialisation was initiated on a large scale. As Japan was thus industrialised in the late nineteenth century, it could defeat Russia in a war (1904–05), which incidentally aroused pride among the colonised people in Asia, including those in India. It was this original initiative taken by the Meiji Emperor that enabled Japan to become a leading industrial power in the twentieth century. It is evident from the example of Japan that industrialisation could be initiated and sustained by the State. In Japan, from the second half of the nineteenth century onwards, large capitalist enterprises similar to cartels or trusts organised around families who were openly patronised. This was known as ‘Zaibatsu’. One Zaibatsu might operate companies in many areas of economic importance. Zaibatsu owned their own banks, which were used for mobilising capital. By the start of World War II, the big four Zaibatsu (Mitsubishi, Sumitomo, Yasuda, and Mitsui) alone had direct control over more than 30 per cent of Japan’s mining, chemical, and metal industries, and almost 50 per cent control over the machinery and equipment market, a significant part of the foreign commercial fleet, and 70 per cent of the commercial stock exchange. After World War II, the Zaibatsu were dissolved, but their remnants managed to survive and reign again with the blessings of the State, albeit in a less blatant form.

The first example of industrialisation, which happened to be set in Britain, influenced capitalist thinking in the textbooks. As a consequence, the textbooks seem to have failed to capture the methods through which industrialisation happened in America, Japan or Germany in the nineteenth century. Bismarck (1815–98), a Prussian statesman and Chancellor, who achieved his goal of political unification of the Prussian-dominated German empire, directed his government to play a bigger and bolder role in starting and strengthening industrialisation. In Germany, the appeal of nationalism was emotionally exploited to promote industry, as can be seen from the promotion of railways under Bismarck. The government’s policy to promote railways was continued even after Bismarck: in 1909, there were 60,000 km of railways in Germany, of which 3,600 km were privately owned. Bismarck used this bureaucratic socialism partly as a safeguard against the pressure of pro-nationalisation socialists. Germany provided protection to its iron and steel industry, as a consequence of which its production of steel went up from 1½ million tonnes in 1880 to 13 million tonnes in 1910 (Russell 1934: 437–39). Only the

United States surpassed Germany in iron and steel production at the beginning of World War I. This strength also applied to the manufacture of dye-stuffs and chemicals, chemical fertilisers, and the electrical industry. In all these sectors, private industry was openly patronised. This model of State-sponsored capitalism was also supported by economists such as Wilhelm Roscher (1817–94), Bruno Hildebrand (1812–78), and Gustav Von Schmoller (1838–1917), who differed from the supporters of the British model and pleaded for the idea of the historical method. The Historical School believed that economics was culture-specific, and was therefore opposed to universal generalisations. It also believed in careful empirical and historical analysis and did not favour ideological positions based on logic and mathematics. It was concerned with social reform and improving the condition of the common man, even during a period of heavy industrialisation. It is contra-distinct from the British system of *laissez-faire*.

Patronage was so effusively showered on private industries that a private monopoly was developed in almost every sector. The steel union (Stahwerksverband), formed in 1904, came to embarrass almost the whole industry. Similarly, the Rhenish-Westphalian syndicate accounted for more than half the coal production of Germany. In other industries, a looser combination called a cartel, which facilitated an agreement on the selling price, was encouraged by the government. This system helped domestic companies in such a manner as to enable them to succeed in foreign markets. This was called 'dumping', a term that remains in prevalence even now. This is exactly what China is currently accused of doing with the private companies. This method of concentration of production by the companies, though after a period of competition, helped Germany enormously at the beginning of the twentieth century. This deliberate pampering of private industry by the State led, in a decade, to achievements in German industry that had taken more than a century in England, and about half a century in America. In Germany, the banks exercised control almost from the beginning of modern industry. As a result, the power of Deutsche Bank was very great, and this power was not confined to Germany, but spread to all places in the world where German finance extended. As Bertrand Russell (1934: 440) pointed out:

> [I]t financed the North-Eastern Pacific Railway, in the United States, until 1893. It controlled the Turkish Railways, and was interested in promoting the Berlin-Bagdad scheme. As time went on, the Deutsche Bank came to have more and more influence on Germany policy. But, the influence was reciprocal if the Bank invested money in Turkey, that is partly because Turkey was important for German diplomacy. Patriotism and finance were in harmony, and the interests of the plutocracy could be furthered without any disloyalty to the State.

According to the book, *Hitler over Europe*, written by Ernst Henri in 1934, this process had reached such a stage that Thyssen, the head of the Steel Trust, had become powerful enough for even Hitler to be considered his megaphone. In other words, the power of the steel magnate Thyssen was so overwhelming as to influence Hitler to the point of articulating his thoughts.

Economic growth in America in the nineteenth century had started earlier than in Germany. Being a bigger country, the American economy by the end of the nineteenth century was more powerful than that of Germany, or, for that matter, Great Britain, which had the biggest empire in the world. During its war of independence, America was inspired by the ideal of liberty, and Jefferson's Declaration of Independence also mentioned that all men are created equal. Being immigrants as a group, they were aggressive and acquisitive. Governments of the day shared this spirit and assisted them in every conceivable way. Although Jefferson had drafted the Declaration of Independence, he was not involved in the drafting of the Constitution of the United States, as he was then serving as the Ambassador in France. As Charles A. Beard pointed out in *An Economic Interpretation of the Constitution of United States* (1925): 'The movement for the Constitution of United States was originated and carried through principally by four groups of personal interest which had been adversely affected under the Articles of Confederation: money, public securities, manufactures, and trade and shipping'. To quote further:

> [T]he members of the Philadelphia Convention which drafted the Constitution were, with a few exceptions, immediately, directly, personally interested in, and derived economic advantages from the establishment of the new system. The Constitution was essentially an economic document based upon the concept that the fundamental private rights of property are anterior to government, and morally beyond the reach of popular majorities. (Russell 1934: 234)

At the very first Congress, the process of making the rich richer commenced. This was gleefully facilitated by Alexander Hamilton (1757–1804), one of the founders of the American Constitution and the first Treasury Secretary under President George Washington. He was no admirer of democracy. In fact, at the constitutional convention, he had proposed that the President and Senators should be chosen for life, and that the President should appoint State Governors, who would have the power of veto over State legislation. Fortunately, he did not succeed in carrying the day with him on this. However, Hamiltonian economics influenced America so deeply as to last forever. Hamilton and Jefferson were great ideological rivals. They were both members of the Washington Cabinet, from 1790–94. Bertrand Russell (1934: 237) observes:

> No two men could have been antithetical. Jefferson stood for democracy and agriculture, Hamilton for aristocracy and urban wealth .... Both in a measure succeeded, and both in a measure failed: Jefferson made America the home of democracy, Hamilton made it the home of millionaires. In politics, the victory went to Jefferson; in economics to Hamilton.

Russell further observes that corruption, deliberately promoted by Hamilton, found plentiful opportunities, first in connection with the allotment of new lands, and then in the financing of railways. As a consequence, the rich in America grew richer than men had ever been.

For all Jefferson's soaring democratic vision, it suffered from the limitation of being unable to see the rising industrial tide of his time. He shared this intellectual limitation with none other than Adam Smith, who belonged to the same period. While Hamilton trampled upon all the norms of public administration as well as the principles of free market in favouring capitalists and capitalism, it must be said, in fairness to him, that a probe following his retirement showed that his decisions had not been prompted by motives of personal corruption.

One of the first things the government did was to pass the Homestead Act in 1862, by which any American, or any foreigner interested in becoming a naturalised citizen, was enabled to obtain 160 acres of public land gratis. To increase the availability of public land, the Federal government started a war against the Native Americans to snatch their lands west of the Mississippi, which had been granted to them by President Jackson. In order to provide labour for cultivation, a legislation was adopted, enabling employers to bring in indentured labour from Europe. The first transcontinental railway was authorised in 1862 by Congress, which granted about 22 million acres of land and government bonds amounting to more than $27 million. The same generous approach was adopted by the government with regard to agriculture, oil wealth, iron ore, and gold towards entrepreneurs in the 1860s. American industry, as compared to Britain, was underdeveloped at the time, and the government therefore limited competition to its national borders as a matter of policy. America being literally a land of opportunity, every section had something to gain, and no one grudged the sudden explosion in inequalities. All of them felt that the most urgent thing was the development of natural resources.

While domestic competition was encouraged, it was utterly unregulated. This phase (the second half of nineteenth-century America) threw up many unscrupulous and ruthless businessmen. Commodore (Cornelius) Vanderbilt (1794–1877) was the most noted amongst them. As a shipping and railroad magnate, he broke every possible rule and built a fortune of over $100 million by 1877, the largest accumulated in the US till then. He, however, gave $1 million to what is now known as the Vanderbilt University, and the rest to his son. Towards the end of his life, Vanderbilt found his rivals in such men as Daniel Drew (1797–1879), James Fisk (1835–72), and Jason 'Jay' Gould (1836–92), who matched him in trickery and bribery. Their game revolved round the Erie Railroad company. In their deadly competition, they stopped short at nothing: they issued a mass of Erie bonds to themselves; they even bought a printing press to convert bonds into shares; they bought judges and managed legislators. In all this, each side tried to win public sympathy by accusing the others of gross irregularities. As they cheated one another, the public authorities were not only mute witnesses, but also active accomplices. This is only illustrative of the state of wild business obtaining in America in the nineteenth century, also known as robber-baron capitalism in the textbooks. This led to huge monopolies. To give a blatant illustration: a self-made businessman, John D. Rockefeller (1839–1937), along with his trusted partner Henry Morrison Flagler (1830–1913), acquired total control over the Standard Oil Company. This company, in time, gained full control not only over the refinery industry, but also the railway lines. Rockefeller faced public wrath, litigation, and every possible democratic agitation, and yet remained on top. The silver lining in his career was his gigantic philanthropy.

American economic historian Ernest L. Bogart (1870–1958) stated that the manufacture of iron and steel was America's key industry. But at the time of the Civil War, Great Britain was much ahead of all other countries in iron and steel. America caught up with England in the year 1890. During 1860–1920, the quantity of iron and steel increased in America by 230 times. Scottish-American industrialist, business magnate, and philanthropist Andrew Carnegie (1835–1913) emerged as the most dominant monopolist of the industry through blatantly illegal practices. While retiring from business, he sold his company for $400 million in 1900 to J. P. Morgan (1837–1913), who congratulated Carnegie on being the richest man in the world.

The growing concern about the evils of industrial and financial monopoly led to the Sherman Anti-trust Act being passed in 1890. However, it remained in limbo for twelve years, in the course of which monopolies grew further. President Theodore Roosevelt (1858–1919), who served as the twenty-sixth President of the US, from 1901–09, took a radical step against the giant railroad complex, the Northern Securities Company, which was under the control of such corporate colossi as J. P. Morgan and John D. Rockefeller. In conformity with the provisions of the Sherman Anti-trust Act, the government succeeded in breaking up the size of the companies. In 1902, President Roosevelt had the Federal Bureau of Corporations endowed with the power to inspect the books of private businesses, to ascertain facts and take action in public interest. He was instrumental in bestowing power on the Interest Rate Commerce Commission to fix railroad rates and forbid discrimination between shippers. He also secured the passage of the Pure Food and Drugs Act 1906, which prohibited the making of adulterated foods, drugs, and medicines. The labour field did not go unnoticed either; he threatened the owners into increasing the pay and granting better working conditions to labour. One of the most notable steps that Roosevelt took as President was converting more than 150 million acres of public land into national forests. President Theodore Roosevelt is rightly regarded in history as the man who first began to regulate capitalism and control monopolies in public interest.

After World War I, pre-war trends such as the expansion of European capitalism, expansion of world markets, and the use of the gold standard suffered serious erosion. Capitalism of the nineteenth century was discredited by World War I and the post-war experience. The Russian Revolution of 1917, one of the results of the war, posed a serious ideological and political threat. The labour was restive, and the Great Depression overshadowed everything else. The free market philosophy retreated in Mussolini's Italy and Hitler's Germany. The economic situation in 1933 was desperate in America. Most of the nation's banks were closed, and industrial production was down to 66 per cent of the 1929 level. More than thirty million people were unemployed, and farmers were no better placed. First, Roosevelt ended the depositors' run on banks by closing all the banks, and then had the Reconstruction Finance Corporation strengthen stronger banks with loans and purchase bank stocks totalling $2 billion. He also introduced radical bank reforms to increase the powers of the Federal Reserve System. On top of them all, he got many bills approved by the Congress, which comprised the early New Deal. These measures, taken in the first 100 days, provided relief to diverse economic groups in the nation. He also had the Congress establish the Federal Emergency Relief Administration (FERA) and appropriate $5 billion for its operation. Congress was also persuaded to establish a Civilian Conservation Corps (CCC) which, at its peak, provided work to young men in reforestation and flood control. Similar measures were undertaken to assist the farmers. A sixth of the nation's home owners, who were threatened by mortgage foreclosure, were rescued. The huge relief money provided through various schemes and agencies stimulated recovery. Other measures included labour, who received guarantees on wages and hours.

In this flurry of reforms, both the Right, represented by businessmen and conservatives, and the Left, who wanted more, were alienated. The Supreme Court also began striking down certain measures, leading President Franklin Roosevelt to threaten to pack the Supreme Court with progressive jurists. In the end, the Supreme Court avoided further confrontation through adjustments with Roosevelt. For those workers still unemployed, the Congress created the Works Programme Administration (WPA), which employed an average of 21,00,000 workers between 1935 and 1941. A new tax measure, criticised by its opponents as anti-rich, raised the levies on people with large incomes and in big corporations, and became a significant factor in redistributing American income. As a result of all these steps, Franklin Roosevelt made America safe for capitalism, although the capitalists of his day loathed him. Roosevelt remained open-minded at all times, and benefited immensely from the advice of J. M. Keynes. Franklin Roosevelt will be remembered as the greatest democratic leader of the developed world in the twentieth century. The *laissez-faire* of the nineteenth century was subjected to strong regulation by Theodore Roosevelt, and was drastically amended to facilitate government intervention by Franklin Roosevelt. The current advocates of capitalism do not like to remember the debts they owe to the two Roosevelts, while the classic leftists, who feel that both Roosevelts pre-empted a socialist revolution, are uncomfortable with their memory.

US economist Thorstein Veblen (1857–1929) took some time to gain recognition because of his unconventional ideas and disorder in his personal life. In 1899, he published his classic work, *The Theory of the Leisure Class*, which applied Darwin's evolutionary theories to the study of modern economic life, highlighting the competitive and predatory nature of the business world. With dry humour, he identified the makers of the American social class, and coined the term 'conspicuous consumption' to describe the display of wealth indulged in by the upper classes. His reputation was strongest in the 1930s, when the Great Depression was seen as a vindication of his criticism of the business system. Veblen, while being a classical capitalist, heaped ridicule on the lavish lifestyle of the rich as no satirist had done before. Through his incisive study of human nature and social structure, he discovered that Marx's prediction that the working class would unite to overthrow the bourgeoisie would never come true for the simple reason that the poor would rather emulate the rich than exterminate them. His second book, *The Theory of Business Enterprise* (1904), is as coruscating and curious as the first. Unlike Smith or Ricardo or Marx, he realised the ascendancy of the machine. He saw society as dominated by the machine, caught up in its standardisation and precision. Economics to him began to mean the machine-like meshing of society as it turned out goods. Such a social machine would need tools like technicians and engineers. The machine was not concerned with values and profits. It only ground out goods. In his examination of productive processes, Veblen's key discovery was the central role of technology.

John Maynard Keynes, British economist, was known for his revolutionary theories on the causes of prolonged unemployment. He served in the British treasury during World War I and attended the Versailles Peace Conference. He resigned in protest over the Treaty of Versailles of 1919, denouncing its provisions in his first book, *The Economic Consequences of the Peace* (1919), and returned to teaching at Cambridge University. His protest against the Treaty of Versailles made him a noted international figure. At Cambridge, he had worked from the beginning with such giants of philosophy and mathematics as Bertrand Russell, A. N. Whitehead, G. E. Moore, Wittgenstein, etc. His early work on mathematical probability earned plaudits from Bertrand Russell and others. Keynes was a man of many parts and was also attached to the 'Bloomsbury Group', comprising English writers, philosophers, and artists, who frequently met to discuss aesthetic and philosophical questions. When he needed money, he played the stock market and won money, thereby proving that he did not only have an academic flair but also a concrete market sense. His private life was equally colourful. He eventually married a noted ballerina, Lydia Lopokova, much to the relief of his friends.

Keynes divagated from mathematical logic into economics, where his genius leapt to its zenith. Having secured his reputation as a public intellectual with his iconoclastic views on the Treaty of Versailles, he foresaw the storm signals of the approaching Depression and began to suggest radical remedies to deal with it. In due course, he met President Roosevelt and advised him on the crisis. President Roosevelt, after meeting Keynes, wrote to Felix Frankfurter: 'I had a grand talk with K, and liked him immensely' (Heilbroner 1999: 261).

Analysing the causes of the Great Depression, he showed how the total demand was influenced by expenditures, and how an equilibrium short of full employment could emerge without setting in operation the force of recovery. He argued that the objective of full employment could be achieved only if governments and central banks deliberately encouraged investments in new capital goods and maintained the cheap money policy and public investment during a recession. His original inventive theory divided the economic community and changed capitalist theory beyond recognition. His impact on Franklin Roosevelt and on the shape of Brettonwood's institutions helped to save the capitalist system, as well as establish welfare states in the West. He turned out to be the greatest bridge-builder between the theories of classical capitalism and social democracy. His policies dominated the West from the 1940s to the 1970s. It was during this period that sharp interpersonal inequalities were alleviated, and the modern middle classes emerged in the West. But the return of the West, more particularly the United States, to neo-classical economics as advocated by Milton Friedman (1912–2006) and others is said to have eventually led to the Great Recession of 2008. What is more, it is also said to have led to an unconscionable rise in economic inequalities. The worst part is that the middle classes have been relatively impoverished, and the lot of the poor has worsened. The world has been rudely reminded of Keynes' remedy, as a result of which there has been a hurried return to Keynesianism. Keynes' legacy is once again being claimed by sections of both pro-capitalist thinkers and left-of-centre economists. Economists like Joseph Stiglitz and Paul Krugman, as admirers of Keynes, are defying ideological pigeonholing, much like Keynes himself. An economist like Thomas Picketty, who is universally credited with empirical sleuthing regarding levels of inequality in even earlier centuries, has suggested remedies beyond Keynes. Keynes is widely regarded as the third greatest economist, after Adam Smith and Karl Marx.

Keynes published his magnum opus, *The General Theory of Employment, Interest and Money*, in 1936, which is considered the greatest economic work of the twentieth century. The prime innovation in general theory was to show that, in severe depressions, monetary policy would not work. Keynes said that economists grounded in classical models were like

> Euclidean geometers in a non-Euclidean world who, discovering that in experience straight lines apparently parallel often meet, rebuke the lines for not keeping straight as the only remedy for the unfortunate collisions that are occurring. Yet, in truth, there is no remedy except to throw over the axiom of parallels and to work a non-Euclidean geometry. Something similar is required today in economics. (Keynes 1964 [1936]: 15)

In the words of Sylvia Nasar (2011: 330):

> ... Keynes ... let money flows (such as income) functionally determine other money flows (such as consumption) .... what made the General Theory ... radical was Keynes's proof that it was possible for a free market economy to settle into states in which workers and machines remained idle for prolonged periods .... only way to revive business confidence ... was by cutting taxes and letting businesses and individuals keep more of their income so ... they could spend it .... the government had to ... act as the spender of last resort ....

Sylvia Nasar further points out that Keynes laid even greater stress on direct investment by government to ensure full expenditure. Keynes emphasised that the government should act as the spender of the last resort.

For all the new and radical ideas that Keynes threw up, he was a proper capitalist thinker. He wrote in 1926, 'I think that Capitalism, wisely managed, can probably be made more efficient for attaining economic ends than any alternative system yet in sight, but that in itself, it is in many ways extremely objectionable' (2004 [1926]). He was very worried about the inflexible influence of outmoded ideologies imbibed by leaders, economists, or even agitators in their twenties, while dealing with new situations. However, he was not so much bothered about the power of vested interests as he was about that of ideology: 'I am sure that the power of vested interests is vastly exaggerated, compared with the gradual encroachment of ideas .... But, soon or late, it's ideas, not vested interests, which are dangerous for good or evil' (Heilbroner 1999: 15). Keynes' peculiar genius lay in his inexplicable ability to put his finger on the pulse of the concrete and the immediate. It is therefore not surprising that he said, 'But this long run is a misleading guide to current affairs. In the long run, we are all dead' (2000 [1923]: Ch. 3). Robert Skidelsky, noted biographer of Keynes, says that Bertrand Russell wrote: 'Keynes' intellect was the sharpest and clearest that I have ever known. When I argued with him, I felt I took my life in my hands, and I seldom emerged without feeling something of a fool' (Skidelsky 2009: 57). No greater tribute can ever be paid.

Joseph Schumpeter described American economist, statistician, and inventor Irving Fisher (1867–1947) as the greatest economist the United States had ever produced. This assessment was later shared by Milton Friedman and James Tobin. Fisher's research on the quantity theory of money started the school of macroeconomic thought known as 'Monetarism'. He was a pioneer in econometrics, including the development of index numbers. Two mistakes led him to suffer, in contrast with Keynes: the first was his false prediction, just prior to the Wall Street crash of 1929, that the market had reached 'a permanently high plateau'; and the second was his theory of debt deflation as an explanation for the 'Great Depression', as well as his advocacy of full-reserve banking and alternative currencies. Keynes also recognised the merit of Irving Fisher's ideas by saying that Fisher had anticipated some of his own ideas.

Friedrich Hayek (1899–1992), Austrian-British economist, took on Keynes, with whom he engaged in heated battles. He criticised government intervention in the free market, arguing that it is destructive of individual values and ultimately ineffective against such economic ailments as inflation, unemployment, and recession. He established his fame with his first book, *The Road to Serfdom* (1944). Two more important books followed—*The Constitution of Liberty* (1960) and *The Political Order of a Free People* (1979). His views were highly influential among conservatives, including former British Prime Minister Margaret Thatcher. Libertarians in America still swear by him.

Joseph Schumpeter (1883–1950), an Austrian-born American economist, first established his reputation as Harvard professor by publishing his two-volume book, *Business Cycles*

(1939), and reached the acme of his fame through his most popular work, *Capitalism, Socialism and Democracy* (1942). He is also known for his posthumous work, *History of Economic Analysis* (1954). Schumpeter belonged to the Historical School of Economics, despite his own criticisms of this School. His ideas about the role of innovation in entrepreneurship can be seen as a continuation of ideas originating in the historical school in the nineteenth century, especially through the works of Gustav Von Schmoller (1838–1917) and Werner Sombart (1863–1941). According to Christopher Freeman, the central point of Schumpeter's work is that capitalism can only be understood as an evolutionary process of continuous innovation and 'creative destruction'. Contrary to Keynes' version, the hero of his story is the entrepreneur. He believed that the institution enabling the entrepreneur to buy the resources needed to realise her/his vision was a well-developed capitalistic financial system, which included a whole range of institutions for granting credit. Schumpeter was pessimistic about the future of capitalism as he believed that capitalism would gradually weaken itself and eventually collapse. Specifically, the success of capitalism would lead to corporatism, and thus to values hostile to capitalism. In the process, unemployment and lack of fulfilling work will lead to the defeat of pro-capitalist parties and the success of social democratic parties. All this will eventually lead to liberal capitalism and 'labourism'.

Schumpeter emphasised that he was analysing trends, not engaging in political advocacy. He laid far greater store by the role of innovation than the invisible hand or price competition in the market. He argued that technological innovation would often create temporary monopolies, allowing abnormal profits that would soon be competed away by rivals and imitators. He also felt that these temporary monopolies were necessary to provide firms with the incentive to develop new products and processes. Although Schumpeter hailed from a relatively aristocratic background, 'elite', for him, was not based on birth, but on intellect and will. He thus envisioned an aristocracy of talent. He was not just a great economist;

he also enriched economics through inputs and insights from various disciplines. Heilbroner therefore described him as a 'historical sociologist' as well.

American economist Paul Samuelson (1915–2009) was the first American to win the Nobel Prize for economics, and is generally regarded as the greatest academic economist of the twentieth century. Samuelson provided the mathematical foundations of economics in his book, *Foundations of Economic Analysis* (1947). He also authored the bestselling economic textbook of all time, *Economics—An Introductory Analysis* (1948). This textbook explained the principles of Keynesian economics and has sold over forty million copies, published in various languages. It is no wonder that Samuelson remarked, 'I don't care who writes the nation's laws or crafts its advanced treaties—if I can write its economics text books'.[1] He wrote his celebrated textbook in the shadow of the Great Depression and World War II. Samuelson wrote: 'It is not too much to say that the widespread creation of dictatorships and the resulting World War II stemmed in no small measure from the world's failure to meet this basic economic problem (The Great Depression) adequately' (Samuelson 2000). After his death, the Massachusetts Institute of Technology (MIT), where he had worked for seventy years, paid the following tribute: 'He transformed everything he touched: the theoretical foundations of his field, the way economics was taught around the world ... as one of the giants on whose shoulders every contemporary economist stands' (Krasny 2009). The Nobel Committee, while awarding its prize, said: 'More than any other contemporary economist, Samuelson has helped to raise the general, analytical and methodological levels in economic science. He has simply rewritten considerable parts

---

[1] 'Paul Anthony Samuelson: The Concise Encyclopedia of Economics | Library of Economics and Liberty', available at http://www.econlib.org/library/Enc/bios/Samuelson.html (accessed 19 February 2017).

of economic theory.'[2] Paul Krugman credited Samuelson with having almost 'created modern economics'.

American economist Milton Friedman (1912–2006) received the 1976 Nobel Prize for economics for his research on consumption analysis, monetary history, and theory of the complexity of stabilisation policy. In the 1960s, he was the main opponent of Keynesian policies. He theorised that there existed a natural rate of unemployment, and argued that employment above this rate would cause inflation to accelerate. He promoted the alternative macroeconomic viewpoint known as 'monetarism', and argued that a steady small expansion of money supply was the preferred policy. He served as advisor to US President Ronald Reagan and Conservative British Prime Minister Margaret Thatcher. A survey of economists ranked Friedman as the second most popular economist of the twentieth century, after Keynes, and *The Economist* described him as the most influential economist of the second half of the twentieth century. He worked for thirty years as professor at the University of Chicago, where he contributed to the establishment of an intellectual community that produced a number of Nobel Prize winners, known collectively as the Chicago School of Economics. From 1968 to 1978, he and Paul Samuelson participated in the Economics Cassette Series by adopting antagonistic positions, with Friedman opposing Keynesian policies and Samuelson supporting neo-Keynesianism. The philosophy of Milton Friedman dominated the economic policies of American Presidents from Ronald Reagan to George W. Bush Jr., and those of Western Europe, starting with Margaret Thatcher. As Chairman of the Federal Bank, Alan Greenspan implemented the monetarism of Milton Friedman.

It is now said that Friedman's policies led to the Great Recession of 2008, which is being alleviated through the

---

[2] 'The Sveriges Riksbank Prize in Economic Sciences in Memory of Alfred Nobel 1970'. Nobelprize.org. Nobel Media AB 2014. Available at <http://www.nobelprize.org/nobel_prizes/economic-sciences/laureates/1970/ (accessed 18 March 2017).

Keynesian medicine. But the tremors of this recession are still being felt. Politics in the US and Western Europe remain polarised, with Bernie Sanders, a self-declared democratic socialist, emerging as the main challenger to Hillary Clinton in the Democratic Party, and Jeremy Corbyn leading a successful internal revolt for the Left within the Labour Party of Britain. Huge sections of the poor and lower middle classes have been feeling alienated in America, leading to the insurgency led by Bernie Sanders within the Democratic Party. The bulk of these classes had no difficulty in supporting Donald Trump as President of the United States, who succeeded in converting their economic alienation into anti-minorityism. This unexpected development is not very different from the phenomena of Fascism in Italy and Nazism in Germany. While the Great Recession of 2008 represented an economic crisis, it has now assumed a political dimension as well.

John Kenneth Galbraith (1908–2006), Canada-born American economist, served as a public official and diplomat. He was active in Democratic Party politics, serving in the administrations of US Presidents Franklin Roosevelt, Harry S. Truman, John Kennedy, and Lyndon Johnson. He was also a prolific author. Among his most famous works was a popular trilogy on economics, *American Capitalism* (1952), *The Affluent Society* (1958), and *The New Industrial State* (1967). He served as professor at Harvard University for about fifty years. As US Ambassador to India, his friendship with Jawaharlal Nehru was well-known. He remained a life-long friend to India and an admirer of Indian democracy. Among the international honours that he received, the Padma Vibhushan, India's second highest civilian award, should be prominently noted. In *The Affluent Society*, he explained that to become successful, post-World War II America as a State should make large investments in such areas as highways and education. Galbraith refused to equate increased production with the economic health of the country. He therefore became a target of all conservatives, led by Friedman. However, American liberals were divided in their estimate. While Joseph Stiglitz felt that 'Galbraith understood capitalism as lived—not as theorized' (2006: 9), Paul Krugman did not think highly of Galbraith as an academic economist. His biographer, Richard Parker, contends that Galbraith was a complex thinker. In his later life, Galbraith was increasingly ignored, as he was perceived to be leaning too much to the Left for American taste. During the Great Recession of 2008, Galbraith was the most talked about American economist, after Keynes. His solutions are considered post-Keynesian, and the Nobel Academy was criticised for denying him the Nobel Prize. His place in history is likely to be determined more by future historians than by contemporary commentators. Galbraith was more than an economist; he was a multidisciplinary thinker.

Indian economist Amartya Sen (1933–) is the only Asian to have won the Nobel Prize in economics. He was also awarded the inaugural Charleston-EFG in recognition of his work on welfare economics in February 2015, during a reception at the Royal Academy in the UK. He is currently the Thomas W. Lamont University Professor and Professor of Economics and Philosophy at Harvard University. In 1998, he was appointed Master of Trinity College, Cambridge, becoming the first Asian head of an Oxbridge college. Sylvia Nasar, in *Grand Pursuit* (2011), included Amartya Sen in her short list of great economists of the twentieth century. Sen defies ideological pigeonholing; early in his career, he ceased to take interest in macroeconomics, focusing instead on social choice theory. He became celebrated for his pioneering work on famines. His searing experience of the Bengal famine in his early teens made him obsessed with the problem of hunger. He propounded that famines occur not only from a lack of food, but also from inequalities built into the mechanisms for distributing food. While focusing on the field of development economics, he exerted considerable influence on the 'Human Development Report', published by the United Nations Development Programme (UNDP). He introduced his original concept of 'capability', interpreting it in terms of 'functionings', in the sense that citizens should be enabled either by the State or by society to realise their inherent potential and exercise the rights enshrined in the statute books. In *Development as Freedom* (1999), Sen outlined five specific types of freedom:

political freedom, economic facilities, social opportunities, transparency guarantees, and protective security.

Sen is perhaps the only modern economist to take as much interest in the problems of ethics as in those of economics. His encounter with John Rawls, famous for his magisterial work, *A Theory of Justice*, was therefore most productive. As a consequence of the impact of Rawls, Sen published his own book, *The Idea of Justice* (2009). Sen is widely described as the 'conscience of economics' for his passionate interest in welfare and ethics. However, going beyond ethics, Sen also covered almost the entire gamut of philosophy. With his knowledge of the ancient Indian classical language, Sanskrit, he is as well-versed in Indian philosophy as he is in that of the West. He was therefore able to proclaim with pardonable patriotic pride: 'Sanskrit had a larger atheistic literature than what exists in any other classical language.' With his love of argument, he interacted with giants like Joan Robinson, Maurice Dobb, Kenneth Arrow, and John Rawls in England and America, and improved on his own thoughts. He had earlier gained through his interactions with distinguished peers such as Dr Manmohan Singh, Jagdish Bhagwati, and Sukumar Chakravarthy, while working as Professor at the Delhi School of Economics. With his command over the areas of economics, ethics, and philosophy, he is rightly regarded as one of the greatest living polymaths in the world.

Joseph Stiglitz was the chief economist at the World Bank till January 2000. He is currently working as professor at Columbia University. He has authored celebrated works like *Globalisation and its Discontents* (2002), *The Roaring Nineties* (2003), *The Price of Inequality* (2012), and *The Great Divide* (2015). He first attracted international attention when he was fired by the World Bank for dissenting with its policies. The thrust of his complaint against the World Bank and the International Monetary Fund (IMF), voiced in *Globalisation and its Discontents*, was that an ideologically inspired programme called the 'Washington Consensus' was being forced on every country, regardless of their stages of growth and socio-economic contexts. Intellectuals in the aid-receiving countries hailed the book for its bold and innovative ideas. He received the Nobel Prize in 2001 for laying the foundations for the theory of markets with asymmetric information. For Stiglitz, there is no such thing as invisible hand. In other words, he differs from Adam Smith's belief that free markets lead to efficiency as if guided by unseen forces. He argued that 'the real debate today is finding the real balance between the market and the government. Both are needed. They can complement each other. This balance will differ from time to time and place to place' (Altman 2006). He showed the limitations not only of Adam Smith's invisible hand, but also those of Pareto optimality. Stiglitz's most important contribution, while serving the Clinton administration in 1995, was helping to define a new economic philosophy, a 'third way', which argued that the government had an important, though limited, role to play.

After his controversial stint at the World Bank, he emerged as the major spokesman of the third way at the global level. In 2012, he described European austerity plans as a 'suicide pact'. Stiglitz has been critical of rating agencies, describing them as the 'key culprit' in the financial crisis, noting that 'they were the party that performed the alchemy from "F" rated to "A" rated'. The banks could not have done what they did without the complicity of rating agencies. In 2008, he co-authored (with Linda Bilmes) the popular *The Three Trillion Dollar War*, in which he examined the full costs of the Iraq war, including many hidden costs. He has, of late, been focusing on the increasing inequalities that developed during the period led by President Ronald Reagan to that of George Bush Jr. During the thirty-year period that followed World War II till the presidency of Reagan, the conditions of the poor improved greatly, with many among the poor joining the ranks of the middle classes. However, from the 1980s to 2010, inequalities increased inordinately, as a result of which the rich became richer, the middle classes became poorer, and the poor was even more impoverished. This new anomalous situation led Stiglitz to coin the famous line, 'one per cent versus ninety nine per cent'. By way of illustration, he drew attention to the wealth of the Walton family:

> The six heirs to the Walmart Empire possess a combined wealth of some $90 billion, which is equivalent to the wealth of the entire bottom thirty per cent of US society (many at the bottom have zero or negative net worth, especially after the housing debacle). Warren Buffet put the matter correctly when he said, there has been a class war going on for the last 20 years, and my class has won. (Stiglitz 2015: 95)

One of the main causes of this galloping inequality, according to Stiglitz, is the 'rent-seeking' problem posed by the dominance of the financial sector. Stiglitz says,

> In recent years, the financial sector has accounted for some 40% of all corporate profits. This does not mean that its social contribution sneaks into the plus column, or comes even close. The crisis shows how it could wreak havoc on the economy. In a rent-seeking economy such as ours has become, private returns and social returns are badly out of whack. (2015: 99)

Stiglitz referred to MF Global as a concrete instance of financial manipulations:

> People were surprised when the financial firm MF Global, headed by Jon Corzine, suddenly collapsed into bankruptcy last year, leaving victims by the thousands as a result of actions that may prove to have been criminal; but given Wall Street's recent history, I am not sure people were all that surprised to learn that several MF Global executives would still be getting their bonuses. (ibid.: 100)

He argued that the rich should pay better wages to the labour in their own interest. He made a political point by saying that,

> Franklin D. Roosevelt, a purebred patrician, understood that the only way to save an essentially capitalist America was not only to spread the wealth through taxation and social programmes, but to put restraints on capitalism itself, through regulation. Roosevelt and the economist John Maynard Keynes, while reviled by the capitalists, succeeded in saving capitalism from the capitalists. (ibid.: 104)

He also pointed out that racial inequalities have widened. Stiglitz is alive to the fact that inequality had always existed. According to him, there are two reasons why inequality is growing beyond an unconscionable and unsustainable limit: first, an increase in rent-seeking, and second, an increase in the inequality of access to quality education and public health. Both negative aspects are accentuated through the perverse tax system, which is stacked against the 99 per cent. Warren Buffet famously pointed out that it was unfair that his tax rate was lower than that of his secretary. While speaking of America's socialism for the rich, he referred to the huge bail-outs to salvage America from the Great Recession. Stiglitz viewed this as a 'new form of ersatz capitalism in which losses are socialised and profits privatised'. He described it as 'socialism with American characteristics', sarcastically reminding people of the pet phrase used by the Government of China to defend any ultra-capitalist programme of its own (Stiglitz 2015: 194).

American economist Paul Krugman (1953–) worked previously as economics professor at MIT and at Princeton University, and now holds the title of Professor Emeritus at Princeton University. In 2008, he was awarded the Nobel Prize in economics for his contributions to New Trade Theory and New Economic Geography. In the words of the Prize Committee, 'By having integrated economies of scale into explicit general equilibrium models, Paul Krugman has deepened our understanding of the determinants of trade and the location of economic activity' (2008: 18). He is arguably the most popular columnist for the world's most prestigious daily, *The New York Times*. In his columns, he not only illumines many a dark patch in economics, but also regales with his political analyses, which are at once biting and incisive. Besides, he continues to write esoteric economic theories in online columns and books. Krugman's *International Economics: Theory and Policy* (1987), co-authored with Maurice Obstfeld, is a standard undergraduate text on international economics. Differing from the previously established trade theory based on the comparative advantage of countries with different characteristics, he explained, in his 1979 paper published in the *Journal of International Economics*, that consumers' preference for diversity and economies of scale in production would favour the model of each country producing a few brands of any given type of product, instead of specialising in different types of products. This is now called the New Trade Theory.

Krugman favours globalisation and trade broadly, but he has reservations about the hyper-globalisation that has occurred since the 1980s. He has also been influential in the field of international finance; his 1979 paper showed that misaligned fixed exchange rate regimes could end in sudden speculative attacks. He has done much to revive discussion of the liquidity trap as a topic in economics by alluding to the bad experience of Japan in the 1990s. Krugman was one of the most prominent advocates of the 2008–09 Keynesian resurgence. His insistent voice on the issue led economics commentator Noah Smith to describe it as the 'Krugman insurgency'. In *The Age of Diminished Expectations* (1990), he drew attention to the increasing inequalities in the US. He attributed this in part to changes in technology, but principally to a change in the political atmosphere caused by Movement Conservatives. In 2007, Krugman published *The Conscience of a Liberal*, in which he discussed over a century of history, from the political economy of the Gilded Age to the Bush (Jr.) era. He stated that a middle-class society with greater prosperity and less inequality was created from the time of Roosevelt to that of Nixon through the New Deal, and through the political mobilisation of the people. He also contends that the new unequal society and the Great Recession of 2008–09 were created not only by neo-conservative economics, but also by the capture of levers of power like the Congress itself. The level of inequality in America today is as high as it was before the New Deal. He quotes the statistics provided by Thomas Picketty and Emmanuel Saez (Krugman 2009: 15):

	Highest-income 10%	*Highest-income 1%*
Average for 1920s	43.6%	17.3%
2005	44.3%	17.4%

The gross inequality prevailing in the 1920s was aggravated by the Great Depression, leading to radicalisation of the mood of the American nation. President Franklin Roosevelt, on the advice of Keynes and others, went in for the New Deal, and created a middle-class society for the first time in history. Observers like John Kenneth Galbraith, Michael Harrington, *Time* magazine, etc., commented that a middle-class society had been created in America in the 1950s, with income inequalities greatly reduced and welfare measures largely in place. By way of illustration, the richest 0.1 per cent of Americans owned more than 20 per cent of the nation's wealth in 1929, but only around 10 per cent in the mid-1950s, thanks to President Roosevelt's tax policy. Krugman further says: 'During the post-war boom, the real income of the typical family roughly doubled, from about $22,000 in today's prices to $44,000. That's a growth rate of 2.7 percent per year. And incomes all through the income distribution grew at about the same rate ...' (Krugman 2007: 54). To emphasise the sharp contrast between the 1950s and 1980s, he points out that, since 1980, the median family income has risen only about 0.7 per cent a year. Krugman explains that this lower inequality came about because of increase in income tax rates, and in the strength of trade union workers.

> The top income tax rate (currently only 35%) rose to 63% during the first FDR term, and 79% by the second. By the mid-fifties, as the United States faced the expenses of the Cold War, it had risen to 91% .... The average federal tax on corporate profits rose from less than 40% to more than 45% in 1955 ... the top estate tax rate rose from 20% to 45, then 60, then 70 and finally 77. (ibid.: 47)

Speaking of the power of the unions, he observes: 'The union membership tripled from 1933 to 1938, then nearly doubled again by 1947. At the end of World War II, more than a third of non-farm workers were members of the unions' (ibid.: 49). As all these radical changes were initiated by President Roosevelt, the affected parties were unitedly ranged against his Presidency. Roosevelt did not mince matters, and took them on. To savour the rhetoric of Roosevelt's election war, we need to note his own words:

> We had to struggle with the old enemies of peace—business and financial monopoly, speculation, reckless banking, class antagonism, sectionalism, war profiteering. They had begun to consider the Government of the United States as a mere appendage to their own affairs. We know now that Government by organized money is just as dangerous as Government by organised mob.
>
> Never before in all our history have these forces been so united against one candidate as they stand today. They are unanimous in their hate for me—and I welcome their hatred. (Krugman 2007: 59)

Despite the intense conflict between the Roosevelt-inspired Democrats and the Republicans, there grew an intellectual consensus relating to the post-Roosevelt tax regime and welfare measures. This relative ideological harmony between the two major parties, accompanied by a less unequal society for thirty years after World War II, was not coincidental. But according to Krugman, it was interrelated. He argues that inequality in American society increased inordinately from the period of Reagan to that of Bush Jr. because of the revival of policies that had ruled the roost in the period preceding the Great Depression. Krugman repeatedly criticised the Bush tax cuts, arguing that they would enlarge the budget deficit, enrich the wealthy and aggravate income distribution. He advocated lower interest rates to promote investment and spending on housing and other durable goods. He also pleaded for increased government spending on infrastructure and unemployment benefits on the ground that they would have a larger stimulus effect than tax cuts. He opposed Bush's proposal to privatise social security.

Paul Krugman was perspicacious enough to sound a warning over housing markets, and had criticised Alan Greenspan's earlier reluctance to regulate the mortgage and related financial markets as early as in 2005. Krugman has repeatedly stated that in his view, Greenspan and Phil Gramm are the two individuals most responsible for causing the subprime crisis. Krugman pointed to the key roles they played in keeping derivatives, financial markets, and investment banks unregulated, and to the Gramm-Leach-Bliley Act, which repealed the Great Depression-era safeguards that prevented commercial banks, investment banks, and insurance companies from merging.

Thomas Picketty (b. 1971) is a French economist, now teaching at the London School of Economics. He is the youngest, and perhaps the most promising, among the noted economists in the world. From the very beginning, he focused on the problem of economic inequality. In his acclaimed work *Capital in the 21st Century* (2013), he showed graphically how the levels of inequality in the last decades of the twentieth century were as high as in the last decades of the nineteenth century. To arrive at this conclusion, he pioneered new statistical methods, which have proved to be precisely correct. *The Economist* of London congratulated him on what it called empirical sleuthing. While faulting him for daring to call his book *Capital*, with a view to inviting comparisons with Marx's *Das Capital*, it conceded that Picketty's work is indeed pathbreaking. The earlier work done by Stiglitz, Paul Krugman, and Anthony Atkinson had already identified inequality as a new economic problem of the highest magnitude. Close on the heels of their work, Thomas Picketty's original research has given this historical depth. Picketty argues that the rate of capital return in developed countries is greater than the rate of economic growth. This is one of Picketty's key discoveries. He argued that the asymmetrical gap between the rate of capital return and that of economic growth has been responsible for the increase in inequality, and will continue to do so in the future. To redress this, he pleads for a progressive global tax on wealth. He further says that this increasing inequality is no accident; rather, it is a feature of capitalism that can be reversed only through state intervention. He also warns that such levels of inequality will jeopardise the democratic system. The essential truth of Picketty's warning can be seen in the triumph of Brexit and Donald Trump. We have witnessed similar trends earlier, too, when the Great Depression enabled Hitler to emerge. Political thinkers must, therefore, take Picketty seriously.

In Europe, Social Democratic parties in France, Germany, and the Scandinavian countries have not only been winning their battles at the hustings repeatedly, but have also succeeded in establishing welfare states. What is more, one paradoxical consequence of welfare states is that a modified capitalism has been able to pacify radical forces and avert political crises. As a result of these processes, the conservative and progressive parties have worked on the basis of a multi-partisan consensus.

In the United States, socialist parties as such did not emerge. But after the Great Depression, through the repeated victories of Franklin Roosevelt, the Democratic Party was transformed into a milder version of the European Socialist parties. The Republican Party, which has been returning to power after Franklin Roosevelt, could never dare to tinker with the prevailing welfare system. Even Ronald Reagan, who was elected on the explicit platform of downsizing the welfare system, could not touch it with a barge pole. Mitt Romney, the Republican candidate in the 2012 Presidential election, publicly bemoaned the fact that welfare beneficiaries in America constituted 47 per cent of the electorate. He enraged not only the beneficiaries, but also progressives by describing them as 'takers'. After Obama's victory, Romney repented his verbal indiscretion. The parties of the Right and the Left in Latin America have been extending their welfare schemes in a competitive manner. The phenomenon of Latin America is more or less true of almost all developing countries in the world.

Against this backdrop, the example of India is both gigantic and glorious. Independent India led by Jawaharlal Nehru, through his stewardship of the Congress Party, was both pragmatic and socialistic right from the start. The mixed economy that he introduced with the assistance of the economist Mahalanobis has withstood the test of time. The mix swung more towards the public sector during Indira Gandhi, and later, under P. V. Narasimha Rao and Manmohan Singh, it shifted back to the private sector. The swings effected by Rao and Singh came rather belatedly, but produced huge positive results. During Nehru's time, the Indian economic pattern was modelled more after Bismarck's Germany or post-Meiji Japan rather than that of the Soviet Union. In the initial stages, the State in Germany and Japan had taken huge initiatives to develop infrastructure and industry, which Nehru followed. It needs to be noted that Nehru started a number of industries in the public sector and did not nationalise private industry, with the exception of the Life Insurance Corporation of India, which was nationalised in the wake of a scam involving Ramakrishna Dalmia, the first big financial scandal in newly independent India. It also needs to be pointed out that the management of TISCO by the Tatas, with only 3–4 per cent of the latter's holding and a more than 70 per cent holding by Public Financial Institutions, shows that private initiative was not discouraged at all in Nehru's time. Nehru's India did not have a smaller private sector than any other country, except perhaps West Germany, which went in for ordoliberalism under the intellectual leadership of Ludwig Erhard. Industry in the UK was largely nationalised under the prime ministership of Clement Attlee. French President Charles de Gaulle went in for large-scale nationalisation in France. Even Jagdish Bhagwati of Columbia University, who is regarded as the high priest of capitalist thinking in India, has always maintained that Nehru's economic model admirably suited India in its initial phase.

Following the split in the Congress Party in 1969, Indira Gandhi went in for land reforms, apart from the nationalisation of banks and other measures. Even during the halcyon days of Indira Gandhi's nationalisation drive, private industries were given huge licences, exemplified by the fact that the Birlas received a fertiliser licence in Goa soon after her left-leaning victory in the 1971 mid-term parliamentary poll. After Indira Gandhi's return to power in 1980, private industry was encouraged by her finance ministers, R. Venkataraman and Pranab Mukherjee. Rajiv Gandhi continued the informal liberalisation of India's economy in a broader way. P. V. Narasimha Rao and his finance minister,

Manmohan Singh, went in for large-scale liberalisation in an open fashion. This major formal ideological change was made politically possible by the severe foreign exchange crunch that India faced at the time. The crunch was graphically demonstrated by the need to mortgage India's gold during Chandrasekhar's prime ministership in 1990. Apart from foreign exchange problems, the change was also facilitated by the coincidental collapse of Soviet Russia, which strengthened the perception that liberalisation was the paramount need of the hour. So much so, that even the minority government of P. V. Narasimha Rao managed to bring about the change with hardly any opposition, either from the socialistically inclined Third Front or from the BJP. Even the Communist parties contented themselves with a verbal protest. It was this unstated consensus that emerged in 1991 that was responsible for the continuation of liberalisation policies by the succeeding governments of the United Front (led by Deve Gowda and I. K. Gujral), the BJP (headed by Vajpayee), and the UPA (led by Dr Manmohan Singh of the Congress). During the tenure of the prime ministership of Dr Manmohan Singh, reformist policies, boldly initiated by Dr Singh as Finance Minister in 1991–96, were further expedited. In this process, Dr Singh was ably assisted by P. Chidambaram and Pranab Mukherjee.

In the meantime, Western countries, which had swung towards unregulated capitalism and globalisation from the late 1970s, have begun to experience a serious backlash since the Great Recession of 2008. Progressive forces (left-of-centre) seem to be asserting themselves so much as to require considerable recalibration in America and Europe. The mere beginning of the assertion of progressive forces seems to have brought out the prejudices against women and minorities. What ought to be an ideological battle between right-of-centre and left-of-centre forces is assuming the dangerous dimension of ethnic conflict. This phenomenon is not new; it was seen in the 1930s when Hitler rode to power on the crest of an ethnic wave. Pope Francis lost no time after Donald Trump's election to the American presidency to remind the people of the world that Hitler had also come to power through the ballot box, implying that democratic election does not by itself guarantee liberal freedoms.

After Roosevelt's New Deal, the formation of the Bretton Woods institution, and the Marshall Aid given by America to Europe after World War II, capitalism in Western Europe underwent a basic transformation. Clement Attlee, who became the Labour Prime Minister of Britain in 1945, nationalised major British industries, and presided over the establishment of a welfare state in Britain. In the post-Roosevelt years, American Presidents from Truman to Nixon strengthened the policies of a welfare state. What is more, they also strengthened the oversight of government institutions of economic activities. France also enhanced the role of the State in the economic sphere to rebuild itself after World War II, under the leadership of Charles De Gaulle. Germany was the only major nation in Western Europe which did not involve the State to the same degree in economic activities. In Japan, private-sector companies were not only deliberately patronised, but also protected from foreign competition by the government, which shows that free trade policies were not practised in Japan. In other Asian economies such as South Korea, the State became the prime patron of private industry. As a consequence, a few companies such as Samsung, Hyundai, etc., were so pampered that they grew to be among the biggest in the world, earning the sobriquet of Chaebols (large industrial conglomerates run or controlled by individuals or families in South Korea). In this process, democratic principles such as the maintenance of individual freedoms and transparency in governance were not observed, either in Japan or in South Korea.

Under Mao, Communist China nationalised industry and agriculture, and promoted literacy, modern industry, and the public health system on a universal scale, but strictly under the aegis of the Chinese communist party. In the first thirty years, the achievements of China in the fields of literacy and public health were stupendous by any standards of history. Such individual liberties as freedom of speech and human rights were trampled upon. Deng Ziao Ping, who eventually succeeded Mao, started privatisation in a big way and patronised private enterprise. He even put Bismarck to shame in this respect; he took the models of Japan and South Korea and beat them to a pulp. Free market, even in the post-Mao period, is alien to China. Through this state-sponsored capitalist process, China has emerged as the second largest economy in the world. It defies pigeonholing into categories such as capitalism and socialism.

It can thus be seen that the capitalist economy that prevailed after World War II was a far cry from the *laissez-faire* that existed in the first half of the nineteenth century in Britain. Even so, the private sector has not become weaker. It should be noted that capitalism in the twentieth century has been rescued by governments through their positive interventions, a quantum jump in industrial technology, and neutralisation of labour unrest through minimum wages and a welfare state. In the developed world, there has emerged a middle-class society, as a consequence of which the inequality between rich and poor did not seem to matter. It is evident from the situation that prevailed in America from Roosevelt to Nixon that the lot of the working class had improved enough to enable it to move into the middle class. The comfort of consensus among intellectuals was so high that as late as in 1997, Irving Kristol published an article in the *Wall Street Journal* which argued:

> Income inequality tends to be swamped by even greater social equality .... In all our major cities, there is not a single restaurant where a CEO can lunch or dine with absolute assurance that he will not run into his secretary. If you fly first class, who will be your travelling companions? You never know. If you go to Paris, you will be lost in a crowd of young people flashing their credit cards. (cited in Krugman 2007: 245)

However, this feeling of social equality did not last long. In *Richistan* (2007), *Wall Street Journal* reporter Robert Frank says:

> Today's rich had formed their own virtual country .... They had built a self-contained world unto themselves, complete with their own health-care system (concierge doctors), separate economy .... The rich were not just getting richer; they were

> becoming financial foreigners, creating their own country within a country, their own society within a society, and their economy within an economy.

The felt social inequalities are manifesting themselves in undesirable ways. Elizabeth Warren, a Harvard School expert on bankruptcy, and Amelia Warren Tyagi, a business consultant, studied the rise of bankruptcy in the United States and made the following observation: 'By 2005, the number of families filing for bankruptcy each year was five times its level in the early 1980s' (cited in Krugman 2007: 247). Paul Krugman summarised their findings thus:

> The proximate reason for this surge in bankruptcies was that families were taking on more debt—and this led to moralistic pronouncements about people spending too much on luxuries they can't afford. What Warren and Tyagi found, however, was that middle-class families were actually spending less on luxuries than they had in the 1970s. Instead, the rise in debt mainly reflected increased spending on housing, largely driven by competition to get into good school districts. (Krugman 2007: 247)

This relative aggravation of middle-class conditions indicates increased inequalities. On top of it, the capitalist economy in the West seems to have been overtaken by internal contradictions. One of the reasons advanced for this problem is the excessive financialisation of the economy. The Great Recession that broke out in 2008, the gravest since the Great Depression, is spectacularly indicative of this crisis. The establishment policymakers, who set aside their favourite economist Milton Friedman and dusted off the classic teachings of Keynes, poured more than a trillion dollars to salvage the situation. This situation came about despite the fact that in the previous three decades, the economy had witnessed far greater growth than at any comparable period in history. Nothing less than the future of capitalism is at stake today. It remains to be seen whether capitalism displays the same radical degree of resilience that it had in the past. In the past eight years since the Great Recession, the Western economy appears to have recovered. But economics as a discipline is still in crisis.

Nothing can summarise the dilemmas of the discipline more objectively than the article titled 'A Less Dismal Science—If Economists Reformed Themselves' (*The Economist* 2016), which stated: 'Economists are accused of being blinkered by mathematical models, of overestimating their predictive powers and churning out narrow-minded graduates .... Related to mathiness is model-mania. Economists are good at reducing a complicated world to a few assumptions.'

The article goes on to say that such simplification through assumptions leads to false consensus, and it was this kind of consensus that had led to the Great Recession of 2008. It points out that the GDP, which was designed as a gauge to measure the size and progress of the economy, was not adequate for a modern world of services, apps, and bots. Above all, it emphasises the need for economists to mingle with historians and sociologists, which would inevitably lead to change in the way economists are trained. In other words, exams would test critical reflection as much as mathematical prowess.

The article reflects the capacity of capitalist intellectuals to rethink their ideology radically. Through such creative self-introspection, capitalism can still discover its new Keynes and reinvent itself.

9

Evolutionary Socialism

Socialism, as British philosopher C. E. M. Joad (1891–1953) observed in the first half of the twentieth century, is a hat that lost its shape as everybody wore it. This witticism is reflective of the zeitgeist not only of Britain, but also of Europe at the time. In Britain, public intellectuals like Sidney Webb, Bernard Shaw, Bertrand Russell, H. G. Wells, and Harold Laski were the leading lights of socialist thought. George Orwell, celebrated author of *Animal Farm* (1945) and *1984* (1949) and bête noire of the Communists, was himself a self-confessed socialist. The philosopher Karl Popper (1902–94), who theoretically argued against the historical prophecies of Karl Marx and described Marx and Plato as 'enemies of open society', was also a champion of socialism. Socialism has been a broad movement as well as a broad spectrum of thought. Intellectuals have studied the past and tried to identify traces of socialism in it. Human heritage is so hoary and heterogeneous that some aspect of every essential trend can be located in it. Dr Sampurnanand (1891–1969), Indian socialist and freedom fighter, talked of Vedic socialism. Every Indian humanist finds in the Buddha a natural and inexhaustible fount of socialist inspiration. Sociologists have even traced the roots of socialism to tribal communism.

The mid-nineteenth century witnessed the social movement of European Christian activists who attempted to combine the aims of socialism with the ethical convictions of Christianity to promote cooperativism over competition as a means to help the poor. Every religious tradition, including that of Judaism and Islam, traced out their respective legacies of charity and sharing. Western historians have gone back to the age of Pericles, who was elected several times through the support of the poor as against the rich, and who can therefore be described as the first elected socialist of the world. After the defeat of democratic Athens against Sparta, Plato said, 'Any city, however small, is in fact divided into two, one the city of the poor, the other of the rich' (Sabine and Thorson 1993: 422). Modern socialist thinkers have tried to trace socialism to Plato's *Republic*, the first political utopia of the world. Plato's *Republic* is no doubt the most inspiring utopia ever composed. Its two supreme aims are: (*i*) to achieve the maximum efficiency of the State; and (*ii*) to bring about harmony between the haves and the have-nots. Plato thought of achieving class harmony through the abolition of private property. As for the maximum efficiency of the State, he planned to entrust despotic power to trained rulers. In the process of achieving these two goals, Plato spared no thought for individual freedom, much less democracy through public participation. Classlessness without political or personal freedom is the opposite of socialism. The definition of democracy given by Aristotle in his epic work *Politics*, against the background of the radical experience of Periclean democracy in Athens, can best serve as the definition of 'socialism' or 'social democracy' even today.

> A democracy is a state where the freemen and the poor, being in the majority, are invested with the power of the state .... The most pure democracy is that which is so called principally from the equality which prevails in it; for this is what the law in that state directs; that the poor shall be in no greater subjection than the rich; nor that the supreme power shall be lodged in either of these, but that both shall share it .... For if liberty and equality, as some persons suppose, are chiefly to be found in a democracy, it must be so by every department of government being alike open to all; but as the people are the majority, and what they vote is law, it follows that such a state must be a democracy .... (Aristotle 2000: Ch. 4)

After noting the timeless topicality of this definition, it is important to remember that Aristotle was no ardent supporter of democracy. However, he was far less of a critic than his master, Plato, or Plato's master, Socrates.

The practices of democracy or the ideas of socialism were confined to ancient Athens. While the former lasted for a short period and rose to their crowning glory during the time of Pericles, they ended with the conquest of Alexander. But the ideas of democracy and socialism unleashed by ancient Athens have since been influencing the political imagination. For more than 1,000 years (at least from the conversion of Constantine I to Christianity in the fourth century till the seventeenth century), however, they remained buried under the debris of religious traditions or scholastic disputations. Their flowering in ancient Athens was nothing more than a flash in the pan. All great ideas, like the Greek mythological bird Phoenix, are resurrected from their ashes. For this resurrection to take place, the Modern Age had to arrive. This Age in politics arrived in the seventeenth century. Despite the ancient echoes that remained muted in mildewed books, these beginnings are essentially modern; democracy, radical socialism, and social democracy had their common beginnings in the seventeenth century. In England, democratic forces began to assert themselves during the English civil wars led by Oliver Cromwell in support of Parliament and against Charles I. Even while Cromwell was fighting the Royalists, he had to suppress a mutiny inspired by the Levellers.

During the anti-Royalist movement, the forces of both democracy and democratic socialism were thrown up. The forces of democratic radicalism were led by a group called the 'Levellers'. The Levellers, in turn, were divided into two ideological groups—Diggers and Levellers. The Diggers were led by the writings of one man, English Protestant religious reformer Gerrard Winstanley (1609–76), who argued that political reform would be hollow unless the inequalities of the economic system were addressed. Winstanley said that he had been ruined in business by the 'cheating art of buying and selling'. The Levellers, who were a larger group, believed in a radical middle-class democracy with political aims. These two groups made their cases in British Parliament through their speeches and pamphlets. The Parliamentary debates of the time represent their ideological division, which, even after three centuries, remain relevant. The Levellers, who overshadowed the Diggers, lasted for a longer while. According to George Sabine, the Levellers 'interpreted the law of nature as endowing human individuals with innate and inalienable rights which legal and political institutions exist only to protect, and construed consent as an individual act which every man is entitled to perform for himself' (1973: 447).

The Levellers formed the left wing of the revolutionists in Cromwell's army, and their position can be understood by the differences they had with the more conservative plans formed by the Officers. In 1647, the revolution was accomplished, but a constitutional settlement was required. Both sides desired the removal of the worst abuses that had led to the war between the King and the Officers. Differences arose between the Officers and Levellers because the former came from the landed gentry and wanted a settlement that would allow political power to remain with their class, whereas the Levellers, who were from a group with small properties, wanted radical economic reforms. The Officers proposed a redistribution of seats on the basis of the proportion of taxes paid by constituencies, while the Levellers desired a distribution of seats based on population. Although the Levellers clarified that the property rights of the people would not be disturbed with franchise being conferred on everybody, the Officers refused to relent. This deadlock was broken through the 'Agreement of the People', under which even Parliament would not be able to repudiate debts, make arbitrary exceptions to the operation of law, or destroy the rights of personal liberty and property. The demands made by the Levellers were absolutely new in history, and definitely radical for the mid-seventeenth century. Their original demands could be described as an early manifestation of socialist urges.

Socialism had to wait almost till the early nineteenth century to develop into a volcano of thoughts and a fount of movements. The French Revolution that shook France between 1787 and 1799 turned out to be the mother of all social movements and socialist revolutions, not only in France but also in the entire modern world. It also turned out to be the nursery of many a political doctrine, ranging from democracy, capitalism, socialism, to communism. The French Revolution was preceded by the French Enlightenment, which shone the floodlight of new knowledge. The French, languishing for centuries in the infernal darkness of absolute monarchy of the Bourbon dynasty, were suddenly confronted with fresh ideas, the most important of which was carried from England by Voltaire, representing the science of Newton and the philosophy of John Locke. The other important tide of ideas was indigenous and represented by Rousseau, who romanticised emotion and inundated the French landscape with radical ideas. The Enlightenment essentially enthroned reason, which subjected every authority in science or religion to the investigation of unfettered minds. It is one of the greatest iconoclastic phenomena in all of history, and unleashed revolutionary ideas in both political and philosophical spheres. In the political sphere, people were exposed to such destabilising concepts as the abolition of monarchy, and the advent of democracy, capitalism, socialism, and communism. In philosophy, they were subjected to equally radical ideas, such as understanding the universe in terms of nature, reason, atheism, deism, etc. It was in this unsettling setting that the French Revolution broke out. While the Revolution led eventually to the anti-climax of the Terror, the rise and fall of Robespierre, and the ascendency of Napoleon, its ripples have since been washing the shores of all oceans and seas.

The French Revolution happened to coincide with the Industrial Revolution. The Industrial Revolution is symbolised by James Watts' steam engine, the railway locomotive, and the factory system in popular imagination. In reality, it was a silent process, and not a thundering event like the French Revolution. The effects of the Industrial Revolution were sweeping enough to transform the modes of production, forms of wealth, character of the classes, and forms of social struggle beyond recognition. In a nutshell, the agrarian civilisation was being replaced by an industrial civilisation in history. Apart from its effect on the economy, the Industrial Revolution helped liberal theorists to emancipate every man from the political institutions and legal restrictions that hampered his growth. Adam Smith, as early as in 1776, gave a call for economic freedom, at a time when the mercantilist age was being replaced by early capitalism. Fortuitously, the rise of capitalism almost coincided with the Industrial Revolution, and industrial capitalism consequently witnessed a quantum jump. The growth of capitalism would have stultified, had it not been simultaneously accompanied by the Industrial Revolution.

The Industrial Revolution, which began in the last quarter of the eighteenth century, received infinite impetus from the Scientific Revolution, which commenced with Copernicus in the early sixteenth century and culminated in Newton in the seventeenth century. The Industrial Revolution, which first took place in Britain, increased the wealth in society. This new wealth strangely led to an increase in the poverty of labour. As a result, in 1779, many textile mills were destroyed during serious riots in Lancashire. Another contradiction created by the factory system is the replacement of labour with machines, and the consequent increase in unemployment. This led to the movement of the Luddites, which began in Nottingham in 1811 and spread to other areas in 1812. The Luddites were charged with surreptitiously destroying textile machinery. The government thereafter resorted to repressive measures, which included a mass trial at York in 1813 that resulted in many hangings and banishments. These contradictions led socialist theorists to claim that the exploitation of workers was inevitable under capitalist competition.

Later scholars, delving into the past, found anticipations of socialist theories in the work of earlier writers. The quest began with Plato himself. As has been clarified in Chapter 6, Plato, in his *Republic*, suggested the communal ownership of land to optimise the competence of the State and avoid class contradictions. It is noteworthy that Plato did not plead for individual freedom. Mere nationalisation, without individual freedom, does not add up to socialism. Plato therefore does not fit the description of a socialist. Thomas More, who wrote his renowned *Utopia* in 1516, is among the modern writers credited with socialist imagination. However, like Plato, he did not bother with freedom, even while championing communal ownership. Among those who participated in the French Revolution, J. P. Brissot (1754–93; the Girondin leader), J. N. Herbert (a French journalist, who took extreme radical positions during the French Revolution and was eventually guillotined), and French political agitator and journalist Gracchus Babeuf (1760–97) are also mentioned as socialist progenitors.

Since socialist thought and movements assumed many dimensions, there is a need to divide socialists into two broad categories, viz., evolutionary socialists and revolutionary socialists, for the purpose of easy analysis. For example, J. P. Brissot was a member of the moderate group known as Girondins in the French Revolution and advocated peaceful socialist changes, whereas Gracchus Babeuf, who led the abortive attempt to overthrow the Directory government in 1796, is regarded as the pioneer of violent socialist movements. They have some essential ideas in common, but it is difficult to treat their approaches on par. William Godwin, in *Political Justice* (1793), pleaded for the abolition of all governments, and for a society where property would go to all those who could make the best use of it. He inspired much of later socialist and anarchist thought. Robert Owen, William Wordsworth, Coleridge, and P. B. Shelley were also influenced by him. Shelley's greatest poem, *Prometheus Unbound,* was largely based on the ideas of Godwin. Shelley himself was an early and empyrean voice of socialism, and his romantic hopes about the future of humanity are reflected in his poetry. The following piece is just one illustration:

> The world's great age begins anew,
> the golden years return,
> the earth doth like a snake renew
> her winter weeds outworn. (*Concise Oxford Dictionary of Quotations* 1964: 213)

British philosopher Thomas Paine influenced people and events in three countries—Britain, the USA, and France. Being British, he participated in the movement for American independence. While supporting the French Revolution, he criticised the 'Reign of Terror', and was therefore imprisoned in France by Robespierre. When he returned to the US, he was criticised for his deist writings. Thomas Paine, while being a pioneering crusader of progressive causes in three countries, was therefore never honoured in any of them in his lifetime. His posthumous influence, however, made him an icon of socialists. While tracing the roots of socialist inspiration in the modern age, scholars can go back to the Levellers and Diggers in Cromwell's army. They can also go back to Rousseau who, in his own chaotic and creative way, unleashed radical social forces. Voltaire and his towering intellectual compeers are not only noted for their contribution to the French Enlightenment, but are also identified as the paladins of liberty. But it is important to recognise that many of them, even while emphasising rights to liberty and property, were alert to the concerns of the poor.

Father Mably, brother of French philosopher Etienne Bonnot de Condillac (1714–80), was a critic of private property. He said: 'What is the principal source of misfortunes which afflict humanity? It is the property of goods .... The state, owning everything, distributes to the individuals, the things which they need. Here, I must say it is a political economy that I like' (Beaud 2004: 58). But Diderot saw protection in the private property of the individual, even while deploring the fact that 'between men, indigence condemns some to work while others get fat from the sweat and toil of those who work' (ibid.: 59). Helvetius observed: 'In most nations, there are only two classes of citizens; one who lacks that what is necessary, the other who is overflowing with excess' (ibid.). He therefore appealed to the government to reduce the wealth of the few, and increase the wealth of the others. De Holbach asked the government to tax luxury, to give to the poor the possibility of living by their work, and to prevent the accumulation of wealth in a few hands. He also proposed that 'all uncultivated land should be returned to commons, in order to be given to those who can make use of it for themselves and for society' (ibid.). Father Raynal, famous for his *Philosophical History of the Two Indes* (1770), said that 'everywhere the rich exploit the poor', and went so far as to write: 'hang them, if need be, these treacherous rich, and recover your dignity'. Linquet, a lawyer and physicist, was no Utopian. He therefore said: 'To want to make everyone happy, in a state, is a project as false in politics as is searching for the philosopher's stone in chemistry' (ibid.: 59–60). Voltaire, leader of the Enlightenment and champion of liberty, asked sarcastically: 'Since you have established yourselves as a people, have you not discovered the secret of obliging all the rich to make all the poor work? (ibid.: 61).

While such radical reservations remained in the air in the eighteenth century, socialist thought and movement could find a foothold and gather momentum only after the creation of material conditions through the establishment of the factory system in the nineteenth century.

The term 'socialist' was used first in Great Britain in 1826 to describe the followers of Robert Owen, and was soon applied to the followers of Saint-Simon and Charles Fourier in France, who attacked the evils of competition and put forward proposals for a new way of life based on cooperative control. Our brief survey of capitalism and socialism shows that both were born together, and not separately or successively.

Robert Owen (1771–1858), a successful master cotton spinner at the head of a great factory at New Lanark (UK), which he turned into a model of good labour conditions, became a severe critic of the manufacturing system and exploitation of labour. He denounced competition, advocating in its place a cooperative system in which men and women would work and live together, on the basis of the communal enjoyment of fruits of labour on the field and in the factory. One of Owen's key insights is that human behaviour is mainly the product of the environment and education, and can be improved through State action. Owen appealed to the government for factory legislation to improve the lot of labour and reduce unemployment. He was also involved in the trade union movement in a big way. Owen believed that labour associations could run industries on a cooperative basis. He tried some of these experiments in 1825 in New Harmony, US, and elsewhere. At New Lanark, Owen proved to be an efficient manager. He also undertook social reforms such as extirpating theft without legal punishment, and tackled drunkenness among workers. New Lanark became so famous that nearly 20,000 persons visited it for their edification.

Owen was such an original thinker as to understand the productive power of machines in the early nineteenth century, as well as their tendency to create unemployment. He therefore felt that free enterprise would be unable to operate on its own, and urged the State to intervene. Owen also took interest in agriculture and believed in intensive cultivation. He therefore preferred the spade to the plough as an implement. Notwithstanding the fact that he was himself an entrepreneur, he believed that labour is the source of all wealth. Although he was very popular as a trade union leader, he avoided intimate relationships with labour radicals. Apart from trade union leadership, his criticism of church practices in particular, and religion in general, cost him considerable social respectability. His brilliance was beautifully balanced, as is evident from his simultaneous emphasis on agriculture and industry; cooperative movement and State intervention; trade union movement and labour reforms; and social reforms and intellectual criticisms. He blazed such a trail that it shone a light even in the twenty-first century. Because of his constructive career and pioneering thought, he is rightly regarded as the founder of British socialism.

Henri de Saint-Simon (1760–1825), French aristocrat, was the first to foresee the emergence of industrial gigantism, and the key role of science in human affairs. He pleaded for planned organisation and control in the general interest, and put forward a series of original ideas: he foresaw the need for technocrats in administration; and envisioned the emergence of an industrialised State under the influence of modern science. In *The New Christianity* (1825), he stated that religion should guide society towards improving the conditions of the poor. According to him, the State should be obliged to provide employment to all. His disciples helped to influence the rise of Christian Socialism. He denounced the exploitation of labour under the prevailing system of property rights, and stood for a non-theological religion for the new unfolding age, based on science. He, in fact, expressed faith in a 'science of sciences', through which he inspired his great disciple, Auguste Comte (1798–1857), the founder of the discipline of Sociology and of 'positivism' in philosophy. Saint-Simon's originality lay in his contribution to socialist thought in terms of his ability to foresee: (*i*) the impending technological leaps; (*ii*) the need for the State to plan and organise the use of the means of production; (*iii*) and the need for technical and business experts.

Charles Fourier (1772–1837), French socialist thinker, was in favour of intensive cultivation, including horticulture. He was opposed to both capitalism and industrialism, and advocated for a form of cooperative settlement which he believed was vital for social organisation. He said that the essential unit of the cooperative organisation should have a minimum of 1,500–1,600 persons living in a single great building. But their incomes would not be equal, as they would depend on the quality of each member's labour contribution and on the extent of the land that each would provide. While the members would retain their property rights, those members investing higher capital would get lower rates of interest. He believed that the formation of such cooperative units should be voluntary, and welcomed by members in their own interest. He was, however, opposed to any State action, and emphasised that society should provide for different types of activities to suit the different moods and tastes of members. According to him, his utopia would suit not only human nature, but also divine dispensation. To use Marx's formulation, Charles Fourier was much more utopian than Robert Owen or Saint-Simon.

Louis Blanc (1811–82), socialist and journalist, was another important figure in France. He believed that workers should take over production and organise self-controlled 'social workshops' until a socialist society came into being. He worked as a member of the provisional government of the Second Republic (1848) and fled to Britain after an unsuccessful revolt by the workers. He stood for socialism that rested on public ownership, combined with workers' control in industry. He is credited with having coined the famous socialist formula, 'From each according to his abilities; to each according to his needs' (Rawls 2008).

Early socialist thought benefited from anti-capitalist writers. In France, Etienne Cabet (1788–1856) authored *Voyage en Icarie* (1840), in which he envisioned the State owning all the major industries and dividing the product on an equal basis. Cabet's rulers were chosen by popular election. Like Saint-Simon, he laid stress on science, and like Fourier, on education. Before the ideal State could be established, he favoured minimum wage laws and high taxation. Apart from being a utopia-maker and leader of the working class, he was a theoretical critic of classical political economy.

P. J. Proudhon (1809–65) distinguished himself as a philosophical anarchist and a great French writer. He is famous for his phrase, 'property is theft'. He wrote a number of books in which he opposed both capitalism and state-supported socialism; he should therefore be treated as a philosophical anarchist. He was a strong advocate of cooperative societies, labour banks, and trade societies. He favoured personal property and inheritance to a limited extent. One of his great books was *The Philosophy of Poverty* (1846), which provoked Marx to not only disagree, but also to write his celebrated riposte, *The Poverty of Philosophy* (1847). Marx described him as a 'petit bourgeois'. Proudhon published radical newspapers, which led to his imprisonment between 1849–52. Police harassment even after his release led him to flee to Belgium in 1858. Upon his return in 1862, he gained influence among the workers, including some of the founders of the First International.

Ferdinand Lassalle (1825–64) was the founder of the German labour movement and a powerful socialist leader. Although he established early contact with Karl Marx and Friedrich Engels during his stay in London, he drifted away from them on ideological grounds. He advocated for an evolutionary approach to socialism through a democratic constitutional State based on universal suffrage. He condemned cooperative societies as useless, and pleaded for the takeover of large-scale industry. Pending the achievement of an industrialised democratic state, he appealed to the existing State to help the workers' associations. Lassalle, who began his career by participating in the Revolution of 1848, went quickly beyond Marxism and led his own trade union movement. He soon became important enough through his trade union movements to be invited by Bismarck to discuss and apply his original ideas. In 1864, he went to Switzerland, fell in love, and was killed in a duel with his lover's former fiancé. His premature demise at the age of thirty-nine dealt a huge blow to both the labour and socialist movements in Germany.

Eduard Bernstein (1850–1932) was a German politician and writer. He joined the German Social Democratic Party in 1872. While spending years in exile in London (brought about by his vehement opposition to Bismarck's government in Germany), he was influenced by Engels and the Fabian Society. Upon returning to Germany in 1901, Bernstein gained fame as a political theorist. He argued that Marxism could and should be revised, which provoked Karl Kautsky (named by Engels as his successor) to call him a 'Revisionist'. The Communists used the phrase 'Revisionist' as a powerful abuse against Bernstein and all other thinkers of his ilk for a century. Bernstein did not agree with Marx that labour would face further impoverishment. Nor did he agree that capitalism would inevitably collapse under the weight of its internal contradictions. He therefore called on the Social Democrats to treat themselves as a party of reform. He was later elected twice as a member of the Reichstag and became a leading member of his party. Despite his political eminence, he had the rare moral courage to go against public opinion in his own country and protest against World War I. In this, he found himself in the celebrated company of European intellectuals such as Bertrand Russell and Bernard Shaw in Britain, Romain Rolland in France, and Benedetto Croce in Italy. Bernstein contributed not only through his liberal Marxism, but also through his unique personality, which represented a blend of humanity, intellect, and authorship.

Jean Jaures (1859–1914) was a French socialist leader and writer, served in the Chamber of Deputies, and adapted Marxism to democratic Socialism. He accepted Marx's theories on surplus value and on the inevitability of capitalist crises, but rejected the theory that increasing pauperisation of the proletariat would inevitably take place, leading to the revolution. For him, socialism would fulfil the spirit of the French Revolution by satisfying the need for liberty and justice. He was opposed to the idea of the dictatorship of the proletariat. While being an internationalist, he appreciated the legitimate nationalist sentiment of the people of his and other countries. For all his patriotism, he was a great liberal who vehemently criticised the wrongful conviction (on charges of treason) of Alfred Dreyfus (1859–1935), a French Captain of Jewish descent. Through his defence of Dreyfus, he displayed a rare liberal outlook in the face of public opposition, and paid the price by losing the next election. He championed the cause of Franco-German reconciliation, which earned him the hatred of French nationalists and led to his assassination in 1914 by a young nationalist fanatic. He was the most noted French orator of his time. He was so concerned about human values that, in criticism of Revolutionary Socialism, he said, 'We are not bound to put ourselves outside humanity, for the sake of remaining inside socialism' (Mehta 1964: 167).

The stream of Socialism started as a flash flood with the pro-poor democracy of Pericles at Parthenon in Athens, but soon dried up in ancient Athens itself and lost its track for about 2,000 years. It resurfaced with the Levellers in Cromwell's army during the English Civil Wars and the Commonwealth, but was once again parched in the heat of the ascendancy of the new middle class. Following the French Revolution, Socialism sprang up again as the labour movement was strengthened with the rise of industry in the nineteenth century.

When evolutionary socialism hit upon the obstacle of revolutionary socialism represented by Marx and others, its further course was facilitated by Louis Blanc, Ferdinand Lassalle, Eduard Bernstein, and Jean Jaures. It was further aided by the founding of the Fabian Society in 1883–84 by a small group of thinkers in London, with the aim of 'reconstructing society in accordance with the highest moral possibilities'. The name refers to the Roman General Fabius Cunctator (Cunctator, in Latin, means delayer), who famously devised delaying tactics to defeat the celebrated Carthaginian General Hannibal, known for his invincible frontal strategy. The Society wanted to adopt Fabian tactics (unlike revolutionary socialists) to defeat the capitalist Hannibal. Important early members included Sidney Webb, Beatrice Webb, Bernard Shaw, Annie Besant, Edward Pease, Graham Wallace, and H. G. Wells. Even Bertrand Russell became a member for a brief period, but disassociated from it on account of differences over foreign policy before World War I. The logo of the Fabian Society included a tortoise, representing 'the group's predilection for a slow, imperceptible transition to socialism'. The rules of the society state that it comprises socialists:

> It therefore aims at the establishment of a society in which equality of opportunity will be assured, and privileges of individuals and classes abolished through the collective ownership and democratic control of the economic sources of the community. It seeks to secure these ends by the methods of political democracy. (Cole 1942: 1)

While publishing tracts, the society permitted individual writers freedom, but asked them to take full responsibility for their views. This freedom attracted almost all progressive intellectuals in Britain to the Fabian Society. In 1889, the Society published *Fabian Essays in Socialism*, edited by Bernard Shaw, which was sold in large numbers.

They believed that the utilitarian aim of greatest happiness of the greatest number could be secured only through extensive State action in the economic field. The society's members played a leading part in founding the London School of Economics and Political Science in 1895, 'for the betterment of society', which became an incubator of influential politicians, economists, prime ministers, and liberal millionaires. The members also played a pre-eminent role in founding the Labour Party in 1900. In the period between the two World Wars, 'Second Generation Fabians' included intellectuals like R. H. Tawney, G. D. H. Cole, and Harold Laski. It was at this time that many future leaders of the Third World, like Jawaharlal Nehru, were exposed to Fabian thought. It is interesting to note that Mohammad Ali Jinnah was a member of the Society at one stage. In the twentieth century, it was natural that all the leaders of the Labour Party, ranging from Ramsay MacDonald, Clement Attlee, Tony Ben, to Harold Wilson, were associated with the Society. The tradition of the Fabian Society and British Labour Party continues to throw up radical thinkers, as is evident from the recent emergence of Jeremy Corbyn as the Labour Party leader.

In the first three decades of the Society's existence, great attention was paid to general arguments against capitalism and in favour of socialism. The tone was rational, practical, and empirical. Many of the programmes adopted by Labour governments owed their origin to the Society. Fabianism exerted its influence through teachers, civil servants, trade union officials, and politicians. The Society's prestige reached its apogee when Attlee was Prime Minister of Great Britain from 1945–51, and established a welfare state along with extensive nationalisation of industry and progressive legislation for the labour. The impact of Fabianism was deeply felt throughout the twentieth century in the whole of Western Europe, and in all colonised countries of the-then British Empire, including India.

Before the arrival of Fabian Socialism in India, Swami Vivekananda, one of the early apostles of Indian nationalism, was the first Indian to use the word 'Socialism' and welcome it. He aroused great pride in the glory of ancient India among Hindus; however, he saw in the caste system the greatest weakness of Hindu society and gave a clarion call for its abolition. He had in fact prophesied in the last decade of the nineteenth century that the twentieth century would herald the age of the Sudras (backward castes). Although he was primarily a spiritual personality, he laid great emphasis on the material prosperity of the nation, and economic justice for the poor. As a consequence of his two-dimensional legacy, he became an icon for both the rightist Hindu forces and

Communist parties. He has remained one of the supreme icons of modern India, cutting across all ideological barriers.

In India, apart from Nehru, socialist thought received spirited support from Subhas Chandra Bose, Jayaprakash Narayan, Acharya Narendra Dev, Lohia, Ashok Mehta, etc. The great martyr of India's freedom struggle, Sardar Bhagat Singh, declared himself a Marxist, but deliberately chose not to join the Communist Party of India. In other words, he expressed sympathy for the revolutionary ideas of Marx, without speaking in favour of communism as such. He should therefore be considered a socialist. Vinoba Bhave, founder of the Bhudan (land donation) movement, needs to be noted as a utopian socialist. Above all, Gandhiji should be regarded as the greatest utopian socialist of India, if not of the world.

Gandhiji was a multidimensional phenomenon, and a bundle of colossal contradictions. Here, we shall confine ourselves to a brief analysis of the utopian aspects of his message. He allowed himself to be influenced by the Bhagwat Gita, Jain philosophy, the Bible, Tolstoy, David Thoreau, etc. Being an organic genius, he formed his own complex synthesis. Gandhiji transcended typecasting and continued to evolve his personality and philosophy so radically, and yet so naturally, that nobody could dare to draw him into doctrinaire disputations. He rose from conservative Hindu positions to those of a social crusader. Nobody from the upper castes has contributed so much to the cause of the untouchables in India. He aroused the empathy of orthodox upper castes by drawing their attention to the historical iniquities heaped on the untouchables. Gandhiji had the supreme moral authority to describe any problem in spiritual terms. In his characteristic manner, he called the untouchables 'Harijans—the children of God', and persuaded upper-caste oppressors to perceive the problem of untouchability in that light. He laid down and enforced the rule that nobody could become a member of his party, the Indian National Congress, without a record of her/his personal service to untouchables. While doing so, he also preserved the unity of the Hindu community by persuading B. R. Ambedkar, the leader of the untouchables, to give up his demand for a separate electorate. What was more, he discreetly bade the leaders of his Party to entrust the crafting of India's new Constitution to Ambedkar, a genius who blended radical ideas with democratic procedures.

Gandhiji reposed faith in free enterprise, but wanted entrepreneurs to be the public trustees of wealth. He did not believe in possession, and in this respect, he owed a direct debt to Jain philosophy, which preaches 'Aparigraha' (non-possession). He almost seemed to agree with Proudhon, who likened property to theft. He can also be likened to Charles Fourier, who had serious reservations about 'industrialism' and preferred agriculture. Gandhiji laid stress on small-scale industry for the purpose of maximising employment. Like all utopian socialists, he was a philosophical anarchist in that he did not set much store by government, or in violent resistance to the government's policies. In fact, he pleaded for civil disobedience, *a la* David Thoreau. Gandhiji has gone down in history as the greatest practitioner of the technique of passive resistance (Satyagraha). Environmentalists now consider him their greatest icon, as he discouraged heavy industrialisation and conspicuous consumption, which would inevitably involve pollution. Like utopian socialists, Gandhiji believed in voluntarism and conversion of the people through moral persuasion.

Vinoba Bhave, Gandhiji's spiritual disciple, launched the Bhudan (voluntary land donation by large landowners) movement soon after India's Independence, and succeeded in getting hundreds of thousands of acres of land distributed among the poor. Vinoba Bhave enrolled thousands of voluntary social workers in this movement. This was possible not only because of his personal efforts, but also because of the moral impact generated by Gandhiji's voluntarism during the freedom struggle.

Gandhiji's political disciple, Jawaharlal Nehru (1889–1964), was the most senior and the most distinguished of all traditional socialists. Nehru, who had been exposed to the philosophy of Marxism and Fabian socialism, was the first socialist to cut through the revivalist appearances of Gandhiji and identify his indefinable political genius. He could also perceive the adamantine will behind Gandhiji's soft words and non-violent teachings. While adopting Gandhiji as his guru, Nehru retained his core beliefs of modern rationalism and democratic socialism.

Netaji Subhas Chandra Bose's (1897–1945) faith in socialism developed while he was a student in Britain. He resigned from the prestigious Indian Civil Service to join the Congress party in order to advance the cause of the freedom struggle. Although he accepted Gandhiji's leadership and admired his unique calibre, he had reservations about Gandhiji's unqualified endorsement of non-violence as the technique of the struggle for freedom. Unlike Nehru, Bose was a great believer in God, but he openly expressed his difficulty with the religious symbolism of Gandhiji's language, fearing that this would alienate religious minorities, including M. A. Jinnah. Netaji, unlike other socialists in India, thought that independent India would need a benevolent dictatorship for a short period, say of ten years, in order to make radical changes and expedite development. This, however, did not mean that he was in favour of any kind of dictatorship as part of his philosophy. He had no organisational problems with Gandhiji or Nehru, but he did with Sardar Patel. He also had an ideological problem with Patel's pro-capitalist stance. He was fond of Nehru because of their ideological like-mindedness, but later developed a problem with the latter's reluctance to distance himself from Gandhiji. These problems assumed a larger ideological character when Bose, as the president of the Congress party, began to advocate support to Hitler's Germany against Britain. It was at this stage that Gandhiji took a strong position against Bose. Bose, who always had reservations about the programme of non-violence, saw an opportunity to clinch the issue of India's freedom in World War II. Although Bose participated in World War II along with his Indian National Army (INA), which he raised on the side of Japan and Germany, he always retained faith in socialism, democracy, and Gandhiji's leadership. It is not surprising, then, that Bose, at the zenith of his glory as the leader of the INA, referred to

Gandhiji as the 'Father of the Nation' through his address on Rangoon Radio.

After Nehru and Bose, Jayaprakash Narayan (1902–79) was the most popular socialist leader during the freedom struggle and in independent India. On principle, JP chose not to study in Britain but in America, where he was converted to the general principles of Marxism. But he joined the Congress party under the leadership of Gandhiji upon his return to India, albeit with strong socialist reservations. JP, along with Acharya Narendra Dev, Ram Manohar Lohia, Ashok Mehta, and other stalwarts, formed the Congress Socialist Party under the umbrella of the Congress party, and strengthened their wing across the country with young recruits. They all voted for Bose when he contested for Congress presidentship against the nominee of the Congress Working Committee, Pattabhi Sitaramaiah, but did not agree with Bose when he differed from Gandhiji and took a position in favour of Hitler's Germany. They believed that Gandhiji's supreme leadership was indispensable, and that the fascism of Germany posed a far greater threat to the world than British imperialism. All of them participated vigorously in the Quit India Movement and suffered long sentences in prison. JP and Lohia escaped from Hazaribagh jail and led the underground movement.

After independence, they developed serious differences with Sardar Patel on both organisational and ideological grounds, and quit the Congress to form their own party. This decision, soon after the death of Gandhiji, was a great mistake, which they later admitted. At any rate, after the 1952 Lok Sabha elections, their new party was divided, with one wing led by Acharya Narendra Dev, Ashok Mehta, etc., and another led by Ram Manohar Lohia. This split prompted JP to quit electoral politics and join the Gandhian movement led by Vinoba Bhave. Jayaprakash Narayan, who started his ideological career with Marxism, turned to utopian socialism and worked in the movement for about twenty years. JP's personal charisma did not diminish even after quitting electoral politics, as people across the party's barriers recognised the selfless way in which he sacrificed greater prospects and high positions. JP pleaded for democracy without political parties, and thus became a philosophical anarchist. His senior colleague, Narendra Dev, stuck with the socialist party through thick and thin. He was noted for his exceptional erudition, particularly on ancient India; he studied the dead Pali language in which the Buddha spoke, and conducted research based on ancient documents. He wrote his original and voluminous account of Buddhist philosophy in Hindi. Unlike JP, Narendra Dev retained a steady propensity for Marxism and made a keen study of the problems of peasants and rural areas. Although he was never charismatic, he was by far the most scholarly and non-controversial leader of the Congress socialist party.

Ram Manohar Lohia (1910–67) and Ashok Mehta (1911–84) were democratic socialists with no sympathy for Marxism as such. Lohia applied socialism to India's peculiar conditions, and theorised that caste in India was a more relevant factor than class. He went on to say that class would be abstract (*nirgun*) and caste concrete (*sagun*) in the Indian context. This theory defined him as a unique socialist thinker and took socialism, at least in north India (more particularly in UP and Bihar), to the masses. Even now, leaders of the backward classes, particularly those belonging to the Yadava and Kurmi castes, swear by Lohia's legacy. Another of Lohia's innovations was his insistence on Indian languages (including Hindi), as he thought that learning a foreign language like English would not only burden children, but also blunt their nationalism. In retrospect, not everybody in India would agree with him, as the world in the meantime has become far more globally interconnected, with English emerging as the most important international language. The third novel idea that Lohia introduced was the encouragement of small-scale industries, on the ground that heavy industrialisation was a Western model not applicable to developing countries in the East, particularly to India, with its vast population. In this respect, he agreed with Gandhiji, and was the first to do so among the socialists. Regardless of the merits of these three innovative ideas, there should be no difficulty in saying that he was the most original thinker in the Congress socialist tradition.

Ashok Mehta, Lohia's principal ideological rival, was an erudite socialist who wrote systematically about the evolution of socialist thought in the modern world. Unlike Lohia, Mehta had no quarrel with the social democrats of Western Europe. He specialised in modern economics as a discipline and wanted to give a new turn to India's socialist policy. He was part of the government responsible for the devaluation of the rupee in 1966 under Indira Gandhi's Prime Ministership. This bold step, which was in a way an anticipation of the liberalisation of the Indian economy in 1991, proved abortive for two reasons. First, the political ground in both the Congress party and the country was not prepared for it. Second, no administrative preparation for economic follow-up had been done.

Both in doctrine and disposition, Ashok Mehta can be somewhat likened to Voltaire and Lohia to Rousseau. Mehta was predictable, for all his erudition. But Lohia, while being equally erudite, was organic in his thinking. Like JP, he refrained from going to England for education, but took his Ph.D. in economics from Berlin University at the age of twenty-four. Lohia was apparently influenced with regard to his language policy by the German philosopher Fichte, who laid heavy stress on the German language. To be fair to Lohia, he did not attribute special divinity to any Indian language, as Fichte had done with German. While Lohia claimed to be on the side of empiricism in philosophy, he appears to have imbibed the German idealist tendency for large formulations and pithy expressions. Lohia had an exceptional flair for coining phrases in both Hindi and English, which enabled him to develop ideologically-oriented workers and mobilise the people for socialist causes in Hindi-speaking India.

M. N. Roy (1887–1954) became a revolutionary in his teens. He was associated with the founding of the Communist party, both in India and in Mexico. After Lenin consolidated his power, he took notice of Roy and invited him to Moscow. In a short time, he rose to the top echelons of the party. When Lenin presented a thesis that Gandhiji, despite his revivalist appearance and non-revolutionary agitation, should be regarded as the leader of the liberal nationalist movement,

M. N. Roy dissented and presented a parallel thesis. According to Roy, Gandhiji was so backward in his thinking and effete in leadership that the communists should have nothing to do with him, and conduct a struggle on their own. Lenin had such regard for Roy that he allowed both the theses to be placed on record without a decision. After Stalin took over, Roy was sent to China as one of the three advisors to the Chinese Communist Party. He spent three years in China when the Communists were in coalition with the Nationalist Party led by Chiang Kai-shek. Even while these three advisors were in China, Chiang Kai-shek broke the coalition and banned the Communist party. Mao Tse Tung did not share the viewpoint of the advisors on strategic issues, because of which all three returned to Moscow. Mao, in an interview to Edgar Snow in 1936, spoke highly of Roy's intellect and added that he was too theoretical. It did not take much time for Roy, upon his return from China, to recognise that he was among Stalin's serious elimination, and had no option but to flee Russia. After spending some time in Europe, he landed in India in disguise. The British police, however, lost no time in recognising Roy and putting him in jail. After his release, he joined the Congress party, but stuck to his negative approach towards Gandhiji's leadership.

M. N. Roy supported the candidature of Subhas Chandra Bose in the crucial election to the Congress Presidentship, but withdrew his support later when Bose refused to go back on his line to back Hitler's Germany. It was at this point that Roy made the famous observation that Netaji's mind was full of Bharat Mata, and nothing else could penetrate it. With the exception of Jawaharlal Nehru, nobody else in India knew the international scene as well as Roy. Roy, in the meantime, was disappointed by Marxism as a theory and propounded his own philosophy, which he called 'Radical Humanism'. He examined the foundations of various aspects of technical philosophy, such as idealism (which he rejected) and materialism (which he stuck to). When matter as the primordial cause of the universe was destabilised by the scientist Dalton, who discovered atomic theory, Roy continued with materialism, saying that he still believed in the philosophy of physical realism. In this, he was a logical positivist in philosophy. However, he lost faith in the Marxian theory of dictatorship of the proletariat. He became a champion of individual liberty to the point of pleading for the abolition of political parties as they would curb the freedom of the individual. He favoured democracy and placed his faith in a radical kind of humanism. He attracted many young intellectuals and educated through his books on the roots of the modern age, and his extensive writings on the Renaissance. Nobody else in India had studied Western philosophy as thoroughly as Roy among political leaders. While Roy rhapsodised over individual liberty, he remained opposed to capitalism. He would, therefore, fall in the category of utopian socialists.

B. R. Ambedkar should be treated as an outstanding social democrat, although he did not declare himself as such. By virtue of his birth on the lowest rung of Hindu society, the Dalit (untouchable) caste, he was a born socialist. But through education and exposure, he grew to be a progressive democrat by conviction. He took his Ph.D. from the UK and another from the US. He was a lawyer and an economist by training, and was a committed historical sociologist besides. Through his enlightened indignation, he became the peerless pioneer of progressive social causes, including that of untouchables. While highlighting the millennial misfortunes that have haunted his community, he rose above its anger and suggested remedial measures for mitigating the injustice in social, economic, and political spheres. He did not confine himself to righting the wrongs of his community alone; he wanted to extend the process to other backward classes as well. For all his soaring egalitarian vision, he was no roaring revolutionary, in a tearing hurry for change. He had the wisdom and the patience for slow change through constitutional democracy. As the leader of the Dalits, he made his inimitable socialist contribution through his role in crafting India's Constitution. While supporting India's struggle for freedom in principle, he refused to join the Congress party on the ground that all Congress party leaders—including its tallest leader, Gandhiji—were from the upper castes, and therefore did not represent the masses of India, who comprised the Other Backward Classes, Scheduled Castes, and Scheduled Tribes.

Ambedkar confronted Gandhiji on this issue at the Round Table Conference in London (1930–32), and Gandhiji responded instantly by stating that India's future constitution would be shaped in a manner that would serve the weaker sections. Ambedkar, through the Poona Pact, secured a commitment from Gandhiji to the scheme of reservations for lower castes in legislative bodies, employment, and education. Gandhiji also gave him the unique opportunity to give appropriate shape to India's new Constitution from the perspective of secular democracy and for the betterment of the weaker sections. Ambedkar, a first-rate political thinker and jurist, rose to the challenge by proving himself the social conscience and democratic watchdog of India's Constitution. He later served as Law Minister under Nehru's Prime Ministership and played his part in giving new shape to the Hindu Code Law. While cooperating with Nehru on the Hindu Code Bill in the face of conservative opposition from sections of the Congress party and the RSS, his reformist thirst for conferring property rights on women remained unquenched, resulting in his resignation from Nehru's Cabinet. Soon after his exit, he embarked on the task of re-establishing the religion of the Buddha. He converted himself to Buddhism on the ground that Hindu society had historically created the caste system and systematically promoted discriminatory social practices, while the Buddha alone, in his majestic moral manner, had sought to undermine the caste system. He was no simple convert to Buddhism, but rose to become its modern apostle and its new exegete. Ambedkar was an agnostic, and believed that the Buddha was the original agnostic. He was therefore opposed to both the main sects of Buddhism, Hinayana and Mahayana, and went on to found his own sect, Navayana. What was more, he wrote a detailed doctrinal interpretation of the Buddha's Dhamma.

As a social revolutionary, he conducted scholarly research to trace the ethnic and historical origins of tribes, untouchables, and the other backward classes. Although

Ambedkar came to be posthumously venerated as a supreme icon by the untouchables, other weaker sections, and progressive intellectuals, he was consciously opposed to the personality cult, believing that it would hamper free thinking and the functioning of democracy. Ambedkar's illuminating essay on the comparative study between the Buddha and Marx highlights his faith in philosophical liberalism and civil liberties. He was thus a unique socialist not only in India, but also in the modern world. Ambedkar was a technocrat par excellence, in that he was an accomplished jurist and economist, besides being a political visionary, Buddhist philosopher, and political theorist. His legend, like that of every other great pioneer in history, loomed larger after his death, and continues to grow. With the exception of Gandhiji, nobody can grow taller than Ambedkar in the history of modern India.

Ramaswamy Naicker (1879–1973), popularly known as Periyar, who started his political career with the Congress party, founded his own movement and party, the Dravidar Kazhagam (DK). He propounded the theory that south Indians were Dravidians, who had been suffused with the false consciousness of being Hindus by the Brahmins of north India. He raised a banner of revolt against Aryanism to the point of identifying Lord Rama as an Aryan deity and Ravana as a Dravidian king. What was more, he openly canvassed for atheism and gave it the shape of a huge movement. In the process, he succeeded in demonising Sanskrit and Hindi as languages of north Indian domination. Since he singled Brahmins out as the ruling class, he succeeded in mobilising the lower castes. However, his own premier disciple, Annadurai, differed from him for personal reasons and formed his own party, the Dravida Munnetra Kazhagam (DMK). Annadurai grew to be more powerful than his guru and became the Chief Minister of Madras state (which would later be called Tamil Nadu) in 1967, riding on the crest of an anti-Hindi wave. After his death, he was succeeded by Karunanidhi as Chief Minister.

This movement became so powerful that today, Tamil Nadu is predominated by two Dravidian parties, the DMK and its breakaway faction, the AIADMK. This entire Dravidian movement, though ethnic in origin and motivation, can be described as socialist on the ground that it stood for the lower castes and weaker sections. Besides, the DMK with Annadurai as Chief Minister was the first to start welfare schemes on a large scale in independent India. In 1967, he offered subsidised rice for the universal consumption of the poor. Later chief ministers of all parties emulated his example by introducing wide-ranging schemes. The ultimate step in this process was the 'Amma Scheme' (started by Jayalalitha as Chief Minister), which included idlis for one rupee. Apart from its brand of socialism, it is important to note that this movement had earlier stood for secession from India. However, the magic wand of Indian democracy put an end to that demand. As with every atheist movement in history, Dravidian rationalism has been snowed under by traditional devotion. Despite the social radicalism that the Dravidian movement unleashed during its early period, its parties are today no better or no worse than other parties in India.

The basic question of socialism continues to haunt us in the twenty-first century. It was raised during the brief period of Pericles in ancient Athens, but vanished without a trace for about two millennia for want of appropriate material conditions. It was resurrected only in the seventeenth century, albeit in fits and starts. Its persistence grew since the Industrial Revolution, which made a visible impact through such new historical phenomena as the quantum jump in industrial growth and seething unrest of the labour class in the nineteenth century. The question of socialism was therefore reframed in the nineteenth century by none other than John Stuart Mill. He struggled throughout his intellectual life to reconcile the needs of liberty and the demands of equality within the framework of capitalism, but was eventually constrained to say, in his 'Autobiography': 'The social problem of the future we considered to be how to unite the greatest individual liberty of action with a common ownership of the raw materials of the globe, and the equal participation of all in the benefits of combined labour' (cited in Mehta 1964: 51).

Instead of concluding the chapter with a question mark, George Bernard Shaw's statement could be offered as a possible response. In *The Intelligent Woman's Guide to Socialism and Capitalism*, Shaw, addressing his intelligent woman, said:

> It would be easy, dear madam, to refer you to the many books on socialism. But, I strongly advise you not to read a line of them until you and your friends have discussed for yourselves 'how wealth should be distributed' in a respectable civilized country, and arrived at the best conclusion you can. For Socialism is nothing but an opinion held by some people on that point. (cited in Mehta 1964: 48)

10

Revolutionary Socialism

Karl Marx is the philosophical Colossus who bestrides the worlds of Socialism, Communism, and, in fact, all realms of social thought that came after the publication of his *Communist Manifesto* (1848), which he wrote in collaboration with Engels. This document is by far the most influential in all socialist literature. Marx imbibed the philosophical thought of Hegel in Germany, absorbed social theories in France, and learnt his economics from Engels in London. Engels not only enlightened him about economics and the working conditions of miners, but also financed the modest living of Marx and his family in London. Marx used the British Library in London to satisfy his insatiable intellectual appetite, and produce his earth-shaking revolutionary theories. London was his base for exporting his explosive theories, as well as for waging ideological battles with capitalist foes and socialist rivals.

Marxism is the only non-religious system that encompasses every aspect of human life. It is therefore derided by critics as totalitarianism. Marx borrowed dialectical philosophy from Hegel, but replaced Hegel's idealism with his own materialism. His materialism is not mechanistic, but takes on a dialectical character, which proceeds even more inexorably than Hegel's idealism. He viewed human history in terms of dialectical stages. The main law emerging from this process is that the ownership of the means of production determines the social superstructure, which subsumes ideas and institutions, laws and politics, religious concepts and artistic forms. All major conflicts in history were influenced and determined by class relations. Except at the primitive stage, class inequality has characterised the historical development of human society. Marxism does not, however, contend that man is exclusively motivated by material interests. In fact, it maintains that altruism, religious devotion, patriotism, etc., are idealistic feelings, but are themselves products of economic conditions.

This Marxian economic interpretation of history has its inadequacies. For example, the Renaissance followed the Middle Ages not just because of improved shipping and other tools of trade, but because men made a deliberate effort to go beyond the mildewed mental and religious stagnation of the Middle Ages to return to the freshness of the bygone Hellenic era. While there is tremendous substance in the Marxian theory of economic causation of social and political phenomena, it does not provide for the intellectual causation of scientific processes. For example, it was the growth of science after the Renaissance that led to the Industrial Revolution. Another Marxian belief that progress is invariably continual, is unhistorical. History provides many examples of more civilised rulers being replaced by barbarian conquerors. At any rate, Marxism argues that capitalism is a necessary interlude to socialism, and is therefore not opposed to capitalism in its initial phases. On the contrary, it accepts classical economics, except that it reconsiders capitalism from a wage-earner's perspective. That is why Marx expressed sympathy for the Prussian monarchy: it was not out of any love for German nationalism, but because he believed that capitalism would be quickly completed under Bismarck's leadership, facilitating the emergence of socialism.

Marx theoretically contended that socialism would arrive first in the most industrialised nations such as England. However, that this was not the case can be seen from the fact that the revolution did not happen in England, but in Russia, an industrially backward society. The high revolutionary hopes of Marx in the nineteenth century were more effectively countered by nationalist, rather than capitalist, forces. Marx did not anticipate that the diversionary strength of nationalist sentiment would be more powerful than the socialist sentiment. In fact, nationalist sentiment came into full play in the nineteenth century, continued into the twentieth century, and assumed the form of imperialist forces in World War I. What was more, it took the wild forms of fascism and Nazism in World War II. Above all, nationalist sentiments were used by capitalist forces to quell labour movements; Germany under Hitler exemplified this aspect.

Marx, however, recognised the way religious sentiments were being exploited to blunt the class sentiment of labour, which prompted him to say that religion was the 'opiate of the masses'. In fact, the capitalist forces, which had been under the impact of rationalism and secularism until the first part of the nineteenth century, began to ally with the Church to counter the labour movements after the revolutions of 1848. It is important to note that this alliance continues to this day in different guises.

Marx accepted the theory of value as propounded by David Ricardo and built his theories of 'exploitation of labour' and surplus value, which inevitably culminate in the total concentration of wealth in just a few hands, thus leading to the complete isolation of capitalists and their eventual capitulation. Such a revolution would happen so naturally that the question of violence would not arise. It is therefore very important to note that Marxism as such did not advocate violence as a means of revolution. Marx's followers used his silence on the issue in different ways. His predictions about such a revolution did not turn out to be true for two important reasons: first, middle classes emerged in Europe in a big way, and second, the conditions of labour improved considerably through labour struggles, which manifested themselves in strikes by the trade unions.

While studying the dire straits of labour, Marx developed a powerful social theory of alienation. The labourer in the pre-industrial phase, in his capacity as craftsman or peasant, had scope for self-expression. But in the industrial phase, he would only become a cog in the machine due to the division of labour, thereby leading to his alienation. Marx's concern, not only for the economic well-being of labour but also for the full flowering of the personality of each labourer, is touching.

While concerning himself with alienation, he was not in any way opposed to technological upgradation. Nevertheless, he was obsessed with the creative leisure that everybody should enjoy. Fortunately, the productivity of industry grew at such an unpredictably fantastic pace in the second half of the twentieth century that the problem of hunger was largely solved for everybody in the developed world. But even in the developed world, such huge disparities exist regarding access to quality education and healthcare that enough scope has not been provided for the full realisation of the potential of relatively poor people. The levels of economic inequality reached their highest point at the end of the nineteenth century. This disparity came to be reduced after the Great Depression and World War II, and the establishment of an extensive welfare state in the developed world. However, the latest data unearthed by Thomas Picketty and others show that inequality is now at the same level as it was at the end of the nineteenth century. This inequality is not academic, but is manifesting itself in the low human development indices of the poor, even in rich countries. It is thus evident that Marx's angst about inequality and its consequent alienation is not a thing of the past. Alienation of human beings seems to manifest itself in different incarnations from time to time. The response to this problem needs to be devised creatively to suit the changing conditions.

As a towering dialectician, Marx had aggressive arguments and altercations with both socialists and revolutionary socialists. Marx politely dismissed such pioneering thinkers as Robert Owen, Saint-Simon, Charles Fourier, etc., as utopian socialists. He had more bitter problems with such revolutionary socialists as Bakunin and Blanqui (philosophical anarchists). For Marx and Engels, dialectical materialism and economic determinism were identical. Marx, at the very start, stated that 'philosophers have only interpreted the world in various ways, but the real task is to alter it' (Russell 1996: 749). He was therefore intuitively seeking a revolutionary theory for altering the future of humanity. According to Marx, the direction of historical process was determined by the mode of production.

He therefore argued that once the stage of capitalism had been reached, socialism would automatically follow. His guarantee of victory for the working class aroused crusading fervour for the communist struggle in the twentieth century.

Marx was in the habit of quoting great European poets to substantiate his postulates. We shall content ourselves with one devastating quotation from Shakespeare's play, *Timon of Athens*.

> Gold? Yellow, glittering, precious gold?
> No, Gods, I am no idle votarist! ...
> Thus much of this will make black white, foul fair,
> Wrong right, base noble, old young, coward valiant ...
> ... Why this
> Will lug your priests and servants from your sides,
> Pluck stout men's pillows from below their heads:
> This yellow slave
> Will knit and break religions, bless the accursed;
> Make the hoar leprosy adored, place thieves
> And give them title, knee and approbation
> With senators on the bench: This is it
> That makes the wappen'd widow wed again;
> She, whom the spital-house and ulcerous sores
> Would cast the gorge at, this embalms and spices
> To the April day again. Come, damned earth,
> Thou common whore of mankind, that put'st odds
> Among the rout of nations.[1]

Explaining the implications of Shakespeare's lines, Marx added the following by way of comment on the omnipotence of money:

> 1. It is the visible divinity—the transformation of all human and natural properties into their contraries, the universal confounding and distorting of things: impossibilities are soldered together by it.
> 2. It is the common whore, the common procurer of people and nations.

[1] Shakespeare, *The Tragedy of Timon of Athens*, Act IV, Scene 3 (Lines 1690–1707). Available at Shakespeare.mit.edu/timon/timon4.3.

> The distorting and confounding of all human and natural qualities, the fraternisation of impossibilities—the divine power of money—lies in its character as men's estranged, alienating and self-disposing species-nature. Money is the alienated ability of mankind.
>
> That which I am unable to do as a man, and of which therefore all my individual essential powers are incapable, I am able to do by means of money. Money thus turns each of these powers into something which in itself it is not—turns it, that is, into its contrary. (Marx 1844)

Like any of the great philosophers from Plato and Aristotle onwards, Marx was a man of supreme intellect. He discovered for the first time that class as a factor determined the nature of all human relations and social institutions. He also discovered that monopoly would inevitably develop through the process of market operations. These two discoveries ensure his everlasting place in history. Despite the failure of the huge experiments conducted in the erstwhile Soviet Russia and China in his name, the egalitarian inspiration of Marx's philosophy will endure forever.

In Marx's time, the distinction between discoveries made in natural sciences and those in social sciences was not appreciated. Now it is recognised that discoveries made in social sciences are more fallible than those in natural sciences. Even in natural sciences, titans like Newton and Einstein are not considered unquestionable. We must therefore show great deference to Marx, without blind reverence.

Friedrich Engels, who survived Marx by twelve years, was the natural successor to Marx as his patron and co-author. Apart from his own works, he completed volumes II and III of *Das Capital* on the basis of Marx's incomplete manuscripts and rough notes. The subtle shades of difference in the thinking of Karl Marx and Engels should be left to scholars. In the public mind and in essential reality, the two have remained indivisible; no two geniuses were ever so intertwined in history. Engels, in his own lifetime, chose Karl Kautsky as his heir. Kautsky was the author of the Erfurt Programme adopted by the German Social Democrat Party in 1891, which committed the party to an evolutionary form of Marxism that rejected both the radicalism of Rosa Luxemburg and the evolutionary socialism of Eduard Bernstein.

Mikhail Bakunin (1814–76), a Russian philosophical anarchist, was a formidable rival of Marx. Bakunin's differences with Marx lay in their conception of the State that follows a successful revolution. Bakunin wanted the State to disappear soon after a successful revolution. Their fight was so fierce that the First International (1872), at which both Marx and Bakunin were inspirational figures, was split, leading to its dissolution in 1876. Bakunin had been active in the revolutions of 1848. After attending the Slav Congress in Prague, he wrote his manifesto, *An Appeal to Slavs* (1848). Arrested for revolutionary intrigues in Germany in 1849, he was sent to Russia and exiled to Siberia. He escaped in 1861. Bakunin had a competent successor in Russia, Peter Kropotkin.

Kropotkin (1842–1921) was the son of a prince, but renounced his aristocratic heritage. He was renowned for his contributions in such varied fields as geography, zoology, sociology, and history. He was imprisoned on political charges (1874–76), but escaped and fled to Western Europe. In France, he was once again imprisoned (1883–86), and in 1886, he settled in London, where he remained until the Russian Revolution of 1917. He was allowed to return to Russia after the Revolution. On his return, Kropotkin was disappointed to find that the Bolsheviks had undertaken the revolution through authoritarian rather than libertarian methods. He therefore retired from politics, but wrote several books in which he attempted to explain anarchism on a scientific basis, arguing in favour of cooperation, rather than conflict, as the chief factor in the evolution of the species.

Auguste Blanqui (1805–81) was perhaps the most romantic revolutionary of the nineteenth century. His activities, including the formation of various secret societies, led to his incarceration in various countries for more than thirty-three years. While being a revolutionary, he was also an ardent French patriot. Like Marx, he believed that a temporary dictatorship after the revolution would eradicate the old order.

He believed in labour agitations, including the general strike, for achieving revolution. His disciples played an important role in the history of the workers' movement even after his death.

Rosa Luxemburg (1871–1919) was a Polish-German radical and intellectual. As a Jew in Russian-controlled Poland, she was drawn into underground political activism. An advocate of the mass strike as the proletariat's most important tool, she was imprisoned in Warsaw. Early in World War I, she co-founded the Spartacus League, and in 1918, she oversaw its transformation into the German Communist Party. She was assassinated less than a month later. She pleaded for a democratic path to socialism, rather than a proletariat dictatorship, after a world revolution. She is therefore considered a libertarian socialist.

Russian Revolution

The philosophy of Marx led to the Russian Revolution of 1917, which inspired working classes throughout the world. Lenin's revolutionary government was the first in history to have been formed on the basis of a theory. It should be mentioned that this government was also the first in history to have lasted for seventy years on the basis of collectivism. While this novel experiment eventually failed, it inspired hundreds of millions of people all over the world, including those who were not communists, during its life span. What is more, it enabled Mao to achieve his revolution. In the 1960s, almost one-third of the world was formally under the red flag. Besides, the rest of the developing world (known as the NAM countries) derived their selective inspiration and varied support from Soviet Russia. The contribution of Soviet Russia to the victory over Hitler was decisive. When Soviet Russia became the first to send Man into outer space, and Khrushchev bragged in the United Nations that this showed the superiority of the socialist system, leaders in the West were demoralised and even non-partisan observers nonplussed.

For all these stupendous successes in the twentieth century, it had its bitter critics, who included social democrats. Social democrats, even while fighting for workers' welfare through labour unions and strikes, kept up their fight for individual freedom, which had been buried in Soviet Russia. Many liberal Marxists argue that Marx had never imagined that a system such as that of Soviet Russia would come about in his name. Marx, like all socialists in the nineteenth century, harboured a soft corner for philosophical anarchism. In fact, Marx theorised that the government following a successful revolution should be deemed socialist, and the socialist phase under proletarian dictatorship would lead to the withering away of the State. Marx considered this post-socialist Statelessness the real communist system. No prediction of his proved more erroneous than this. Although proletarianism ended in Soviet Russia and Communist China, the dictatorship has not ended. How diametrically different the systems that obtain now in Russia and China are from the utopian picture that Marx envisioned for communist society can be imagined from the words of Marx himself:

> In Communist society, where nobody has one exclusive sphere of activity but each can become accomplished in any branch he wishes, society regulates the general production and thus makes it possible for me to do one thing today and another tomorrow, to hunt in the morning, fish in the afternoon, rear cattle in the evening, criticise after dinner, just as I have a mind, without ever becoming hunter, fisherman, cowherd, or critic. (Marx 1977: 169)

Freedom without fetters and prosperity without inequality were to characterise the ideal society of Marx. But the path of proletarian dictatorship that he chose for these grand goals (albeit for temporary purposes) has proved to be erroneous.

Lenin (1872–1924)

Although Marx had philosophically opined that personalities would not matter, Lenin's decisive role shows that the Russian Revolution would not have been possible without his supreme revolutionary talent. Lenin's young and open mind was turned revolutionary with the execution of his elder brother

Aleksander, a member of Narodnik, for his part in a plot to assassinate Aleksander III. Later, Lenin described the Narodniks as 'infantile leftists' and turned to Marxism as his guide. Lenin soon decided to apply Marxism to Russian conditions. He criticised the struggles of labour leaders of his time on the ground that they were more interested in the incremental welfare of workers than in revolution. He pioneered the concept of a cadre-based party to inoculate it against the infiltration of police agents, which was one of the bones of contention between him and the Mensheviks. As the Russian Revolution of 1905 failed, Lenin went into exile, and formed his Bolshevik party in a firm and formal way. When World War I broke out, Lenin saw an opportunity for a revolution in Russia, and criticised other socialist parties for supporting their respective governments on the basis of nationalist sentiment. He therefore had no problem in obtaining the support of the German government to enter Russia after the fall of the Czar. He pleaded for an immediate revolution in Russia, even at the risk of Russia's defeat at the hands of Germany in World War I. As capitalist development in Russia was at a very backward stage, he had to bypass Marx's prescription that capitalism must reach an advanced stage before it could move into the socialist stage. For this purpose, he wrote a thesis, 'Imperialism, the Highest Stage of Capitalism', according to which Czarist Russia represented imperialism, because of which it attained the most advanced phase of capitalism, despite its industrial backwardness. On this basis, he sought an immediate revolution in Russia which, according to the Mensheviks, amounted to deviation from Marxist lines. Lenin thus pursued his independent Bolshevik strategy and successfully accomplished his October Revolution.

In order to consolidate his revolutionary power, he adopted flexible tactics. Departing tactically from the Marxist line, he utilised the peasants (in addition to industrial workers) as a class on the side of the revolution by promising to distribute the lands belonging to landlords amongst them. He thus lured the peasants, who were working as soldiers in the trenches during World War I, back to their villages with this offer, thereby achieving a measure of unity between the proletariat (industrial labour) and peasants for his revolutionary objectives. His main aim was the seizure and consolidation of the power of the State, and slogans were just tactical means, not doctrinal nostrums. Through such a resilient strategy, he could overthrow Kerensky's unstable government and form his own. He always believed that his Russian Revolution would be partial, but wished for it to survive until social revolution in the West had been achieved. To stabilise his October Revolution, he settled on a peace accord with Germany in March 1918, even though the terms were not exactly honourable for his country. In conformity with his doctrine, he went in for a complete abolition of markets, of exchange, and of money. However, he soon realised that this abolition was not working, and initiated the 'new Economic Policy' which allowed peasants to sell their surplus in the open market. He also reverted to an economy based on money, and partly on exchange. Both his peace pact with Germany and adoption of the new economic policy demonstrate his famed flexibility. Lenin's legend came to a premature end with his death in 1924, but it left much to the historical imagination of scholars.

If Marx is the most important revolutionary philosopher in history, Lenin can be described as the most important revolutionary. Lenin was an original thinker who adapted Marxian theory to Russian conditions. He split the Russian Social Democratic Workers' Party and formed his own faction, known as the Bolsheviks, parting ways with the other faction, the Mensheviks. The Mensheviks played an active role in both the Russian Revolution of 1905, and in the St. Petersburg Soviet. Lenin participated in the Russian Revolution of 1905, but resumed his exile in 1907. He saw World War I as an opportunity for a revolution in Russia. In February 1917, Czar Nicholas II had to abdicate his throne for three reasons, viz., (*i*) disastrous losses in World War I; (*ii*) riots over food scarcity in Petersburg; and (*iii*) mutiny by the Army. After the abdication, a provisional government was organised four times between March and October of 1917. A socialist, Aleksander Kerensky, became its head in July and put down a coup, but was unable to halt Russia's slide into political and military chaos. Lenin, who returned to Russia after the Czar's abdication, deployed his unique genius to stage his own October Revolution against the Kerensky government. This last fight between Kerensky and Lenin widened and embittered the pre-existing ideological split between Communists and Socialists throughout the world, and lasted for more than half a century.

Stalin (1879–1953)

Contrary to general expectations, Joseph Stalin, rather than the charismatic Trotsky, emerged as the successor to Lenin. Stalin, born in Georgia to a poor family, was being prepared for an ecclesiastical career, but was soon drawn to a Georgian patriotic and socialist organisation and came under the influence of Marxism. He was also drawn to Lenin and his Bolshevik faction. From 1902, he was imprisoned and deported more than once. He met Lenin only in 1905, and after the failure of the 1905 revolution, he distinguished himself as the Bolshevik leader of Baku. Stalin's role in the October Revolution of 1917 was overshadowed by Trotsky as well as by other leaders. His career achieved prominence when he became Secretary General of the party's Central Committee from 1922, which gave him the power base for his ultimate rise. It also enabled him to overcome his principal rival, Trotsky, after Lenin's death. By 1929, Stalin managed to expel Trotsky from the party and banished him from the USSR. He subdued all other rivals by various means. From the early 1930s, he went in for large-scale industrialisation and collective farming in the process of which he resorted to extreme methods, including sending hundreds of thousands of peasants to the notorious labour camps by terming them kulaks (a category of affluent peasants who were opposed to collectivisation). He also shifted hundreds of thousands of farmers forcibly from the rural areas to industrial centres. He simultaneously carried out great purges in the course of which most of the old Bolsheviks and some military leaders were compelled to recant or be eliminated. These ruthless methods, on the plea of discipline and progress, gave his regime a peculiar terroristic character.

Stalin displayed amazing strategic resilience to counteract Hitler: in the first place, he reached a non-aggression pact with Hitler to give himself breathing space, and prepare properly for World War II. When Germany invaded Russia in 1941, Stalin took control of military operations. He allied Russia with Britain and the US. At the Tehran, Yalta, and Potsdam conferences, he demonstrated his negotiating skills. Soviet Russia's contribution to World War II was as high as that of any other country, if not more. After the war, he consolidated Soviet power in Eastern Europe and built up Soviet Union as a world military and atomic power. By the time of his death in 1953, Soviet Russia had emerged as the parallel superpower to the USA.

Stalin's legacy is a terribly mixed one. His achievements are monumental by any standard of history. But his excesses were so outrageous that they alienated many communist intellectuals and further embittered many socialists. This situation does not only reflect the personal temperament of Stalin, but is also taken as proof of the proposition that all dictatorships would ineluctably lead to intolerable authoritarian situations. In Soviet Russia itself, he was disowned by his successor Nikita Khrushchev (1894–1971). At any rate, the Soviet Union itself came to an end in 1991 for a variety of reasons.

The story of the Soviet Union would be incomplete without a brief reference to Leon Trotsky (1879–1940), the tallest revolutionary leader next to Lenin. He was an able Marxist theoretician, an outstanding writer and orator, and the chief organiser of the primitive Red Army. Outwitted by Stalin's low cunning and isolated by his own grandstanding, Trotsky failed to succeed Lenin and became the worst target of Stalin's fury. After being banished from Russia in 1929, Trotsky lived in Turkey and France, where he wrote his memoirs as well as a history of the Russian Revolution. He moved from country to country in Europe for his security, and eventually found asylum in 1936 in Mexico. During Stalin's Great Purge of 1936–38, Trotsky was officially accused of having organised subversive activities, carried out by his adherents inside the USSR. An international commission under the Chairmanship of eminent American philosopher, John Dewey, was set up to inquire into the Stalin government's charges against Trotsky, and rejected them as untrue. Be that as it may, Trotsky was murdered by a Spanish communist in 1940. Trotsky is important not only for his chequered career, but also for his philosophy, known as Trotskyism. Joseph Stalin propagated the theory of 'Socialism in one country', but Trotsky theorised in favour of 'permanent revolution'. Trotsky believed that as the economic development of all nations was influenced by the laws of the world market, a revolution in one nation would not be stable. He therefore pleaded for urgent attempts for revolutions in all other nations. Trotsky continued to attack the Soviet bureaucracy as Bonapartist (based on the dictatorship of one man). After Trotsky's murder, Trotskyism became a generic term for various revolutionary doctrines that opposed the Soviet form of communism. However, Trotsky's theory did not gain much traction because of its inbuilt contradictions. It also believed in complete state ownership and control, which would inevitably lead to dictatorship. It failed to clarify how a dictatorship based on his theory would be different from that of Stalin. At the doctrinal level, it is a distinction without difference.

Mao Tse-Tung (1893–1976)

Mao provided new dimensions to the revolution in China and made several innovations on Marxism-Leninism. Born to a well-to-do farmer's family in Hunan province, he was briefly drawn to various political theories such as constitutional monarchism, English idealism and utopian socialism, but soon adopted a Chinese nationalist and anti-imperialist outlook. He helped to found the Chinese Communist Party in Hunan province in 1920 and soon discovered the latent strength of peasants, through their galvanisation for action. In the process, he made his original discovery that in the objective conditions of China, peasants would have to play a much greater role than proletarians. Until 1927, the Kuomintang (Nationalist) remained an ally of the Communists. Mao served in various positions, including that of chief propagandist. When the alliance fell apart, he fled to the mountains in 1927. After three years of roaming and regrouping, he succeeded in setting up red enclaves in the Southeastern hinterland and proclaimed a Chinese 'Soviet Republic'. Although he became Chairman, he shared the actual power with a Soviet-trained group of leaders, which included Indian Communist intellectual, M. N. Roy. He developed differences with the Soviet group members, who grew distrustful of Mao's guerrilla tactics. By this time, Mao had made two definite alterations in the strategy of Marxism-Leninism: one, he used peasants for staging rebellions, and two, he engaged the Kuomintang forces in guerrilla tactics. Mao's advice for combating the Kuomintang in 1928 can be had through the following limerick:

> When the enemy advances, we retreat.
> When the enemy rests, we harass him.
> When the enemy avoids a battle, we attack.
> When the enemy retreats, we advance. (MaoTse-Tung 1930)

With new tactics such as these, he inflicted several setbacks on the Kuomintang. He also had to deal with Japanese incursions into China. When the Kuomintang forces returned to encircle the Red Army—they gave greater priority to the containment of the Red Army than to the resistance to Japanese incursions—Mao thereafter strategically decided to evacuate with 85,000 soldiers and 15,000 cadres, and embarked on the 'Long March' in 1934. After waging many a heroic battle on the way, the Red Army reached the Shensi Soviet in 1936 with only 78,000 surviving members. The historic Long March made Mao the undisputed leader of the Communist Party of China. Mao showed himself to be an intense nationalist and a flexible strategist when he allied with the Kuomintang government headed by Chiang Kai-shek during World War II to fight against Japan. In the process, he won much liberal sympathy in China. After the defeat of Japan, the Civil War resumed, leading to the defeat of Chiang Kai-shek's forces, which withdrew to Taiwan.

On 1 October 1949, Mao proclaimed the foundation of the Peoples' Republic of China and went on to solidify his control through land reform campaigns. This collectivisation programme was accused of ruthlessness. Mao's critics allege that during the land reforms, a huge number of peasants were beaten to death by the Communist Party. The campaign to suppress counter-revolutionaries involved public executions that targeted former Kuomintang officials, suspect businessmen, and others. Mao himself admitted that 700,000 people were killed in these campaigns during 1950–52, although Western reports claim that the deaths ran into millions. In 1957, he launched the 'Great Leap Forward' campaign that aimed to rapidly transform China's agrarian economy into an industrial one. The campaign led to a great famine in China, whose death toll is alleged to have run into millions. Even after capturing power and consolidating his revolution, Mao's streak of nationalism manifested itself through Chinese expansions even after the revolution. It was most evident when China continued to make claims on India's land, backing these up with aggression on India's soil in 1962. The bias against India continued to the point of supporting Pakistan on the issue of Bangladesh in 1971.

In 1966, Mao started the Great Proletarian Cultural Revolution, a programme to rid Chinese society of 'counter-revolutionary' elements that lasted for a decade. It was marked by indiscriminate attacks on numerous individuals and destruction of cultural artefacts. Above all, it was characterised by the promotion of Mao's personality cult. His own international stature began to grow rapidly after Stalin's death in 1953. Even during Stalin's lifetime, the gap between China and Russia began to grow on ideological questions. But it was widened further in Khrushchev's time. At any rate, Mao's personal image grew rapidly across the world. Mao gained in his romantic appeal because of his cultural revolution. It was, however, viewed in two different ways: while critics called it an unrestrained murderous anarchy, admirers argued that it was a new way of destroying the last vestiges of feudal, bourgeois, and bureaucratic structures. When Mao gave a call for bombarding the headquarters of the Communist Party of China, he attracted positive notice even among non-communist liberals, as this was seen to be attacking the Party's apparatchiks. Even a section of traditional communists were excited enough to say that Mao was tackling Soviet Russia's bureaucratic evils in a revolutionary way. What is not understood is that concentration of power, either in a Communist State or in a faction of the Communist party, would inevitably breed hierarchical structures. Although Mao's admirers across the world have declined, the old division of opinion persists.

Before Mao's death in 1976, he went in for a radical change in foreign policy and welcomed American President Richard Nixon in 1972 in Beijing, signalling a policy of opening up China. This last foreign policy change was strengthened further under the rule of Deng Xiaoping (1978–92). We also need to note that under his leadership, China went in for its own radical mix of privatisation and globalisation, eventually emerging as the second largest economic power in the world. While the economic programme of Communism has been abandoned, two of its distinctive political features continue. First, the dictatorship, though not of the proletariat, remains as strong as ever. Second, the mantra of Mao's name is routinely recited by way of deference to the collective memory of the Chinese masses. Mao's admirers outside China, however, condemn the current Chinese system as neo-capitalist.

Ho Chi Minh (1890–1969)

Ho Chi Minh was the son of a Confucian scholar and teacher. In deference to his father's wishes, he received French education. He chose to leave school in order to go abroad, as his father, at that time, was facing a number of difficulties. He worked as a kitchen help on a French steamer and visited many countries from 1911–17. In 1912, while working as the cook's helper on a ship, he travelled to the United States, where he worked in many menial jobs. From 1919–23, while living in France, he developed interest in politics and joined a group of Vietnamese nationalists in Paris. Following World War I, the group petitioned for the recognition of the civil rights of Vietnamese people in China to Western powers at the Versailles talks, but was ignored. US President Woodrow Wilson also belied their hopes. In 1923, Ho Chi Minh left Paris for Moscow, where he was employed by the Comintern, the Communist International, and participated in the fifth Comintern Congress in June 1924 before going to Canton, China. However, Chiang Kai-Shek's 1927 anti-Communist coup forced him to return to Moscow. He soon returned to Vietnam via China to lead the Viet Minh independence movement. He oversaw many successful military actions against the Vichy French and during the Japanese occupation of Vietnam in World War II. He was later jailed in China by Chiang Kai-Shek's local authorities before being rescued by Chinese communists.

Following his release in 1943, he returned to Vietnam, where he became Chairman of the provisional government of Vietnam. In his capacity as Chairman, he repeatedly petitioned American President Harry S. Truman to support Vietnam independence, citing the Atlantic Charter, but there was no response. Following the victory of America and its allies in World War II, Vietnam was vacated by Japan, only to be reoccupied by French colonial forces. The Viet Minh, led by Ho Chi Minh along with General Giap (1911–2013), had to fight a long war for independence from the French, finally defeating them at the battle of Dien Bien Phu in 1954.

Following an international conference at Geneva, Vietnam was partitioned along the 17th parallel, with the northern part under Ho Chi Minh and the southern part under Bao Dai. This partition was to be temporary, but the reunification elections were never held. Bao Dai declared the independence of South Vietnam (Republic of Vietnam). The most important reason for avoiding the election was the fear that Ho Chi Minh's popular Viet Min party would win it. Since the election was avoided in a malafide manner, North Vietnamese guerrillas and pro-Communist rebels in South Vietnam began working towards uniting Vietnam, which led to the US intervention and the Vietnam War. In the war that ensued, fighters trained in the north (the Viet Cong) fought a guerrilla war against the US-supported South Vietnamese forces. At the height of US involvement, there were more than half a million US military personnel in Vietnam. The Tet Offensive of 1968, in which the Viet Cong attacked thirty-six major South Vietnamese cities and towns, marked a turning point in the war. Many in the US had come to oppose the war on moral and practical grounds, and President Lyndon B. Johnson (1908–73) decided to shift to a policy of 'de-escalation'.

The US war in Vietnam was met with an international outcry. An international war tribunal headed by philosopher Bertrand Russell (1872–1970) kept up the campaign against the US administration. But the war continued till 1976, when North Vietnam's forces finally trounced the US-backed South Vietnam, leading to the reunification of the country. More than two million people (including 58,000 Americans) died over the course of the war (1955–76), half of them civilians. The Vietnam War left an indelible negative imprint on the American psyche. Twenty-five years later, cool heads in America opposed the war in Iraq. After yet another bitter lesson in Iraq, American public opinion seems to have turned against America's international interventions, at least for the moment.

The Vietnamese war taught an important historical lesson: that is, American forces, which represented the greatest military might in history, could be defeated by a highly motivated and well-organised people. Through the trials and tribulations of the Vietnamese people, Ho Chi Minh emerged as the most gentle of all Communist giants, and General Giap arguably as the greatest military genius of the twentieth century. After their victory against America, the Vietnamese had to fight one more war against China to defend their national prestige, thereby proving their fierce nationalist spirit once again.

Marshal Tito (1892–1980)

Marshal Tito (originally Joseph Broz; 1945–53), Yugoslav politician, premier, and President (1953–80), was born in

Croatia to a peasant family. He fought in the Astro-Hungarian Army in World War I and was captured by the Russians in 1915. While in Russia, he took part in the July Day demonstrations of 1917 and joined the Bolsheviks. In 1920, he returned to Croatia, where he became a local leader of the Communist Party of Yugoslavia. He rose in the Party hierarchy (interrupted by a prison term [1928–34]) to become its Secretary General in 1939. In World War II, Tito (a pseudonym adopted around 1935), proved to be an effective leader of the Yugoslav partisans. As Marshal from 1943, he strengthened the communist control of Yugoslavia as Premier and President; he developed an independent form of socialist rule in defiance of Stalin's Soviet Union, pursued a policy of non-alignment, and built ties with other non-aligned States, including India led by Nehru. He also improved relations with Western powers in the teeth of opposition from Soviet Russia. His defiance of Stalin marked him out as an international hero. Within Yugoslavia, he set up a system of 'symmetrical federalism' (1974) that established equality among the six republics and Serbia's autonomous provinces (including Kosovo), while maintaining tight control to prevent separatist movements. After his death, both the federal system and Yugoslavia came apart, leading to civil wars and international crises. Like Ho Chi Minh, Marshal Tito is another non-controversial communist hero.

Fidel Castro (1926–2016)

Fidel Castro was a political leader of Cuba from 1959 and President from 1976–2008. The son of a prosperous sugar planter, he became a lawyer and worked on behalf of the poor in Havana. He was a candidate for Cuba's legislature when General Fulgencio Batista overthrew the government in 1952. If this initial attempt of Castro to participate in the elections had not been frustrated, he would have probably evolved as a great social democrat. As it happened, he organised a rebellion against Batista in 1953, but failed. He was captured, served time in prison, and then went to Mexico, where along with others (including Che Guevara), he continued to plot

Batista's overthrow. He led an armed rebellion back to Cuba in 1956, which also failed. Finally, after organising guerrillas throughout the island, Castro managed to capture power. He nationalised private commerce and industry and expropriated US-owned land; vastly expanded health services and eliminated illiteracy; and also suppressed all opposition. The US attempted to overthrow his government through the Bay of Pigs invasion (17 April 1961), in which Cuban exiles participated. The invasion was intended to spark a rebellion against Castro, but did not materialise. The result was a huge propaganda victory for Castro and severe embarrassment for the administration of John F. Kennedy, which precipitated the Cuban Missile Crisis and led to major confrontation over the presence of Soviet nuclear-armed missiles in Cuba. In October 1962, a US spy plane detected a ballistic missile on a launching site in Cuba. President Kennedy placed a naval blockade around the island and for several days, the US and the Soviet Union hovered on the brink of war. Nikita Khrushchev finally agreed to remove the missiles in return for a secret commitment from the US to withdraw US missiles from Turkey and never to invade Cuba. While this incident frightened the world, it further fuelled the nuclear arms race between the superpowers. Tensions between the US and Cuba continued to run high until President Obama recognised Cuba and tried to normalise relations through his visit in 2016.

After the collapse of communism in the USSR, Cuba lost important financial backing and its economy suffered greatly. Cuba gradually improved in the 1990s with the encouragement of tourism. After capturing Cuba, Castro emerged as a charismatic international hero, particularly for the countries of Latin America, and demonstrated his political stamina by ruling for more than fifty-five years in the face of American hostility. His is the longest regime headed by a fiery revolutionary in the modern age. He retired from office on health grounds, and was succeeded by his brother, Raul Castro. Fidel Castro remained the most popular leader of the Cuban people even after his exit, despite the economic troubles of the country. These economic problems were created by the limitations of the communist system, compounded by the merciless economic blockade imposed by America for more than half a century. President Obama eventually accorded diplomatic recognition to Cuba, and improved relations between Cuba and America. President Obama's visit to Cuba and his meeting with the ailing Fidel Castro were welcomed by the world. Within months of Obama's visit, Castro passed away. Donald Trump, who succeeded Obama, had no kind words to say about Castro, even on the day of his death. Despite the ruthless pressures exerted by America for over sixty years, Castro's personality retained enough appeal to be favourably compared to that of Ho Chi Minh.

Che Guevara (1928–67)

Che Guevara was born in Argentina to a middle-class family. Widespread poverty and American interventionism led to his study of Marxism, and convinced him that the only solution to South and Central America's problems lay in armed revolution. He met Cuban leader Fidel Castro, and played a key role in the eventual success of the latter's guerrilla war against Cuban dictator Batista. He served as minister and in other positions in Cuba, but soon quit all official positions to spread the revolution in other parts of the developing world. He spent several months in Africa, particularly the Congo, attempting to train rebel forces. He eventually landed in Bolivia to lead rebel forces against the government of Rene Barriaentos Ortuno. With US assistance, the Bolivian army captured Guevara and executed him on 9 October 1967. His martyrdom turned him into a quintessential icon for various leftist-inspired movements. His birth in Argentina, struggles in Cuba, and death in Bolivia were incidents that lent romance to his name. He could be compared to the English poet Byron, who died in Greece for its freedom in the nineteenth century. Che Guevara was known for his wide literary and intellectual interests, as well as for his ruthless revolutionary actions. He should be regarded as one of the charismatic revolutionary heroes in history.

Communism also spread to Western Europe. Its presence was felt in Italy in a big way, where the communist unit was led by Palmiro Togliatti (1893–1964). He served as Vice-Premier in a coalition government in Italy, advocated a national, democratically oriented form of communism, and made the Italian Communist Party the largest in Western Europe. Togliatti tried to dissociate the Italian Communist Party from the Soviet Union after the revelation of Stalin's excesses. Enrico Berlinguer, as party leader (1972–84), became a leading proponent of what came to be known as Euro-Communism. In 1991, in order to consolidate left-wing forces and broaden its base, the party's name was changed to Democratic Party of the Left. Most European communist parties trod the path of Euro-communism. However, these parties declined after the break-up of the Soviet Union.

Next to China in Asia, communism spread through the Communist Party of India. Some of its leading lights included P. C. Joshi, S. A. Dange, P. Sundaraiah, and E. M. S. Namboodiripad. Namboodiripad and Sundariah became members of the Congress party through one of the latter's platforms, the Congress Socialist Party (as the Communist Party of India was banned at the time). However, the split between Congress Socialist party members and those of the Communist Group came to a head in 1942, when members of the latter decided to support the British war effort following the German declaration of war on Russia. This decision turned out to be controversial, for it ran counter to the nationalist sentiment in India. Even after India attained independence, the Communist Party of India remained a banned organisation as it was supporting the Telangana Armed Movement. However, in 1950, the ban was lifted after the CPI agreed to withdraw the armed movement on the instructions of Stalin and participate in elections. The CPI emerged as a strong party in many parts of India, including the then composite Madras state, then Hyderabad state, West Bengal, etc. However, the party itself came to be ideologically divided when China's aggression took place on India's territory in 1962. This ideological division led to a formal split in 1964, when a major faction broke away from the CPI and was formed into CPI (M).

The CPI (M) suffered another major split in 1968 when a group broke away and formed its own party, known initially as CPI (ML), on the ground that the parliamentary path would kill the revolutionary spirit and never lead to a Communist revolution. The CPI (M) in what was then Andhra Pradesh was severely eroded, with some of its tall leaders, such as Tarimila Nagireddy, Chandra Pulla Reddy, Kolla Venkaiah, Devulapalli Venkateswara Rao, etc., opting for the extra-parliamentary path. The CPI (ML) and its various factions were all inspired by Maoism. The extra-parliamentary left movement started in Naxalbari in West Bengal under the leadership of Charu Majumdar manifested itself in many parts of the country. Its presence was felt in all states where the communist party had been historically dominant. Of all its breakaway factions, the PWG (Peoples War Group) has emerged as the most influential. Ultra-left violence is one of the most urgent concerns of the Central government in India, as it operates across various states. Although its overall impact has declined in rural areas, it continues to call the shots in most areas inhabited by hill tribes. While containing the problem of insurrectionary violence, the Indian State has been charged with resorting to extra-judicial killings.

The electoral record of communist parties in India is not unimpressive. The CPI government was formed in Kerala under the leadership of Namboodiripad in 1958. Left-led governments have been formed in Kerala ever since, although they were never elected for two successive terms. However, they rarely failed to defeat the Congress-led governments in Kerala after one term. In West Bengal, the CPI (M) government remained in power for a record thirty-four years, with Jyoti Basu as Chief Minister for twenty-four consecutive years. The influence of communist parties has remained stagnant for a number of reasons. First, they were split more than twice. Second, Nehru's socialist image and Indira Gandhi's land reforms and other pro-poor programmes have checkmated their growth.

Third, the levels of rural poverty have declined substantially. Fourth, the number of people belonging to the middle classes has increased enormously, with the status of the lower classes and trade union workers being upgraded. Finally, the collapse of the Soviet Union and the crypto-capitalist character of the current Chinese Republic have disappointed the left-leaning intelligentsia. Despite all these setbacks, the CPI(M) manages to lead the formidable factors in West Bengal and Tripura, and continues to be the main opposition in West Bengal and a considerable electoral factor in several other states. The CPI, although weaker than the CPI (M), also continues to be an electoral force to be reckoned with in various parts of the country. The CPI (ML) factions, notwithstanding the erosion of their strength, remain a cause for concern for various state governments and the Government of India.

In Nepal, the influence of communist parties has remained steady over a long period. The Maoist-centre led by Prachanda is a redoutable electoral force. There are other communist parties, with varying strengths, working in Nepal within the framework of a democratic constitution. The future of the communist parties and that of democracy itself in Nepal needs to be closely watched.

The Revolutionary Socialism set the whole world on fire, which raged for more than 150 years. It made inestimable contributions through anti-colonial struggles throughout the world; varied forms of support, such as economic, diplomatic, and military to non-aligned countries; boosting labour and peasants' struggle and the Soviet bulwark against all forms of neo-imperialism. Above all, it offered an effective counter-force to Western nations, thus providing some space for smaller countries to enjoy their modest independence for half-a-century. But it has its own seamy record, which includes brutal suppression of the democratic freedoms of not only peoples and enemies of Socialism, but also its own erstwhile leaders, and theoretical sanction to gory violence.

11

Feminism

Women, like all weaker sections such as slaves, serfs, and people from the lower castes in India, were subjected to routine discrimination during the entire agrarian phase in history. This was the case in every religious or racial civilisation. While other forms of discrimination based on slavery or caste system witnessed some protests from time to time, however effete or ephemeral, voices of dissent were seldom raised in the case of women. This silence or lack of gender consciousness was because of their co-option as part of systemic subordination. Women belonging to elite or royal households enjoyed a superior status to other women or men in their societies; such women could become crowned empresses, like Cleopatra, Elizabeth I, Victoria, Mary, Queen of Scots, and Mary Tudor outside India. Likewise, within India there were warrior queens like Laxmi Bai of Jhansi, Rani Rundrama Devi of the Kakatiya empire, and Rani Velu Nachiyar of Shivganga, who led armies into battle because of their family affiliations, and not because of their gender (or rather, despite their gender).

Such examples abound in every part of the world, but they do not speak to women's gender status. The posthumous glorification of a precocious genius like St. Joan of Arc is a rare exception, even so, her canonisation came 500 years too late. That apart, St. Joan fell martyr to the cause of the French nation, but not to that of her gender. Women as a class seem to have been reconciled to their inferior gender status, even seemingly enjoying the amour or adulation of their husbands or lovers. Poetry and arts have sublimated the subjection of women to such an extent that they have themselves been revelling in their objectification, not only historically but also contemporaneously. It is enough to go through the titillating accounts of female stars in Hollywood or Bollywood, recounted in glossy magazines or anonymous websites, to learn about the continuing discrimination against women.

Ironically, in some ways women from the upper classes seemed to have enjoyed less security or liberty as compared to their lower-class counterparts. For instance, barriers in matters of divorce and remarriage were far less rigorous among the lower classes. Men of the lower classes or castes did not possess the economic levers of property or social status to ensure their superiority to the women in their households.

In every religious or cultural tradition, some verbal obeisance was invariably paid from time to time, and from scripture to scripture, to confer special status on women. But when judged against the empirical evidence of women's situation, these could be seen as mere redeeming exercises in tokenism. In all societies, male chauvinism asserted and perpetuated itself through entrenched institutions and customs in subtle or crude ways. The victims of these time-honoured traditions were blissfully ignorant of their collective suppression. This does not mean, however, that clever or strong women did not exercise disproportionate influence through their husbands or lovers. Such influence was vicarious and individual-specific, but never part of the system. These severe limitations that women laboured under for thousands of years stemmed from the structure and nature of agrarian society.

Things had to change in the modern age. Even there, however, the change had to wait from the Renaissance to the French Revolution. It was only in 1792, when the French Revolution was at its height, that Mary Wollstonecraft (1759–97), the eighteenth-century British proto-feminist, wrote *A Vindication of the Rights of Women*, arguing that women should be educated rationally to give them the opportunity to contribute to society. She further argued in her Preface:

'My main argument is built on this simple principle, that if she be not prepared by education to become the companion of man, she will stop the progress of knowledge, for truth must be common to all.' She also contended that society would degenerate if it did not educate women, particularly because mothers are the primary educators of young children. She attributed the problems of uneducated women to men, and to a false system of education gathered from the books written on the subject by men who considered the problems of women through the prism of men. She attacked even the radical philosopher Rousseau for arguing in his famous work *Emile* (1762) that women should be educated for the pleasure of men.

Wollstonecraft further wrote, 'Taught from their infancy that beauty is woman's sceptre, the mind shapes itself to the body, and roaming round its gilt cage, only seeks to adorn its prison' (Wollstonecraft 1996: 43). She argued that women should not only be able to focus on their beauty, but also be the rational companions of their husbands. She wanted women to study politics and business of various kinds, and pleaded for free school education for children between the ages of five to nine. These schools should be co-educational, with the same curriculum for boys and girls. She exposed the sexual double standards of the late eighteenth century and demanded that men adhere to the same virtues as expected of women. She warned women not to fall 'prey' to their senses and 'not to be' blown about by every momentary gust of feeling. She therefore pleaded that women should try and succeed in blending sexual love with self-esteem, with a view to avoiding exploitation by men. *A Vindication* was considered so radical that it was not published in the first part of the nineteenth century. Later, both the book and the author (whose private life was considered scandalous by conservatives for a century) became the icons of feminism.

In 1790, Marquis De Condorcet, a mathematician and pillar of the French Revolution, published *For the Admission to Rights of Citizenship for Women*. The statement of French playwright Olympe de Gouges (1748–93)—'if a woman has the right to be guillotined, she has the right to debate'—proved too much for patriarchy. She was arrested and sentenced to death in 1793. As she walked up to the guillotine, she declared that the children of her fatherland would avenge her death.

As we noted earlier, Wollstonecraft's plea for women's education did not bear fruit for long decades. It was only in the middle of the nineteenth century that Queen's College and Bedford College in London started offering a few courses to women (in 1848), and the 'Ladies of Langham Place'[1] took up the cause and set up Girton College, Cambridge, in 1869. However, women were consistently denied degrees till the twentieth century. Oxford finally opened its gates to women in 1920, while Cambridge kept its doors firmly shut till 1948. The Ladies of Langham Place, it must be noted here, were fighting not only for women's right to education, but also for marital and divorce reforms and the right of women to work outside their homes.

The turn of the nineteenth century had not brought much succour to the rights of women. By law women remained firmly under the male thumb, as nineteenth-century society continued to adhere to the concept of *pater familias*—the man as master of the house. Women not only lost all control over property, income, and wealth to their husbands upon marriage, but they also lost ownership of their bodies, which were considered the property of their spouses. Even after divorce, the husband retained complete legal control over his former wife's income. Women were barred from opening bank accounts and married women were not allowed to conclude a business contract without legal approval from their husbands. Worse still, the domestic abuse of wives and children was sanctioned by the law. It was under these circumstances that the nineteenth-century voices for women's rights were raised. A year after French socialist Fourier introduced the word 'feminisme', British writer and social reformist Caroline Norton (1808–77)

[1] The Langham Place Circle was a feminist activist network that advocated changes in women's employment, education, and marital law.

left her husband, George Chapple Norton, an unsuccessful barrister and MP from Guildford. By all accounts, Norton was an abusive husband who tortured his wife, both physically and mentally. Caroline subsisted on her earnings as a writer, until Norton decided he was legally entitled to them. To make matters worse, he refused her access to her children and accused her of committing adultery with Lord Melbourne, then Prime Minister of Great Britain. Caroline Norton took him to court, but the case was thrown out after a nine-day trial. The Norton case was to become pivotal to the reform of marriage laws. Caroline's open letter to Queen Victoria, nineteen years after her separation, was placed and read out before the House. Mrs Norton's letter was instrumental to the successful passage of the Custody of Infants Act 1839 and the Matrimonial Causes Act of 1857. But Britain's divorce laws continued to be ridiculous and male-friendly well into the twentieth century. The big change came only in 1969 when the Divorce Reform Act was passed, allowing couples to divorce after they had been separated for two years (or five years if only one of them wanted a divorce).

In the nineteenth century, the great philosopher John Stuart Mill took up the cause of women and their right to vote. He wrote a famous essay, 'The Subjection of Women', in 1869, which pleaded for equal treatment for both sexes. Mill credited his wife, Harriet Taylor Mill, with co-writing the essay. Mill was not only a respected philosopher, but also belonged to a reputed family. He therefore raised many an eyebrow for his views, which were radical for the time in Britain. He argued that human beings of both sexes were capable of being educated and civilised, and that everybody should have a right to vote, including women, but with the exception of barbarians and the uneducated. Mill further argued that the concept of inequality of women was a relic of the past. He went so far as to say: '[T]he legal subordination of one sex to the other—is wrong in itself and now one of the chief hindrances to human improvement; and that it ought to be replaced by a principle of perfect equality, admitting no power or privilege on the one side, nor disability on the other' (Mill 1869: 1). He dismissed the argument that women were naturally unable to do certain things. In his words:

> What women by nature cannot do, it is quite superfluous to forbid them from doing .... I deny that anyone knows or can know, the nature of the two sexes, as long as they have only been seen in their present relation to one another. Until conditions of equality exist, no one can possibly assess the natural differences between women and men, distorted as they have been. What is natural to the two sexes can only be found out by allowing both to develop and use their faculties freely. (Mill 1869: 12)

Mill attacked marriage laws by saying, '[T]here remain no legal slaves save the mistress of every house' (ibid.: 47). He pleaded for the reform of marriage laws whereby they were reduced to a business agreement, placing no restriction on either party. He also pleaded for allowing women to keep their own property and work outside the home to gain independent financial status. In the context of women's suffrage, he said: 'Under whatever conditions and within whatever limits, men are admitted to the suffrage, there is not a shadow of justification for not admitting women under the same' (ibid.: 30).

Mill wrote in favour of women's rights and campaigned for their rights as an MP; he was also the President of the National Society for women's suffrage. It is important to note that Mill was advocating for women's suffrage at a time when even men of the lower classes did not have it. At that time, England was still going through the Chartist Movement, which only advocated for universal adult male suffrage.

The idea of women's suffrage was so radical even in the last quarter of the nineteenth century that the highbrow French magazine, *Le Figaro*, commented in its editorial in 1883 that if women were given the right to vote, a demand for the right to vote for cattle would soon be made. It is instructive to note that this comment was made in Paris, 100 years after the French Revolution and a decade after the Paris Commune. England, which was the first to start and develop democracy in the modern age, was no exception either. Women in England had to wait till 1928 to get the franchise extended to all women over twenty-one, without property limitations. Emmeline Pankhurst was the most notable woman activist in England, with *Time* naming her as one of the 100 most important people of the twentieth century. In France, women obtained the right to vote only for the provisional government with the French Republic of 21 April 1944. In Switzerland, women of all strata gained the right to vote as late as in 1971. But in the canton of Appenzell Innerrhoden, women obtained the right to vote on local issues only in 1991, when the canton was forced to do so by the Federal Supreme Court of Switzerland. In Liechtenstein, women were given the right to vote by the women's suffrage referendum of 1984. Three referendums, held earlier in 1968, 1971, and 1973, had failed to secure women's right to vote. In Western Europe, The Netherlands was the first to have granted the right to vote after the successful movement led by Wilhelmina Drucker (1847–1925).

Meanwhile, the United States, which had witnessed a parallel suffragist movement, granted women the right to vote in 1919. Prominent among the suffragist leaders of the United States were Lucretia Mott, Elizabeth Cady Stanton, and Susan B. Anthony, who each campaigned for the abolition of slavery before championing female franchise. The leaders of the women's campaign on both sides of the Atlantic stayed in touch, and were aware of the activities taking place on the other side of the ocean. An important moment in American feminism was the Seneca Falls Convention in New York (1848), during which the Declaration of Independence for Women was drafted.

Despite France's rich history of liberalism and radicalism, women obtained the right to vote as late as 21 April 1944. This brief account of the struggle for women's suffrage even in the West will suffice to show how slow and agonising it was for women to get the right to vote even in the twentieth century.

In India, the women's movement was different from that in the West. The initial campaign for the emancipation of women was started by men; in the nineteenth century, social reformers like Raja Ram Mohan Roy (1772–1833) fought for the abolition of Sati and Ishwar Chandra Vidyasagar (1820–91) championed the cause of widow remarriage. Mahatma Jyotiba Phule raised the crime for women's education and proceeded to educate his wife Savitribai Phule. She ran around schools to provide education for women. However, in *Mapping the Women's Movement in India* (2009), De Souza disagrees with the general perception that women were passive recipients in the fight for their liberation. She cites cases of 'exceptional' women who rebelled against their assigned roles. For example, Basundari Devi, a housewife in Bengal, wrote an autobiography in 1876 (*Amar Jibon* or *My Life*) describing the oppression of women. She mentions the example of Swarnakumari Devi, sister of Rabindranath Tagore, founder of the Ladies' Theosophical Society, and later, member of the Indian National Congress. She and her daughter, Sarala Devi, went so far as to train women in martial arts. She also refers to Pandita Ramabai, whose father educated her mother, Lakshmibai, even at the cost of being exiled by his own community. Pandita Ramabai was one of the ten women delegates to the Indian National Congress in 1889. Then there was the Begum of Bhopal, who founded the All India Muslim Women's Conference with women's education as the prime agenda, along with campaigning against polygamy and other regressive practices (De Souza 2009: 73–74).

The World Bank Policy Research Report on Gender and Development stated:

> The women's movement in India took off in the 1920s, building on the 19th century social reform movement. The women's movement progressed during the period of high nationalism and the freedom struggle, both of which shaped its contours. Among the many achievements of the movement, the most significant were the constitutional guarantees of equal rights for women and universal adult suffrage in independent India. (Sen 2000)

In its 1917 session, the Indian National Congress, presided over by Annie Besant (one of the founders of the Women's Indian Association), supported the demand for voting for women, as did the Muslim League.

Travancore-Cochin, then a princely state, led the way by giving women voting rights in 1920, followed by Madras and Bombay in 1921, and other states thereafter. However, enfranchisement remained limited to women who were married, owned properties, or were educated. The Government of India Act, 1935, did not change the situation much, as the restrictions of property and education remained. Women in India achieved full suffrage only in 1950.

The first wave of the women's movement in India began with reformist campaigns in the late nineteenth and early twentieth centuries, but it was Mahatma Gandhi who brought women out of their homes and into the public sphere in droves. Gandhi transcended patriarchal norms to mobilise women, although the target was the colonial government and not social oppression. Sarojini Naidu, Lado Rani Zutshi, Rani Gudiallo, Kamala Nehru, Hansa Mehta, Anantikabai Gokhale, Satyavati, Parvathibai, Rukmini Lakshmipaty, Lilavati Munshi, Durgabai Deshmukh, Kamaladevi Chattopadhyaya, and thousands of others joined Congress leaders in making and selling salt. 'This is remembered as the turning point for women's participation in struggle .... Of all the leaders and reforms, Gandhiji was the most forceful in his conviction that women should and have the right to individuality and freedom from violation of their personal dignity' (De Souza 2009: 77–78).

However, the momentum built up during the freedom struggle was not carried over to post-independence India. Political scientist Zoya Hasan sees a certain instrumentalism in the deployment of women against colonial rule. She says:

> Women more or less went into retreat after Independence, in part because of the nationalist ideology and in part because the Congress Party, in the first two decades, focussed on the role of the state, believing that state intervention would bring about social change and contribute to the overall improvement of all vulnerable and disadvantaged groups within the country, including women. (Hasan 2012)

This mindset was to change only in the 1970s, with the Report of the Committee on the Status of Women, which drew attention to the gross underrepresentation of women in all spheres.

The feminist movement should not be confined to the struggle for suffrage, but should naturally cover other aspects of equal entitlement. Even in democratic countries where women have been granted the right to vote, the struggle for many other rights continues. During the late Qing period (which was soon followed by the democratic regime led by Sun Yatsen) and reform movements such as the Hundred Days' Reform, Chinese feminists called for women's liberation from traditional roles and Neo-Confucian gender segregation. Later, the Chinese Communist Party launched schemes to integrate women into the workforce, and claimed that the revolution had successfully achieved women's liberation. This tall claim has not been borne out by ground reality. Arab feminism was closely connected with Arab nationalism. In 1899, Qasim Amin, considered the father of Arab feminism, argued for the legal and social reforms of women. His leadership led to the development of Cairo University and to the National Movement. In 1923, Hodashaarawi founded the Egyptian feminist union and emerged as a symbol of the Arab women's rights movement. The Iranian Constitutional Revolution in 1905 triggered the Iranian women's movement, which worked to achieve women's equality in education, marriage, careers, and legal rights. However, during the Iranian revolution of 1979, many of the rights that women had gained earlier through their movements were abolished.

In many European countries, women did not have many rights even in the twentieth century. For instance, in France, married women did not get the right to work without their husbands' permission until 1965.

Simone De Beauvoir (1908–86) was a pre-eminent French feminist, existentialist philosopher, and writer in the mid-twentieth century. She was famous also for her friendship with Jean Paul Sartre (1905–80), with whom she maintained a life-long intellectual and romantic bond. They both rejected the institution of marriage. Sartre was one of the greatest philosophers and writers of the twentieth century, who refused the Nobel Prize for literature on the ground that he did not approve of the institutionalisation of the Nobel Prize. He was also a public activist and led the 1968 student revolt in France against the government of De Gaulle. Beauvoir is known for her treatise, *The Second Sex* (1949), an erudite and passionate plea for the abolition of what she called the myth of the 'eternal feminine', which became a major classic of feminist literature. Beauvoir's distinctive contributions combined a synthesis of Marxism and Existentialism.

Beauvoir largely identified what is known in the West as 'second wave feminism', with the first wave being equated with the fight for franchise. The second wave is concerned with issues of equality beyond the right to vote, such as gender discrimination. Second-wave feminists see women's cultural and political inequalities as inextricably intertwined. They understand aspects of personal lives as deeply politicised, and as reflecting sexist power structures. It was feminist author Carol Hanisch who wrote a famous essay in 1969, titled 'The Personal is Political', which became both a slogan and a battle-cry. It also became synonymous with second-wave feminism.

In the early 1990s in the USA, third-wave feminism distinguished itself from the second wave around issues of sexuality. It challenged female heterosexuality and celebrated sexuality as a means of female empowerment. It also attempted to avoid the second wave's essentialist definitions of femininity, which, it argued, over-emphasises the experiences of upper middle-class white women. To be fair to the second-wave feminists, they also sought to negotiate space within feminist thought for consideration of race-related subjectivities. Third-wave feminists can be divided into two groups—one relates to those who believe there are important differences between the sexes, and the other to those who believe that there are no such inherent differences, arguing instead that gender roles are produced by social conditioning.

According to the standpoint theory, women's social position determines their knowledge levels, skills, and perspectives. This theory refuses to see traditional science as unbiased. An international controversy broke out when the then president of Harvard University, Lawrence Summers, made a statement about the relative difficulties of women vis-a-vis the sciences. The standpoint theorists condemned this statement as unscientific, and Lawrence Summers was forced to make amends. Since the 1980s, standpoint feminists have taken up such global issues as rape, incest, and prostitution, and culturally specific issues such as female genital mutilations in some parts of Africa and the Middle East. They have also taken up the issue of limitations imposed on women's development by glass-ceiling practices in developed economies. All such issues highlight the manner in which gender equality interacts with racism, homophobia, classism, and colonisation.

Feminist theory has been extended to a variety of disciplines, including anthropology, sociology, economics, women's studies, literary criticism, art history, psychoanalysis, and philosophy. Themes explored in feminist theory include discrimination, stereotyping, sexual objectification, oppression, and patriarchy.

More recent feminist theory, such as that of Lisa Lucile Owens, has focused on feminism as a universal emancipatory movement. Generally, the various branches of feminism closely track the political leanings of the larger society. But Liberal (Capitalist) Feminism seeks the individualistic equality of men and women through political and legal reform without altering the structure of society. Catherine Rottenberg has argued that the pro-capitalist bias divests liberal feminism of the consideration of problems of economic and social inequality. Due to this, liberal feminism cannot offer a sustained analysis of the structures of male dominance, power, or privilege. Radical feminism regards the male-controlled capitalist hierarchy as the defining feature of women's oppression, and seeks to reconstruct society. Conservative feminism is dependent upon the nature of the society to which it belongs.

Feminist views on sexuality vary, and have depended on historical period or cultural context. Matters such as the sex industry, sexual interpretations in the media, and issues regarding consent to sex under conditions of male dominance have been controversial among feminists. This debate culminated in the late 1970s and 1980s in the West in what came to be known as the feminist sex wars, which pitted anti-pornography feminism against sex-positive feminism, and divided the feminist movement. Over the course of the 1970s, a large number of influential women in the West came to accept lesbian and bisexual women as part of feminism.

Opinions on the sex industry are diverse. Some feminists see it as the exploitative result of patriarchal social structures, which reinforce the sexual and cultural attitudes implicit in rape and sexual harassment. There are also feminists who argue that it can be a medium of feminist expression and the means for women to take control of their sexuality.

Feminists such as Catherine MacKinnon argue that women have very little control over their bodies, with female sexuality being largely controlled and defined by men in patriarchal societies. They argue that sexual violence is rooted in the ideologies of male sexual entitlement, and that these systems grant women very few easy options to refuse sexual advances.

Advocates of feminism have been struggling to rid every walk of life, such as science (biology in particular), psychology, culture, music, art, literature, and cinema of notions of male superiority since the beginning of the twentieth century.

Feminism has had its impact on major political movements. Since the late nineteenth century, some feminists have allied with socialism. August Bebel (1840–1913), an early activist of the German Social Democrat party, argued that the struggle for equal rights between the sexes is part of the movement for social equality in general. In 1907, an International Conference of Socialist Women in Stuttgart described suffrage as a tool of class struggle. Clara Zetkin of the SPD called for women's suffrage to build a 'socialist order, the only one that allows a radical solution to the women's question'. In Britain, the women's movement was allied with the Labour Party. Hitler and Mussolini not only glorified traditional notions of patriarchal society, but also declared themselves as opposed to feminism. After the rise of Nazism in Germany in 1933, there was a rapid dissolution of the political rights and economic opportunities that feminists had earlier fought for and obtained.

The civil rights movement in America influenced the feminist movement, and vice versa. The feminist movement brought about changes in all democratic societies, including women's suffrage; greater access to education; near equitable pay with men; the right to initiate divorce proceedings; the right of women to take individual decisions regarding pregnancy (including access to contraceptives and abortion), and the right to own property. Women came to occupy prominent political positions. Margaret Thatcher and Indira Gandhi were among the prominent examples of women who emerged as powerful political leaders on the international stage. Angela Merkel and Theresa May are now dominating the European stage. Hillary Clinton missed the incumbency at the White House by a whisker, partly because women in America were not yet conscious enough to appreciate the importance of a woman becoming the President of their country. In India, women leaders such as Sonia Gandhi, Mayawati, and Mamata Banerjee are currently dominating on the political stage. Fifty per cent of political offices in local bodies have been reserved for women in India, in addition to the proposal for reserving 33 per cent of seats in Parliament and state legislatures. Such political empowerment is taking place in various degrees in all democracies of the world.

Despite considerable progress, there is still a long way to go before women are given equal opportunities to realise their full potential. It is not only a question of providing legal rights, but also a stubborn problem of creating the material conditions for women to rise to their full height. To delay this process is nothing short of denying the utilisation of 50 per cent of human talent. Entrenched sexist prejudices reinforced subtly by outdated social traditions are the invisible stumbling blocks. A conscious purging of the political system and social psyche, rather than a dependence on trickle-down effects, is the way forward.

12

Environmentalism

Environmentalism is now a snowballing global movement. The climate of the earth has been changing continually since the inception of the planet. The changes that occurred in history were the handiwork of nature itself. For example, the glaciers of the Himalayas were at their maximum 20,000 years ago. But as the Holocene dawned about 12,000 years ago, ushering in a warmer era on the planet, the Himalayan glaciers retreated. This retreat must, in all probability, have left its own climatic impact on the region. Herodotus of ancient Greece, regarded as the first great historian in the West, observed while writing about the conditions of the Persian Empire in the fifth century BC that the territory north of the Indus river (then part of the Persian empire) was the most prosperous part of the empire. The current desert conditions of this region show how the climate has changed radically in the meantime. Apart from this, it is known through excavations made in the 1920s that Harappa and Mohenjodaro were among the flourishing cities of South Asia. One speculation concerning the destruction of the cities refers to possible changes in the climate of their time. Similar climatic changes have taken place throughout the history of civilisation in other parts of the world.

Aboriginal humans, while entering the Agrarian Society, may have made their own (however insignificant in quantitative terms) contribution to the change in climate, as they deployed their newly acquired weapons of bronze or iron to clear the forests for their settlement. These climatic changes were of a minor nature. However, the changes effected in the wake of the Industrial Revolution have been immense and incessant enough to cause concern bordering on alarm. This post-industrial phenomenon is the direct result of large-scale human intervention. Environmentalists have been raising a hue and cry almost from the nineteenth century about the deleterious effects of this new, yet little-noted catastrophe looming on the horizon.

The first large-scale environmental laws came in the form of Britain's Alkali Acts, passed in 1863 to regulate the aggravating air pollution (gaseous hydrochloric acid) caused by the Leblanc process used to produce soda ash. The responsibilities of the Inspectorate established then for the purpose were gradually expanded, culminating in the Alkali Order 1958, which placed all major heavy industries that emitted smoke, grit, dust, and fumes under supervision. Many other steps were initiated to eliminate water and air pollution. It was, however, under the impetus of the Great Smog of 1952 in London, which almost brought the city to a standstill and caused thousands of deaths, that the Clean Air Act 1956 was passed. The Act provided a powerful fillip to modern environmentalism, and prompted a rethinking of the threat of environmental degradation to people's quality of life. Even in the nineteenth century, zoologist Alfred Newton published a series of investigations titled 'On the Desirability of Establishing a Close Time for the Preservation of Indigenous Animals' between 1872 and 1903. His advocacy for legislation led to the formation of the Royal Society for the Protection of Birds, and exerted influence for the passage of the Sea Birds Preservation Act in 1869 as the first nature protection law in the world. Romantic poet William Wordsworth (1770–1850), writing about the Lake District, said that it is a 'sort of national property in which every man has a right and interest who has an eye to perceive and a heart to enjoy' (Wordsworth 1906: 92). However, systematic efforts grew out of the amenity movement in Britain in the 1870s, which was a reaction to industrialisation, the growth of cities, and worsening air and water pollution. This new consciousness led to the formation of organisations like The Friends of the Lake District, National Trust for Places of Historic Interest or Natural Beauty, etc.

In 1893, Octavia Hill (1838–1912), Sir Robert Hunter (1844–1913), and Canon Hardwicke Rawnsley (1851–1920) agreed to set up a national body to coordinate environmental conservation efforts across the country, and consequently the 'National Trust for Places of Historic Interest or Natural Beauty' was formally inaugurated in 1894, and given statutory status in 1907.

An early 'Back-to-Nature' movement was advocated by intellectuals such as art critic and philanthropist John Ruskin (1819–1900), writer and socialist activist William Morris (1834–96), playwright George Bernard Shaw (1856–1950), and socialist poet and philosopher Edward Carpenter (1844–1929), who were all against consumerism, pollution, and such other activities that were harmful to the natural world.

John Ruskin argued that people should return to a 'small piece of English ground, beautiful, peaceful and fruitful. We will have no steam engines upon it ... we will have plenty of flowers and vegetables ... we will have some music and poetry; the children will learn to dance to it and sing it' (Dearden 1999: 206).

The movement in the United States began in the late nineteenth century under the leadership of Scottish-American naturalist John Muir (1838–1914) and Henry David Thoreau (1817–62). Thoreau led a simple life by living close to nature. He published his experiences in *Walden, or, Life in the Woods* (1854), which argued that people should get closer to nature. Muir came to believe in nature's inherent right and successfully lobbied the Congress to form the Yosemite National Park, and went on to set up the Sierra Club in 1892. In the twentieth century, efforts were made to save some wildlife, particularly the American Bison. In 1916, the National Park Service was founded by US President Woodrow Wilson.

In Britain, the Forestry Commission was set up in 1919, and by 1939, it was the largest landowner in Britain.

During the 1930s, even among the Nazis, there were some forces that were supportive of animal rights, zoos, and wildlife. In 1933, the government in Germany created a stringent animal protection law. In 1934–35, the regime enacted a law which can be translated into English as the 'perpetual forest'. In the second part of the twentieth century, the Sierra Club used photography as a weapon to spread consciousness about the need to preserve beautiful natural spots. The Sierra Club Exhibit Format Series galvanised public opposition to building dams in the Grand Canyon. It also succeeded in getting protection for many other national treasures.

Until now, we have mainly discussed the deleterious effects of industrialisation on rare natural treasures. A mathematician-philosopher like Bertrand Russell began to note the ongoing exhaustion of non-renewable natural resources through industrialisation. In his *New Hopes for a Changing World* (1951), he stated:

> Modern industry, in fact, is a kind of rape .... All Industry depends upon irreversible processes; it all uses up the earth's capital .... sooner or later, owing to the exhaustion of raw material, its capacity to supply human needs will diminish, not suddenly, but gradually. This could ... be prevented if men exercised any restraint or foresight in their present frenzied exploitation .... the matter is far more grave as regards soil, which is the raw material of food .... Apart from the question of food, there is the question of energy .... (Russell 1951: 31–33)

In 1962, American biologist Rachel Carson published *Silent Spring*, which described the harmful effects of the indiscriminate spraying of DDT. The public concern that ensued led to the creation of the United States Environmental Protection Agency in 1970, which banned the agricultural use of DDT in 1972. This new interest in the environment led to the recognition of problems such as air pollution, petroleum spills, etc. In the 1970s, the movement gained momentum around the world as a productive outgrowth of the counter-culture movement.

Protection of the environment also became important in the developing world. In the 1970s, the Chipko movement was started by Sunderlal Bahuguna in India under the ideological inspiration of Gandhiji, and set up a peaceful resistance to deforestation by literally hugging the trees (leading to the coining of the term 'tree huggers'). More recently, India has witnessed the Narmada Bachao Andolan led by Medha Patkar, which highlighted the dangers of huge dams. India has also been experiencing mass protests against nuclear power plants and other hazardous chemical units.

Earth Day was first observed in San Francisco and other cities on 21 March 1970, the first day of spring. On 21 March 1971, United Nations Secretary-General U. Thant spoke of a 'spaceship Earth'.

By the mid-1970s, the back-to-the-land movement had started to form, and ideas of environmental ethics were synergised with anti-Vietnam war sentiments and other political issues. Individuals living on the fringes of mainstream society started to champion some of the more radical environmental theories, such as deep ecology. Around this time, a more mainstream environmentalism began to assert itself with the signing of the Endangered Species Act in 1973 in the USA.

In 1979, James Lovelock, a British scientist, published *Gaia, a new look at life on Earth*, which proposed that life on earth can be understood as a single organism. This became an important part of the 'Deep Green' ideology. There has since been debate and argument between the more radical followers of this 'Deep Green' ideology and mainstream environmentalists.

Environmentalism, with its all-embracing ideological and ethical perspectives, was bound to manifest itself in political movements. The world's first political parties to campaign on an environmental platform were the United Tasmania Group, Australia and the Values Party of New Zealand. The first Green Party was founded in 1972 in the Swiss canton of Neuchatel. In erstwhile West Germany, Petra Karin Kelly (1947–92) emerged as the most important political leader espousing environmental causes, not only in her country but also in the whole of Western Europe. She helped to found the West German Green Party in 1980. Even after entering the German parliament (the Bundestag chamber) in 1973, she persisted with her direct action protests, and even strengthened her grassroots contacts across countries. She mounted a direct action within the Bundestag chamber as well as in front of the White House, in Berlin's Alexanderplatz and in the West German chamber in Pretoria. She was utilising her parliamentary mandate to further her causes, even as some of her colleagues felt that her steps were contrary to the serious behaviour expected of an MP. Be that as it may, she left an indelible imprint on the Green movement. The Greens are now an electoral factor not only through their parties, but also through other fora.

At an ideological level, the Club of Rome, founded in 1968 in Rome and comprising current and former heads of State, UN bureaucrats, high-level politicians, government officials, diplomats, scientists, and economists, garnered considerable public attention in 1972 with its report, 'The limits to growth'. This report has sold thirty million copies in more than thirty translations. It predicted that economic growth could not continue indefinitely because of the limited availability of natural resources, particularly oil. The 1973 oil crisis illustrated the point graphically. The Club of Rome, in collaboration with academic researchers, supported another publication, 'Mankind at the Turning Point' (1974), which noted that since several factors are within human control, possible environmental and economic catastrophes are preventable. In a 1991 publication of the Club, 'The First Global Revolution', it pointed out that pollution and global warming constitute a common threat, leading to water shortages, famines, etc. It has further pointed out that all these dangers are caused by human intervention in natural processes, and only through changed attitudes and behaviour can they be overcome. In the meantime, a study by Graham Turner of the CSIRO, Australia, found in 2008 that '30 years of historical data compare favourably with key features of a business-as-usual scenario', called the 'standard run scenario', which will result in a collapse in the global system midway through the twenty-first century. Even if this study is viewed as alarmist, one thing that emerges indisputably is that the current system of production and consumption is utterly unsustainable.

Mahesh Rangarajan stated (2007: xiv):

> The number of people in the world grew four-fold between 1900 and 2000 .... There was a concurrent expansion in ... world economy .... the kind of growth that took place was ... more

> intensive in use of energy and raw materials, and generated more waste .... carbon dioxide emissions rose thirteen-fold and energy use increased sixteen-fold .... It marked a new phase of human existence on the planet .... While the increases ... were not distributed evenly across nations, the ecological consequences ... did cross borders .... Nor was the proportion of people to land and resources equitably spread out across the globe.

As historian John McNeill has calculated, the energy used by humans in that 100-year run (between 1900 and 2000) was more than that used by all our ancestors in the past 10,000 years. Such prodigal consumption of energy was bound to affect the climatic equilibrium on the planet, and it has. Gandhiji was always convinced of the inapplicability of the Western model to India. He wrote in 'Young India' of 20 December 1928:

> God forbid that India should ever take to industrialization after the manner of the West. The economic imperialism of a single tiny island kingdom [England] is today keeping the world in chains. If an entire nation of 300 million [India's population at the time] took to similar economic exploitation, it would strip the world bare like locusts. (Guha 2007: 114–15)

As we have seen in Chapter 9, French socialist pioneers Charles Fourier and Proudhon also had serious reservations about heavy industrialisation. Gandhiji's ideas are comparable to theirs.

Ramachandra Guha points out that Gandhiji paid attention to the crucial problem of soil. He was an enthusiastic supporter of organic manure, which enriched the soil through the effective disposal of waste. Gandhiji also supported the methods of organic agriculture that Albert Howard developed at his Institute of Plant Industry in Indore.

Indira Gandhi was among the international leaders who voiced an early concern about the pollution problem. While speaking at the UN Conference on the Environment held at Stockholm, Sweden, in 1972, she said:

> On the one hand, the rich look askance at our continuing poverty—on the other, they warn against their own methods. We do not wish to impoverish the environment any further and

> yet we cannot for a moment forget the grim poverty of large numbers of people. Are not poverty and need the greatest polluters? The environment cannot be improved in conditions of poverty. Nor can poverty be eradicated without the use of science and technology. (Rangarajan 2007: xviii)

This historic speech of Indira Gandhi is noted in two different ways: one is that she pleaded passionately for the protection of the environment, and two is that she entered a serious caveat on behalf of developing countries to the effect that they should not be allowed to pay the same high price for protecting the environment as the developed countries, which had thus far impoverished the environment by indiscriminately using modern technology for the hungry pursuit of their wealth. Both aspects of her speech continue to be relevant to this day, as they are figuring in every environment conference that has since been held. Despite her caveat at the Stockholm Conference, Indira Gandhi utilised every opportunity to improve the environment and ecology in our country.

After this conference, Indira Gandhi launched 'Project Tiger' in April 1973, the single largest wildlife conservation scheme in the world at the time. This Project was preceded by The Wildlife (Protection) Act in 1972 and followed by the Forest Conservation Act in 1980. Apart from forests, the methods and uses of water, fisheries, grazing lands and commons, and city spaces need to be taken care of from the conservation angle in India. Industrialisation, urbanisation, and the growing consumerism of an increasing number of Indians are not only compounding contradictions, but also dividing intellectuals. This situation is true of the whole world in differing proportions.

The expression 'Spaceship Earth' was used by Richard Buckminster Fuller (1895–1983) to highlight the fact that the resources of our planet are limited. M. S. Swaminathan graphically illustrated the point when he said:

> One can see Earth as an extra-large, very efficient, Nature-designed spaceship, carrying its full load of three billion passengers through space at 18.5 miles per second, equipped with its own energy, refuelling, recycling and life-support systems. A

> thin envelop of air, soil and water around the Earth, together with energy from the Sun, provide the major ingredients for the evolution and survival of the large number of living things, including man, on Earth, and all are closely interrelated. This complex and delicately balanced web of relationships together constitutes the biosphere within which man has his place. (Swaminathan 2007: 161)

Lester R. Brown argues in *Eco-economy: Building an Economy for the Earth* (2001) that the environment was not part of the economy, as many corporate planners and economists believe; instead, the economy was part of the environment. He further argues that the economy must be designed in a way that makes it compatible with the ecosystem of which it is a part, and there is now the technology to build it.

The question is: Does the world leadership have the will and the wisdom to summon and deploy the appropriate technology—although it may entail some passing economic dislocations (region-wise or sector-wise)—to salvage nothing less than human life, nay, all forms of life? The resources on the planet are in peril because more is being asked of them than they can give on an ongoing basis. Lester Brown (2006: 3) further stated:

> We are cutting trees faster than they can regenerate, overgrazing rangelands and converting them into deserts, over-pumping aquifers, and draining rivers dry. On our cropland, soil erosion exceeds new soil formation ....
>
> We are taking fish from the ocean faster than they can reproduce. We are releasing carbon dioxide (CO2) into the atmosphere faster than nature absorbs it .... As ... CO2 levels rise, so does the earth's temperature. Habitat destruction and climate change are destroying plant and animal species ... faster than new species can evolve, launching the first mass extinction since the one that eradicated the dinosaurs 65 million years ago.

> Overfishing is not the only problem. Pollution, notably fertilizer run-off, damages a lot of marine ecosystems. There are estimated to be 5 trillion bits of plastic in the ocean .... By the middle of the century, the sea could contain more plastic than fish by weight. (*The Economist* 27 June 2017)

Apart from the oceans and land, harm comes via the sky through the accumulation of carbon dioxide in the atmosphere, leading to acidification of the ocean's chemistry, which in turn adversely affects not just crabs and oysters, but quite a lot of larvae. It also damages coral reefs. The few facts mentioned above show that the oceans, which are the biggest thing on Earth, are being irreparably destroyed by humble humans in a fit of both amnesia and avarice.

Lester Brown further says: 'Throughout history, humans have lived on the Earth's sustainable yield—the interest from its natural endowment. But now we are consuming the endowment itself' (2006: 3). He disclosed that a scientific study led by Mathis Wackernagel had concluded that humans' demands first surpassed the earth's regenerative capacity around 1980. The study also said that humanity's demands exceeded the capacity in 1999 by 20 per cent.

One of the vulnerable economic sectors is food, where the bubble is most obvious. Food availability grew constantly in the nineteenth and twentieth centuries, thanks to technology. However, grain production has been declining of late in some smaller countries, but the shocking thing is that even China's grain harvest dropped from 390 million to 340 million tonnes over a five-year period (1997–2002) because of a fall in underground water levels caused by over-pumping of its aquifers. At this rate, China will have to enter the world grain market for massive imports, which will place heavy pressure on exportable grain supplies in the world food market. Apart from the falling water tables, soil erosion, deteriorating rangelands, collapsing fisheries, and rising temperatures are together ranging themselves against an effort to accelerate food supplies. Above all, we are exceeding the earth's natural capacities. Farmers currently on the land may face higher temperatures than any generation since agriculture began about 10,000 years ago. Higher temperatures reduce crop yields through their effect on photosynthesis, moisture balance, and fertilisation. As per the Inter-governmental Panel on Climate Change, grain harvests in tropical regions could be reduced by an average of 5 per cent by 2020 and 46 per cent by 2050. Avoiding these declines will be difficult, unless scientists can develop crop strains that are not vulnerable to thermal stress.

As water availability has been declining in China, India, the United States, and elsewhere in the world, the water consumption curve has been climbing. In other words, cutbacks in grain harvests and water tables will occur soon, and together, even as the world's population keeps growing. As these global disasters loom large, there is a need to pause and view our recent growth rates from a historical perspective. The world population grew from 2.5 billion in 1950 to 6.1 billion in 2000. The growth during these fifty years was greater than during the four million years since we emerged as a distinct species. However, incomes rose even faster. The income per person worldwide nearly tripled from 1950 to 2000. Together, growth in population and rise in incomes expanded the global economic output from just under $7 trillion (in 2001 dollar rates) of goods and services in 1950 to $46 trillion in 2000, a gain of nearly seven-fold. The demand growth caused by the rise in population and incomes could so far be met by farmers resorting to ploughing land that was not only arable, but erodible, leading to the loss of billions of tonnes of top soil each year. The thin layer of top soil that covers much of the earth's land surface is the foundation of civilisation. Now more than a third of that foundation, the world's crop land, is losing top soil through erosion at a faster rate than new soil can form itself, leading to a reduction in the land's productivity—nay, to a transformation of the land into desert. This, in turn, has resulted in rivers being drained dry, to the detriment of wildlife and ecosystems. This apart, fossil fuel use also quadrupled, setting in motion a rise in carbon emissions. Atmospheric CO_2 concentrations climbed from 316 parts per million (ppm) in 1959 (when official measurements began) to 369 ppm in 2000.

Apart from desertification, land is being taken away from farming by urbanisation and highway and railway networks. While much can be extended by science and technology, land is obviously not such an elastic factor. Mark Twain is reputed to have remarked that the problem with land is that they do not make it any more.

In addition to facing water shortages, eroding soils, and shrinking green land, Earth is also being bombarded by rising temperatures and rising seas. This change in climate will mean more intense and frequent heat waves and more devastating storms, which have already been felt and recorded in various parts of the world. It will also lead to melting ice and rising seas. Above all, it will shrink the snowfields and glaciers, which feed most of the world's major river systems. Scientists are alarmed by the ice melting because of its effect on the sea level. Rising seas can shrink the habitable land area while the population is growing, leading to twin tragedies. It was during the 1930s that the rise in temperatures was first noticed, when it brought record temperatures and drought to the US Great Plains, leading to the creation of the Dust Bowl. But from 1977 onwards, the temperature began to climb routinely. During the 1980s, the average global temperature was 0.26 degrees Celsius above the norm; during the 1990s, it averaged 0.40 degrees above the norm; and during the first three years of the new century, the average temperature was 0.55 degrees above the norm. Against this backdrop of record increases, the projections of the Inter-governmental Panel on Climate Change (IPCC), which state that Earth's average temperature will rise 1.4–5.8 degrees Celsius (2.5–10.4 degrees Fahrenheit) during the twenty-first century appear probable. The IPCC upper-end projected increase of 5.8 degrees Celsius during this century is comparable to the change registered between the last Ice Age and today.

At a practical level, this projected rise of 1.4–5.8 degrees Celsius is a global average. In reality, it will be much greater over land than over oceans, in the higher latitudes than over the equator, in the continental interior than in coastal regions. According to James J. McCarthy, Harvard professor of biological oceanography, while the global average temperature rose roughly 1 degree Fahrenheit during the twentieth century, on Alaska's northslope and in northwestern Canada, it rose by 4–7 degrees Fahrenheit (2.2–3.9 degrees

Celsius), which is several times the global average. The first major victim of rising temperatures is agriculture. If we permit atmospheric CO_2 levels to continue to rise, we will be headed for a world far warmer than any since farming began. Snow/ice masses in mountains, which are considered nature's fresh water reservoirs and romantically described as 'reservoirs in the sky', are being threatened by the rise in temperature.

The IPCC projected that the sea level would rise during this century by 0.09–0.88 metres (4–35") as a result of thermal expansion and ice melting. The vast snow/ice mass in the Himalayas is also retreating. Both the North and the South poles are showing the effects of rising temperatures. According to a report submitted in 2002, the Arctic Ocean ice cover had shrunk to its smallest area since 1978. In addition to shrinking, the Arctic sea ice had thinned by 42 per cent from 1965 to 2000—from an average of 3.1 metres to 1.8 metres. This combination of shrinking and thinning has reduced the mass of sea ice by half. At this rate, the Arctic sea could be entirely ice-free during the summer within a matter of decades, in which case the Arctic heat balance would be altered. Similar changes are noticed at the other end of the earth, the Antarctic ice sheet. The accelerated melting of ice is of immediate concern in low-lying regions of coastal countries, which could include half of Bangladesh's rice land. This will possibly lead to the migration of millions of Bangladeshis. Apart from Bangladesh, rice-growing river flood plains would also be affected, including in India, Thailand, Vietnam, Indonesia, and China. With a 1 metre rise in sea level, more than a third of Shanghai city would be under water. For China as a whole, 70 million people would be vulnerable to a 100-year storm surge.

Despite such terrible threats to humanity, policymaking elites remain undisturbed. What is worse, they are encouraging the fossil fuel industry through concealed subsidies. Oil and gas companies have been among the most powerful lobbyists in the world. More than $200 billion are being annually distributed as subsidy to this sector, in the name of consumers, by governments across the world. Even the intense knowledge of existential issues cannot translate itself into policymaking wisdom in the face of vested interests. In this case, the vested interests have been conveniently allied to the consumerist vices of the rich.

The silver lining is the voluntarism that has been sprouting at all levels, from the local to the global, and its extension to politics. Pressure groups such as Greenpeace, Friends of the Earth (US), the Wyoming Outdoor Council, etc., have been working for the past half a century. In various Western countries, political parties with a Green ideology have become forces to be reckoned with, but they have a long way to go before becoming mainstream parties.

Anti-Green forces have a multi-pronged strategy. They first deny climate change by arguing that the changes noticed are of a historical kind, and that scientific evidence about the post-industrial changes is not decisive. Although the numbers of nay-sayers are declining slowly, they still remain significant. They also argue that all these problems can in due course be fixed by new technology. While techno-optimism is not misplaced, as the record of recent history shows, the issues at stake for the species as a whole are so catastrophic in nature that blind faith in future technology will be suicidal. What is demanded is nothing less than the invention of new forms of energy that can replace fossil fuels. The prospects of such a fundamental technological revolution have been tantalising for decades, but have proved elusive and may prove to be illusory. There have been, of course, some innovations in such non-renewable forms of energy as solar panels, wind energy, etc. But they do not as yet come close to mitigating the problem. In desperation, we are rushing back to nuclear energy, which is naturally accompanied by huge controversies. We should be focusing on fresh and fundamental techniques of energy instead. Since technological breakthroughs cannot be taken for granted, humanity, in the meantime, needs to economise on depletable sources of nature rigorously.

Developed countries led by the United States should embark upon a monumental research product, such as the Manhattan project, which was launched during World War II to produce the atom bomb. Such political will is not only a far cry, but also appears to be a cry in the wilderness of our disoriented world.

While huge environmental projects should always haunt our dreams, we should in the meantime pursue rescue missions to meet such aggravating problems as food and water shortages, eroding soils and shrinking crop lands, rising temperatures and rising seas. The United Nations has been trying to persuade nations to agree to a package of emission cuts. Its efforts resulted in a modest agreement at the United Nations Climate Change Conference in 2016. The agreement calls for zero net anthropogenic greenhouse emissions to be reached during the second half of the twenty-first century. It achieved, for the first time in over twenty years of UN negotiations, a binding universal agreement on climate from all the nations of the world. The US and China, by far the two largest national emitters, should be persuaded to sign up. For the first time ever, America—then led by President Obama—played a positive role, as it had earlier been denying or downplaying the problem of climate change. This agreement is just a beginning, albeit a good beginning, considering the past history of disagreements. The environmentalists, however, were not satisfied. Unremitting pressure across nations through education and agitation will need to be exerted on all governments for much stronger agreements and equally effective enforcement. It is going to be a long and laborious process; it will not be a series of romantic crusades like the struggles in the past for justice for the lower classes or freedom for colonised nations. And yet, this will be more crucial for the future of humankind than any in history.

13

Nuclear Pacifism

> *Non-violence is the only thing the atom bomb cannot destroy. I did not move a muscle when I first heard that the atom bomb had wiped out Hiroshima. On the contrary, I said to myself 'unless now the world adopts non-violence, it will spell certain suicide for mankind'.*
>
> Gandhiji

History has always been marked by bloody wars for survival and power, as well as persuasive movements for peace and compassion. The ancient Greek philosopher Heraclitus (540–480 BC) said, 'war is the father of all and the king of all: and some he has made gods and some men, some bond and some free' (Russell 1996: 60). He further stated: 'We must know that war is common to all and strife is justice; that all things come into being and pass away through strife' (ibid.). Heraclitus was describing the raw processes of nature as well as the ruthless affairs of human history. But such portrayals were contemporaneously accompanied by feelings of love and fraternity. 'Om Shanthi' (call for peace) figures in the Vedic lore. The founding leaders of Jainism were so obsessed with non-violence that they called upon their devotees to eat their supper before dusk, so that they could avoid hurting small insects. This ancient Jain custom is still followed by its adherents in India. The Buddha, contemporary of Heraclitus, stressed the supreme significance of peace. Jesus, who came 600 years after the Buddha, was born in Bethlehem (West Asia) and died a martyr to peace. Quite apart from such contradictory philosophical trends, conquerors like Alexander, Genghis Khan, Julius Caesar, Napoleon, etc., were dominating and determining the course of history. But the experiences of war in the twentieth century were very different.

The total casualties of World War I were estimated at 10 million dead, 21 million wounded, and 7.7 million missing or imprisoned. These numbers were so incomparably huge as to make all previous wars in history look like skirmishes. The devastation caused was gargantuan, not only because of the numbers but also because of such new weaponry as tanks, submarines, aircraft, etc. Many pacifist intellectuals like Bertrand Russell in Britain, Romain Rolland and Jean Jaures in France, and Benedetto Croce in Italy had warned against World War I because of its profound pointlessness, and incurred the nationalist indignation of their respective countrymen for their alleged lack of patriotism. The revulsion against the War was so universal that victorious nations were compelled to form the League of Nations in 1919 to prevent wars in the future. But the seeds of World War II were sown by the peace agreements themselves. The Treaty of Versailles, concluded at the end of the War, had such provocative and punitive provisions against the vanquished nations, particularly Germany, that it turned out to be self-defeating. Intellectuals like J. M. Keynes publicly warned against the Treaty of Versailles. However, the statesmen of victorious nations did not predictably pay heed to such calls for wisdom.

The inevitable World War II had been preceded by a perceptible gathering of storms. Unlike World War I, it seemed to be a moral and ideological war, although among imperialist nations. Hitler, as the leader of Nazi Germany, the perpetrator of the anti-Jew pogrom, and ally of fascist Italy, made all the ideological difference from the inception of World War II. Despite the relative righteousness of the Allied Powers (France, Britain, the US, and the Soviet Union), the costs of World War II were much greater than those of even World War I. Estimates of the total military and civilian casualties varied from 35 million to 60 million killed, including the six million Jews who died in the Holocaust, and millions more civilians injured. But the most frightening feature of World War II was not its incomparable casualties nor its untold devastation, but the dropping of the atom bomb on Hiroshima.

The idea of developing an atom bomb had coincided with the very beginning of World War II. Albert Einstein and physicist Leo Szilard wrote a letter to United States President Franklin Roosevelt on 2 August 1939, warning that:

> In the course of the last four months it has been made probable through the work of Joliot in France as well as Fermi and Szilard in America—that it may become possible to set up a nuclear chain reaction in a large mass of uranium, by which vast amounts of power and large quantities of new radium-like elements would be generated. Now it appears almost certain that this could be achieved in the immediate future.
>
> This new phenomenon would also lead to the construction of bombs, and it is conceivable—though much less certain—that extremely powerful bombs of this type may thus be constructed. A single bomb of this type, carried by boat and exploded in a port, might very well destroy the whole port together with some of the surrounding territory. However, such bombs might very well prove too heavy for transportation by air.

The letter also specifically warned about Germany:

> I understand that Germany has actually stopped the sale of uranium from the Czechoslovakian mines which she has taken over. That she should have taken such early action might perhaps be understood on the ground that the son of the German Under-Secretary of State, von Weizsacker, is attached to the Kaiser-Wilhelm Institute in Berlin, where some of the American work on uranium is now being repeated.[1]

This letter was followed by President Roosevelt launching the Manhattan Project, which eventually developed the atom bomb. It is interesting to note that Einstein did not work on the Manhattan Project as the Army had denied him work clearance, stating that his pacifist leanings made him a security risk. But he was allowed to work as a consultant to

---

[1] Einstein's letter, dated 2 August 1939, to President Franklin D. Roosevelt. Available at http://www.atomicarchive.com/Docs/Begin/Einstein.shtml (accessed 3 March 2018).

the United States Navy's Bureau of Ordinance. According to Linus Pauling (1901–94), who won two Nobel prizes, one for Medicine and the second for Peace, Einstein later regretted signing the letter because it led to the development and use of the atomic bomb in combat, adding that Einstein had believed the decision justified because of the greater danger of Nazi Germany developing the bomb first. In 1947, Einstein told *Newsweek* magazine: 'Had I known that the Germans would not succeed in developing an atomic bomb, I would have done nothing.' Theoretical physicist J. Robert Oppenheimer (1904–67) headed the Manhattan Project. The first artificial atomic test was held on 16 July 1945, on a site that Oppenheimer codenamed 'Trinity' in mid-1944. He later said that this name was from one of John Donne's Holy Sonnets. As Oppenheimer watched the explosion on Hiroshima, he simply exclaimed, according to his brother, 'It worked'! A contemporary account by Brigadier General Thomas Farrell, who was present in the control bunker at the site with Oppenheimer, summarised his reaction as follows:

> Oppenheimer, on whom had rested a very heavy burden, grew tenser as the last seconds ticked off. He scarcely breathed. He held on to a post to steady himself. For the last few seconds, he stared directly ahead and then when the announcer shouted 'Now!' and there came this tremendous burst of light followed shortly thereafter by the deep growling roar of the explosion, his face relaxed into an expression of tremendous relief.[2]

Oppenheimer later recalled that, while witnessing the explosion, he thought of a verse from the Hindu holy book, the *Bhagavad Gita* (XI, 12): 'If the radiance of a thousand suns were to burst at once into the sky, that would be like the splendour of the mighty one.'

On the evening of the actual explosion, he expressed regret that the weapon had not been available in time to use

---

[2] Paper 1305, Diplomatic Papers, The Conference of Berlin (The Potsdam Conference), 1945 Vol. II, dtd. 18 July 1945, Office of the Historian Department of State, USA. Available at https://history.state.gov/hitoricaldocuments/frus1945BerlinV02/d1305.

against Nazi Germany. He was, however, upset about the bombing of Nagasaki, as he did not consider it necessary from a military point of view. When he expressed this view at a personal meeting with President Harry S. Truman in October 1945, and further remarked that he felt he had 'blood on my hands', he did not ingratiate himself with the President. After the meeting, Truman told his Under-Secretary of State Dean Acheson, 'I don't want to see that son of a b**** in this office ever again.' However, for his services, Oppenheimer was awarded the Medal for Merit from President Truman in 1946. After attaining supreme stature upon the completion of the Manhattan Project, Oppenheimer spent the rest of his life under the shadow of the charge of having harboured pro-communist sympathies in his youth.

Soon after World War II, the forbidding implications of atomic weapons dawned on scientists and intellectuals. After learning of the bombing of Hiroshima and seeing the impending nuclear arms race, Joseph Rotblat (1908–2005), the only scientist to quit the Manhattan Project on moral grounds, remarked that 'he became worried about the whole future of mankind'. Over the years that followed, Bertrand Russell and Rotblat worked on efforts to curb nuclear proliferation, collaborating with Albert Einstein and other scientists to compose what became known as the 'Russell–Einstein Manifesto'. Russell, while releasing the Manifesto, said: 'I am bringing the warning pronounced by the signatories to the notice of all the powerful Governments in the world in the earnest hope that they may agree to allow their citizens to survive.'[3]

Joseph Rotblat, who received the Nobel Peace Prize in 1995, came to be famous for his epigrammatic statement, 'Remember your humanity, and forget the rest'. After the release of the Russell–Einstein Manifesto, the philanthropist Cyrus S. Eaton hosted a conference in July 1957, which came

[3] Russell-Einstein Manifesto, issued on 9 July 1955 at the Press Conference at Caxton Hall, London.

to be considered the first of the Pugwash Conferences on Science and World Affairs.

Gandhiji, the modern prophet of peace, reacting to Hiroshima and Nagasaki, wrote in 1946: 'The atomic bomb has deadened the finest feeling that has sustained mankind for ages. There used to be the so-called laws of war which made it tolerable. Now, we know the naked truth. War knows no law except that of might.'[4] While talking to a British journalist in 1946, Gandhiji reiterated this conviction by saying, 'I regard the employment of the atom bomb for the wholesale destruction of men, women and children as the most diabolical use of science.'[5] Nehru, the first Prime Minister of India and foremost disciple of Gandhiji, articulated and contributed more than any other ruling statesman in the world to highlight the ultimate threat that nuclear weapons pose to humanity.

A poem written by Hiroshima-born Sadakuri (1913–2006), who lived in the city and was exposed to radiation, captured the situation beautifully:

It may have been a mistake for the first time;
But it is a betrayal the second time.
We will not forget;
The promise you have made to the dead.

The poem is obviously referring to Hiroshima as the first mistake and Nagasaki as the second, and wishfully hoping that the mistake would not be repeated a third time.

With nuclear weapons today in the hands of nine nations, this wish is now sounding like nothing more than pious platitude. Even as the Nuclear Non-Proliferation Treaty (NPT) was concluded in 1970, five nations, the United States, Russia, UK, France and China, were treated as nuclear-weapon States. India and Pakistan, which did not sign the NPT, have since become nuclear-weapon States. North Korea was a party to NPT, but withdrew in 2003 from it, and has since been

---

[4] 'Gandhiji's reactions on Atom Bomb on Hiroshima and Nagasaki'. Available at https://quora.com H, 29–9–1946, 335.

[5] 'Gandhiji's reactions on Atom Bomb on Hiroshima and Nagasaki'. Available at https://quora.com H, 7–7–1946, 212.

believed to have developed atomic weapons, and is openly testing nuclear missiles. Israel, which did not sign the NPT, is believed to possess about eighty nuclear warheads, although it observes a policy of deliberate ambiguity for diplomatic reasons. According to the Bulletin of the Atomic Scientists Nuclear Notebook 2014, the total number of nuclear weapons worldwide is estimated at 10,144. South Africa is the only country that dismantled its nuclear arsenal before joining the NPT, as its last white regime did not want to bequeath them to its black heirs. With the exception of Russia and the United States (which have subjected their nuclear forces to independent verification under various treaties), these figures are no better than rough estimates. It is important to note that the delivery methods of nuclear weapon states have evolved to varying degrees of sophistication, with some achieving a nuclear triad. Although the number of active warheads has declined in absolute terms, the power of warheads and their delivery systems has been augmented multi-fold, as a consequence of which their destructive potential is much greater than it ever was. All this camouflaging seems to be nothing but a gigantic exercise in collective self-deception.

The question arises: Can the world afford such short-sighted leadership? As the original conscientious objectors, right from Albert Einstein, pointed out, it is the total proscription of nuclear weapons rather than any plan to prevent their misuse or spread that should be aimed at. But the appetite for nuclear power is insatiable. Many countries like Iran are determined to acquire the weapons through force or fraud. Some countries like Germany and Japan are maintaining their nuclear chastity, not because of any lack of capacity, but because of their total confidence in the American nuclear umbrella and their instant capacity to develop these weapons. In the meantime, North Korea, which represents the black nadir of medieval ages, claims to have developed nuclear weapons and blackmails not only its prosperous neighbour, South Korea, but also threatens to attack the United States. Nobody in the world knows how to handle this wild card. Even China, which abetted this nuclear development of North Korea, does not seem to have a clue. Nuclear Pakistan, which is teetering on the edge of a failed State, does not seem to be much better placed than North Korea. The world is depending on America to rein in Pakistan, and America, in turn, seems to turn to China for the purpose. Matters appeared to worsen when Donald Trump, as the presidential candidate of the Republican Party, said that Germany and Japan should develop their own nuclear weapons to protect themselves, instead of depending on the United States.

This depressing scenario continues to exist, despite all the diplomatic efforts made in the past half-a-century to contain the nuclear threat. On 11 May 1995, the Nuclear Non-Proliferation Treaty was extended indefinitely. The NPT is widely seen to be based on a central bargain: 'The NPT non-nuclear-weapon states agree never to acquire nuclear weapons and the NPT nuclear-weapon states in exchange agree to share the benefits of peaceful nuclear technology and to pursue nuclear disarmament aimed at the ultimate elimination of their nuclear arsenals.'

Several additional measures have been adopted to strengthen the NPT and make it difficult for States to acquire the capability to produce nuclear weapons, including the export controls of the Nuclear Suppliers Group and the enhanced verification measures of the IAEA Additional Protocol.

Nuclear pacifists argue that the NPT cannot stop the proliferation of nuclear weapons or the motivation to acquire them. The efficacy of the Treaty seems to depend on the strength or will of the nations desirous of acquiring them. The Treaty is three-pronged, as it comprises non-proliferation, disarmament, and the peaceful use of nuclear energy. The second prong, disarmament, is the weakest of all, and getting weaker with passing time.

In the meantime, America and the then USSR entered into a bilateral treaty, START (Strategic Arms Reduction Treaty). On the advice of Andrei Sakharov, father of the Soviet bomb—who later turned into a peace activist, as well as a leading civil rights activist in erstwhile Soviet Russia—the Soviet Union withdrew its objection to the US SDI (Strategic Defence

Initiative) and signed the Treaty on 31 July 1991. The treaty barred its signatories from deploying more than 6,000 nuclear warheads atop a total of 1,600 intercontinental ballistic missiles (ICBMs) and bombers. START negotiated the largest and most complex arms control treaty in history, and its final implementation in late 2001 resulted in the removal of about 80 per cent of all strategic nuclear weapons then in existence.

The START I treaty expired on 5 December 2009. On 8 April 2010, the replacement New START treaty was signed in Prague by US President Barack Obama and Russian President Dmitry Medvedev. START II was to be a bilateral treaty between the USA and Russia on the Reduction and Limitation of Strategic Offensive Arms. It was to ban the use of Multiple Independently Targetable Re-entry Vehicles (MIRVs). It is described as the De-MIRV-ing Agreement, although it never entered into effect. MIRV land-based ICBMs are considered destabilising because of their ability to carry 3–12 warheads and deliver them to separate targets. This special ability possibly destroys many of the enemy's missile sites if used as a first strike. In such a situation, the balance of terror, which is otherwise sought to be maintained to prevent first strike by rivals, would be critically lost. START II did not enter into force for another reason. For the Russians, the signing of the ABM (The Anti-ballistic Missile) Treaty by the Americans became the most critical thing. The ABM Treaty was supposed to preserve the long-standing principle of Mutually Assured Destruction (MAD). No acronym has ever been so appropriately named. At any rate, START II eventually failed to take off. The fate of START III did not fare any better. The future of any further talks between America and Russia appears to be bleaker than ever because of the revival of the Cold War between the two countries.

When the world's attention should be more sharply focused on the reduction of nuclear weapons and their delivery systems, it is currently focused on threats from non-State actors such as the ISIS, Al-Qaeda, etc.

The world seemed safer during the Cold War, as the heads of the two superpowers, America and erstwhile Soviet

Russia, were always on the hotline. What was more, they were as engaged in diplomatic contacts as in war games. Such a dialectical approach could save the world during misadventures like the Cuban missile crisis. Now the world is far more volatile because of multiple players. The worst part is that non-State actors like the Al-Qaeda or the ISIS, with their potential access to dirty nuclear bombs, have become unpredictable and uncontrollable factors. Such destabilising developments highlight the current fragility of the fate of humankind. Efforts to prevent the worst should therefore continue with far greater vigour than ever before.

The situation is getting worse not only because of an incalculable increase in the destructive capacity of nuclear weapon systems, but also because the lofty idealism that immediately followed World War II has now given way to feckless cynicism. As a result, nuclear pacifism is now a laughable idea for practical statesmen, and a distant dream for liberal idealists.

14

GLOBALISM

An ancient Hindu scripture speaks of '*Vasudaika Kutumbakam*' (literally, 'the world is a family'). Such sublime sentiments were voiced in almost all ancient traditions. However, even then, there was a colossal chasm between the feelings of noble souls and the deeds of ambitious rulers. At any rate, much of pre-history is lost in the mist without dependable chronicles. Such history that is available for the past few thousand years is a mixed record, full of embellished memories and poetic exaggerations. Epics and such other literary compositions contain facts shrouded in myths and mythologies. Even so, these are valuable sources, which show that humans have been capable of both lofty thoughts and atrocious actions. It is therefore not easy to learn from even recorded history without rejecting some happenings and accepting others. This process of inevitable selection from the available historical material does entail philosophical, religious, moral, cultural, geographical, and historical choices. Such choices would always be *appeles* of discord. Literary compositions, religious scriptures, etc., testify to the terrible truth that these choices have led to wars, ranging from epic battles to little skirmishes.

Apart from the natural human tendency to pick on bones of contention, history also seems to divide people in numerous ways. For example, race has always been invoked to unify people or to engage in wars. Even the facts of recorded history demonstrate that racial purity cannot be claimed for any people in the world. As Bertrand Russell pointed out in *New Hopes for a Changing World* (1951), which he wrote soon after

World War II, as Hitler had made his Aryan race a pretext for persecuting Jews:

> The Nazis and their ideological precursors made a vigorous propaganda for racial purity, but the facts are against them. The purest races on earth are the Australian aborigines, the Hottentots, and the Pygmies. All the historically great races have resulted from a mixture. The Germans themselves are largely Slav; the Russians are largely Mongol. All the Mediterranean nations are mixed. The British are a combination of Germanic, Celtic and pre-Celtic elements. The Athenians were mongrels, resulting from a mixture of northern barbarian conquerors with the old pre-Hellenic stock. (ibid.: 109)

The current nationalist theories of race are generally motivated by nationalism, and are consequently controversial.

We should therefore turn to incontrovertible sources for guidance by taking advantage of the advances in science. From biology, we know that humans have been evolving for millions of years, as the earlier *Homo erectus*, followed by the *Homo sapiens*. The latest research shows that humans migrated from Africa about 1,50,000 years ago. Recent study based on DNA shows that Africans reached south India between 60,000–70,000 years ago, and proceeded to Gujarat by sea. It also reveals that they pushed forward on land via Afghanistan to Europe. One of the interesting things pointed out is that the Roma Gypsies in Europe have the same DNA as south Indians. Yet another interesting fact is that the DNA of Australian aboriginals is comparable to those of south India. Aside from scholarly differences on the details, science establishes that the oneness of the human race is a genetic fact. Humans later developed into distinct races through pigmentation and other processes in the course of evolution and numerous migrations over thousands of years. The current cultural diversity that characterises humanity is the result of the impact of various climatic, ethnic, geographical, and cultural factors that played their part after the commencement of the original migrations. The soaring aspirations towards human unity among noble souls in both ancient and later times can now rest on an unshakable scientific footing. The original migrants from

Africa, travelling from continent to continent, eked out their living for millennia in various parts of the planet through fruit-gathering or animal-hunting for want of an appropriate climate.

It was not until roughly 11,000 years ago, when the Holocene period dawned throwing certain geographical regions in the eastern hemisphere into warmer conditions. This change in climatic conditions enabled humans to settle down in river valleys to develop cultivation, thus ushering in the Agrarian Society. This Agrarian Society lasted for about 10,000 years. However, long before the dawn of agrarian civilisation, human history had witnessed many distinct periods.

One of these is known as the Palaeolithic period (Old Stone Age). The last phase of this period, termed 'Upper Palaeolithic' (40,000–10,000 BC), saw the emergence of a more complex, specialised, and diverse regional stone-tool industries. The two principal forms of Palaeolithic art are small sculptures such as the 'Venus' figurines and various carved or shaped animal and other figures, and monumental paintings, incised designs, and relics on the walls of caves such as Altamira and Lascaux. The end of the Palaeolithic period was marked by the emergence of the settled agricultural villages of the Neolithic period.

The Neolithic period (New Stone Age) marked the final stage of technological development and cultural evolution among pre-historic humans, characterised by stone-tools shaped by polishing or grinding, domestication of plants or animals, permanent villages, and such crafts as pottery and weaving. Its beginnings are associated with the villages that emerged in South Asia (9000 BC) and flourished in the Tigris and Euphrates river valleys from 7000 BC. Farming spread northward throughout Eurasia, and reached Britain and Scandinavia after 3000 BC.

The New Stone Age was followed by the Bronze Age. The beginning of this period is sometimes called the Chalcolithic (copper stone) Age, implying the initial use of pure copper along with stone. It was only in the second millennium BC that true bronze came to be used. This Age was also noted for the invention of the wheel and the ox-drawn plough. At any rate, the Bronze Age yielded place to the Iron Age by 1000 BC.

The Iron Age marked the final technological and cultural stage in the Stone-Bronze-Iron Age sequence (or Three-Age System), in which iron largely replaced bronze in implements and weapons. The start of the Iron Age varied geographically, beginning in the Middle East and Southeastern Europe in 1200 BC, but not until 600 BC in China. Although the large-scale production of iron implements ushered in new patterns of more permanent settlement, the use of iron for weapons placed arms in the hands of the masses for the first time and set up a series of large-scale movements and conquests.

This brief narration of pre-history shows that the Old and New Stone Ages preceded Agrarian Society, but that both bronze and iron came to be used only after the start of Agrarian Society. The Agrarian Society, which predominated in history for about ten millennia, came to be replaced by Industrial Society only in the nineteenth century.

Elementary facts about the phases of history have been presented here to place the human story in a global perspective, as contra-distinct from that of race, religion, nation, region, etc. A global perspective, even about the pre-industrial phases, has become an intellectual imperative to highlight the blunt scientific fact that all humans share a common genetic past (however remote it may seem), and that cultural conflicts in the world today are all based upon partial and distorted versions of history. We shall now proceed (leapfrogging over the Old and New Stone Ages, Bronze and Iron Ages, as well as the Agrarian Society) to the start and development of the current Industrial Society.

Industrial Society began to take shape and gather speed only in the nineteenth century. Its foundations had been laid by the Scientific Revolution, which began in the second half of the sixteenth century and culminated in Newton's discoveries in the seventeenth century. An illustrative list of discoveries relating to the second half of the sixteenth as well as the seventeenth century has already been mentioned in Chapter 4.

To this, we can add some of the discoveries and inventions that occurred in the eighteenth century:

1. d'Alembert systematised the principles of mechanics;
2. Lavoisier analysed, first, the composition of air (1770–71), and then of water (1783);
3. Berthollet studied chlorine, and demonstrated the bleaching action of chlorine gas (1772);
4. Lagrange established the principles of analytical mechanics (1787).

The Scientific Revolution of the seventeenth century was followed not just by the above-mentioned discoveries of the eighteenth century, but by many important inventions in the nineteenth century as well. British historian G. M. Young wrote that of all the decades in history, a wise man would choose the 1850s to be young in. Young said so not only because of the simultaneous revolutions that broke out in various countries in Europe in 1848, but also because this decade witnessed a number of major inventions. Ben Wilson, in *Heyday* (2016), mentioned the arrival and proliferation of telegraphy, Henry Bessemer's 'cheap steel', spherical trigonometry, detailed logs of ocean waves, the Colt pistol, McCormick's reaping machines, and Charles Goodyear's vulcanised rubber, all of which occurred in this short period. Karl Marx, after witnessing the Great Exhibition in London's Hyde Park, was so impressed by the radical inventions that he wrote in 1851 that there was no more splendid time to enter the world than the present.

We need to refer to some of the more important inventions from the last quarter of the eighteenth century onwards.

James Watt improved on the steam-pumping engine and made it available for the driving of machinery. It was first used in cotton mills. In 1804, Trevithick adapted the Watt engine to transportation, and built the first locomotive. From 1830 onwards, this engine was used extensively for railways. The first steamship put to sea was American, which travelled from New York to Philadelphia. It was followed by the trans-Atlantic crossing. Apart from railways and steamships, the electric telegraph came into existence in 1835. The first undersea cable was laid in 1851 between France and England, and soon spread to various parts of the world.

Man's power, in the meantime, extended to various structural materials. The Bessemer and the open-hearth processes came into operation by 1864, through which steel and every sort of iron could be melted. As in the case of the metallurgy of steel, there was a parallel development in the metallurgy of copper, tin, nickel, aluminium, and a multitude of other metals. Concurrently, the science of electricity developed, leading to the invention of the electric light and electric traction.

American inventor Thomas Alva Edison (1847–1931) has gone down in history as the greatest representative of technical inventions. He (singly and jointly) held the world record for 1,093 patents, nearly 400 of them for electric light and power. He created the world's first industrial research laboratory in which he invented a carbon-button transmitter, still used in telephones, speakers, and microphones today, the phonograph, and the incandescent light bulb. He supervised the installation of the world's first commercial central power system. He built a new laboratory in West Orange, NJ, whose first major endeavour was the commercialisation of the phonograph, while Alexander Graham Bell (1847–1922) improved on Edison's initial invention. At the new laboratory, Edison and his team developed an early movie camera and an instrument for moving pictures. They also developed the alkaline storage battery.

The Scientific Revolution, followed by these inventions, gave birth to the Industrial Revolution (the term 'Revolution' is routinely used for want of another word). The supreme significance of the Industrial Revolution has no precedent or parallel in all of history. Its effects are so all-pervading that all the human tools used until the eighteenth century have since become obsolete. It should be emphasised that the Industrial Revolution led to the current globalism. The Industrial Society has now reached every corner of the earth, and has even enabled humans to see the earth veritably as a speck of dust from distant space. Astronomers and cosmonauts from various countries took a global view and spoke about Earth from outer space, and not about their nations, races, or religions. The global view of some of our noble ancestors was the product of their soaring imaginations, often articulated in figurative language. However, the globe has now become one entity today, either through fast travel on the planet or through a sighting from the sky. These technological feats have reduced Earth to a village at the physical plane. But our cultural vision remains constricted. One could hope, in the words of Rabindranath Tagore: 'Where the world has not been broken up into fragments by narrow domestic walls'. Tagore's prayer of over 100 years ago still remains unrealised. Philosophy and poetry have always been flying like free birds for millennia, beyond all borders and barriers, in all times and climes. But technology had to wait until the nineteenth century to lend physical reality to ancient philosophy and poetry. Culture, on the other hand, has been unable to keep pace with technology, thereby creating a gargantuan gulf. The supreme need of the hour is to bridge this gulf, and world statesmanship needs to address this as its only task.

Charles Darwin (1809–82), in founding modern biology in the nineteenth century, added a startling new dimension to our scientific education. No scientist in history has exploded our beliefs of the Agrarian Society and paved the way for our new industrial culture as much as Darwin. The zoological and geological knowledge he gleaned on his voyages enabled him to publish his celebrated theory: 'On the Origins of Species by Means of Natural Selection'. Seeing the competition between individuals of a single species, he recognised that within a local population, the individual with, for example, the sharper beak might have a better chance of survival and reproduction, and that such traits, if passed on to new generations, would be predominant in future populations. He saw this natural selection as the mechanism by which advantageous variations were passed on to later generations, while less advantageous traits gradually disappeared. Although Darwin's ideas were modified by later developments in genetics and molecular biology, his work remains central to modern evolutionary theory. Thomas Henry Huxley (1825–95), British biologist, was one of the earliest supporters of Darwinism. He took on the religious critics of Darwin with superb success. As a result of fierce debate between those who supported Darwinism and those favouring Christian theology, the intelligentsia of the time found itself facing a philosophical dilemma, best expressed by English poet Mathew Arnold:

> Wandering between two worlds, one
> dead.
> The other powerless to be born. (*Concise Oxford Dictionary of Quotations* 1977: 11)

This is an archetypal illustration of the unintended impact of science on religion and philosophy. The process of discoveries led by Einstein continued into the twentieth century, gaining in new qualitative dimensions with the advent of nuclear weapons, intercontinental migrations through aircraft, space exploration, information technology, etc. Humans, as discussed earlier, were born in Africa and spread to various parts of the world through migrations. In the process, they began to divide themselves into races, religions, etc. The current Industrial Society has brought humans together in terms of geographical reach (as they can now travel and interact with peoples through telecommunications, the Internet, air travel, etc.). But such intimate interactions have not proved capable of bridging cultural, religious, racial, and linguistic distances. The world has thus been globalised in merely physical terms, and not in psychological or cultural terms.

Such un-bridged cultural distances manifested themselves through recourse to the post-industrial weapon systems in the two world wars. The unprecedented destruction caused by the world wars, and even the invention of the ultimate weapon, the atom bomb, during World War II, has taught us no lesson. The atom bomb, too, failed to dissuade the world leadership from seeking to dominate the world, either on the pretext of political ideology or social identity. The atom bombs dropped on Hiroshima and Nagasaki were comparatively very small, and have since been developed into huge ones.

Even at the end of World War I, leaders and intellectuals were worried about the need for a world government to negotiate areas of conflict and avoid further international wars. H. G. Wells, in *The Outline of History*, wrote the following, which reflected the mood of the most enlightened after World War I:

> Our true State ... is already beginning ... to which every man owes his utmost political effort, must be now this nascent Federal World State .... Our true God now is the God of all men .... Our true nationality is mankind. How far will modern men ... identify themselves with this necessity and ... revise their ideas, remake their institutions, and educate the coming generations to this final extension of citizenship? How far will they remain dark, obdurate, habitual, and traditional ...? Sooner or later that unity must come or else plainly men must perish by their own inventions. (Wells 1920: 580)

As a result of the consensus for a world body, the League of Nations was established by the Allied Powers at the end of World War I. Headquartered at Geneva, the League was discredited by its failure to prevent Japanese expansion in Manchuria and China, Italy's conquest of Ethiopia, and Germany's seizure of Austria. The League of Nations was replaced in 1946 by the United Nations, which has since been converted into a spineless wonder by the superpowers. It should be stated in fairness, though, that the United Nations has rendered remarkable service in many spheres, such as education and humanitarian work. Above all, it serves the purpose of enabling rivals to not only dabble in adversarial debate, but also make discreet contacts to explore new areas of agreement. Every sane person will pray for a better fate for the United Nations than its predecessor, the League of Nations, met with.

The invention of atomic weapons has made war absolutely antediluvian. As Arnold J. Toynbee stated in *A Study of History*: 'To die for a country or a cause becomes a gratuitous and meaningless act of heroism if it has become demonstrably certain that the country will perish together with the patriot, and the cause together with the devotee, in one all-comprehending catastrophe' (1987: 325).

He further added: 'The progress of technology has no power to diminish the sway of human feelings over the course of human affairs. Militarism is a matter not of technology, but of psychology—the will to fight' (ibid.: 323). Despite the invention of technology to annihilate the human species, human psychology remains stubborn. As we have seen before, idealists throughout history had pleaded for peace and against war, even before modern weapons were forged. Even a traditional Victorian poet as Tennyson prayed in the nineteenth century for a constructive debate on the common destiny of humanity in a world organisation that he described as 'In the Parliament of man, the Federation of the world' (*The Concise Oxford Dictionary of Quotations* 1964: 228).

After the devastating experiences of the two world wars, the Cold War, and the confusing proliferation of current conflicts, it is necessary to descend from the heady heights of that optimism and contemplate upon concrete and gradual steps towards globalism, without losing sight of the ultimate dream.

From this perspective, the imperative is to develop a sense of human unity based on the evidence of science and the culture of tolerance promoted by great seers and scientists from ancient epochs to modern times. In other words, it should be a globalism based both on science and tolerance. Instead of globalism, economic globalisation through technology, commerce, and finance has spread to all parts of the planet. It has led to considerable cultural integration only of the elites of all countries, leaving the masses everywhere in the lurch, in terms of indigence, illiteracy, and disease. Critics view this global corporatism as nothing but a euphemistic reincarnation of bygone colonialism. The most visible aspect of cultural globalisation is the diffusion of certain cuisines, such as American fast food chains. The two most successful global food and beverage outlets, McDonald's and Starbucks, are American companies, with over 36,000 and 27,000 locations operating worldwide, respectively, as of 2018. Such cultural globalisation may lead to a human monoculture, rather than to a global multiculture. Terms such as 'coca-colonisation' have been coined to refer not only to the dominance of American culture, but also to the dominance of American companies. These processes have modernised certain sectors of the economy in developing countries.

These modernised sectors of developing countries such as China and India have themselves become the manufacturing hubs of multinational companies belonging to the developed West, especially America. This outsourcing to developing countries has been accompanied by the immigration of trained personnel to the developed world. This kind of selective globalisation has not only aggravated inequalities within the developing world, but has also generated tensions in the developed world. The latter has been giving vent to this new discomfort in two different ways: first, through straightforward agitation against inequalities (such as the 'Occupy Wall Street' movement), and second, through diversion of the resentment of the indigenous poor towards ethnic minorities and migrant groups. The first method is not strong enough to shake their societies; the second, however, has caused serious disturbances. This reaction against minorities and immigrants is visible through processes such as Brexit and the triumph of Donald Trump. The anti-globalisation movement, which began in developing countries, has since spread to developed countries. The selective absorption of trained personnel from developing countries was bad enough for the relatively poor in rich countries. But it has been further compounded by the vast immigrations caused by the conflicts in West Asia. These conflicts may have originated in the erroneous diplomacy of Western countries. However, the people of these Western countries are not willing to bear the economic and cultural brunt of the sins of their own rulers.

As a consequence, three complex phenomena: (*i*) negative developments in the form of increased inequalities in developed countries; (*ii*) diversion of the anger of the economically backward towards ethnic minorities; and (*iii*) the unceasing asylum-seeking by refugees of West Asia, are confronting the leaders of North America and Western Europe. Western leaders are divided among themselves regarding the solutions to these new problems. The cumulative impact of such processes is widening the cultural chasm within countries, and among countries. While new inventions have increased the physical intimacy of the people, old xenophobic feelings are resurfacing and increasing the psychological distance.

There is a strong view among critics that economic globalisation by companies is generating unmanageable tensions among countries and cultures. They argue that the wars in West Asia, such as the invasions of Iraq by George Bush Sr. and George Bush Jr., were prompted by pressure from the oil lobbies. They further argue that the Israeli lobby and the oil lobby have joined hands to force the pace of wars. The leadership of the West needs to learn proper lessons from these experiences. While economic globalisation is inevitable because of international connectivity, there is a need to look at its pace and sequencing. The exclusive focus on economic aspects, at the cost of the neglect of egalitarian and cultural issues, needs to be revisited. A conscious emphasis should be laid on the need to bridge the gap between the cultural capacity to interact with peoples other than one's own, and the technological potency to augment the physical proximity of various peoples of the world.

15

The Great Asymmetry

The unleashed power of the atom has changed everything save our modes of thinking and we thus drift toward unparalled catastrophe.

Einstein (*The Oxford Dictionary of Modern Quotations*: 99)

In the preceding chapters, we have seen how the current state of globalisation has been achieved through progress in science and commerce. However, studies in philosophy, psychology, history, etc., have not made the same degree of contribution to the process of globalisation. Even in science, the inquisitive spirit of Copernicus, which paved the way for the Scientific Revolution in the seventeenth century, has since been subjected to sad neglect. We are so dazzled by the devices of modern technology that we no longer remember their recent historical origins. For instance, mobile phone technology could not have come into being without the discovery of telegraphy in the nineteenth century. Similarly, very few software experts are aware of the great mathematician Alan Turing (1912–54), who through his 'Turing Machine', presented in 1936 at the age of twenty-four, made a critical contribution to the invention of the modern computer. This ignorance leads to intellectual shallowness, which is afflicting the new generations. It shows that we need to enrich education with the approach of getting imported modern technology from the perspective of history. Otherwise, the new generations will know about the current heights to which technology has risen, but without any idea of its foundations. The same historical approach should be extended to cover the evolution of humankind. It is through such an overarching process that innumerable subsidiary memories (false or real) of various peoples in the world can be seen in their wider context.

In other words, a history based on science and technology will enable humans to view themselves from a different prism, and thus outgrow the ground rules and gut feelings developed during the Agrarian Society. It is this overall mental growth that will make humans distrust people of other countries, creeds, etc., less, and might even make them trust more. This psychic transfiguration will make them more deserving of the facilities and fruits of Industrial Society, while remaining wary of the seamy side of exploding technology, such as destructive weapons. Today, humanity finds itself in the position of Bhasmasura, a character in Hindu mythology, who is granted a boon by Lord Shiva (one of the three supreme deities in the Hindu religion)—he (the former) can reduce anything to ashes by merely placing his hand on it. According to the legend, Bhasmasura goes on to destroy all his enemies and then turns to place his hand on Lord Shiva himself. Lord Shiva, who cannot undo his own boon, rushes to Lord Vishnu for rescue. Lord Vishnu (another supreme deity of the Hindu trinity) manages to trick Bhasmasura into placing his hand on his own head, thereby leading to his self-destruction. This simile is not inapt in that humans have won the boon of technology but are tending to destroy themselves and their new luxuries through their old prejudices and new weapons. We do not have a divine saviour like Lord Vishnu to save us from this collective hara-kiri. Bhasmasura's suicidal mentality, which also afflicts our species, needs to be transformed into an altruistic attitude. The task we are to perform is more complex than the one Lord Vishnu performed, as transformation of thought is more difficult than the destruction of being.

Einstein's observation that our modes of thinking have not changed at all, despite the invention of the atom bomb, needs to be particularly noted. His thought is even more poignantly applicable to current times, given the development of far more powerful weapons of mass destruction. Even Einstein could not have foreseen the perils of environmental annihilation, the unregulated augmentation of Artificial Intelligence, etc. For instance, our planet passed a dismal, if significant, milestone in September 2016. For the first time since the Pliocene Epoch (which began 1.8 million years ago and ended 10,000 years ago), carbon dioxide concentrations of 400 parts per million were recorded at Mauna Loa in Hawaii, a sentinel site for atmospheric measurements. In April 2017, the figure jumped to 410 ppm, dissipating the optimism generated by the Paris agreement and prompting *Scientific American* to warn that even if industrial emissions of greenhouse gases decrease to the levels mandated by the UN-sponsored pact, carbon dioxide would continue to increase and would level off only when emissions were cut in half. 'Even when concentrations of carbon dioxide level off, the impact of climate change will extend centuries into the future,' it observed.

The Economist of London (27 May–2 June 2017) dealt with the worsening problem of ocean warming. Its editorial stated:

> The ocean provides 3bn people with almost a fifth of their protein (making fish a bigger source of the stuff than beef). Fishing and aquaculture assure the livelihoods of one in ten of the world's people. Climate and weather systems depend on the temperature patterns of the ocean and its interactions with the atmosphere. If anything ought to be too big to fail, it is the ocean.

The Editorial went on to say that humans mistook the size of the ocean for its capacity to absorb anything, but mechanical fishing and pollution have altered its temperatures and chemistry and aggravated its ecosystem. What is worse, the fish itself get polluted in the ocean, leading eventually to an adverse impact on human health. The Paris agreement provides a solution for the protection of ocean resources. But the irony is that the Paris agreement is itself in peril, as President Trump has withdrawn America from it.

This recent withdrawal of the United States government from the Climate Change agreement of Paris has engendered fears about the durability of the Paris pact. At a time when scientists are calling for accelerated timelines for actions laid down in Paris, this retrogression can only be viewed from the perspectives described in this book: the resurgence of nativism, protectionism, and isolationism, which stand in stark contrast to the current realities of economic globalisation, the international footprint of terrorism, the ubiquitous nature of the Internet, and climate change.

Our predicament is as follows: first, we need to continue exploring the frontiers of science in our pursuit of knowledge while concurrently using the fruits of that knowledge for the betterment of the world, and second, we have to ensure that our quest for technological innovation does not occur at the cost of our environment. A balance needs to be struck, and urgently so. This gap between scientific and technological advancement, on the one hand, and our failure to adapt ourselves emotionally and intellectually to bridge it on the other may be termed the 'great asymmetry' of our Age.

Stephen Jay Gould (1998) presents this incongruity thus: 'The essence of human tragedy lies in the power of politics, reaction, and irrationality to overwhelm the still, small voice of science, and even to use its tools of intended benevolence for perverse ends'. Here, Gould echoes the fears that Alfred Russel Wallace had aired in his book, *The Wonderful Century*, in 1898. Wallace had expressed alarm at the fact that human moral progress had not kept pace with the advancement of science:

> The more we realise the vast possibilities of human welfare which science has given us, the more we must recognise our total failure to make any adequate use of them .... Instead of devoting the highest powers of our greatest men to remedy these evils, we see the governments of the most advanced nations arming their people to the teeth, and expending much of their wealth and all the resources of their science, in preparation for the destruction of life, of property, and of happiness. (Wallace 2011 [1898]: 378–79)

Gould employed an anecdote from the French Revolution to illustrate the misuse of science for human destruction. In March 1792, Charles-Henri Sanson, the public executioner of Paris, requested the French National Assembly to commission a new device that would expedite the execution of condemned prisoners. Gould (1998) adds:

> The Assembly therefore commissioned Joseph-Ignace Guillotin to build a 'humane' device to 'separate the head from the body in the twinkling of an eye' (to quote Guillotin's own instructions for use). The doctor's eponymous machine performed as specified—and France lost, among 'many thousands gone', in the Reign of Terror, her greatest scientist, Antoine-Laurent Lavoisier.

The technology required for Guillotin's invention has snowballed to the point where the atom bomb was invented. The history of technology, from the inventions of the 'Old Stone Age' to those of 'Artificial Intelligence', shows that their effects have been beneficent to begin with, but have invariably lent themselves to abuse. The most negative use of inventions have always manifested themselves in the destructive sophistication of weapons. The monstrous misuse of nuclear energy for weapons is only the latest illustration of this historical trend. Keeping this in mind, we need to note that there has always been some chasm between value-neutral technology and hidebound psychology. But the source of the latest asymmetry lies in the ethos of agrarian roots, which failed to evolve in tandem with the technological miracles of the Industrial Revolution. This hiatus between ongoing tectonic transformations and the stagnant mindset of the Agrarian Society is the greatest source of contemporary challenges.

We have already noted in earlier chapters the technological changes that led to the replacement of the Agrarian Society by the Industrial Society. We have also noted the unique historical setting in which the Scientific Revolution occurred, leading to the Industrial Revolution through the practical application of scientific discoveries. Modern ideologies that preceded or followed the Industrial Revolution have been briefly discussed. The new wealth showered bountiful benedictions on humanity in the form of the universalisation of prosperity, minimisation of disease, optimisation of educational opportunities, prolonging the lifespan, etc. However, it has now become a double-edged sword in that it can 'wipe every tear from every eye' (to put it in the words of Gandhiji), if used positively, or 'it would strip the world bare like locusts' (to quote Gandhiji again), if used in a negative way. While industrial wealth is a mixed blessing, the new weapon-systems are an unmixed curse. We are revelling in the rewards of the Industrial Revolution without soberly assimilating the wisdom that would keep our minds alive to its flip side.

As the great English poet T. S. Eliot despairingly exclaimed in the early twentieth century:

> Where is the life we have lost in living?
> Where is the wisdom we have lost in
> Knowledge?
> Where is the knowledge we have lost in
> Information? (*Oxford Dictionary of Modern Quotations* 1996: 104)

Poet Alfred Tennyson belonged to the nineteenth century, which was characterised by Victorian optimism. He said: '*Knowledge comes, but wisdom lingers*' (*The Concise Oxford Dictionary of Quotations* 1977: 228).

New science has been spreading knowledge ceaselessly since the seventeenth century, but wisdom has not even started on its slow journey. The first sparks of wisdom will be illuminated, not when we master new sciences and their applications, but when we begin to unlearn and distance ourselves from the past of the Agrarian Society. This is not to say that all the past can be jettisoned. The lofty morality of the ancient sages remains relevant for all ages. It is difficult to choose between what can be discarded and what cannot be; a choice can be made only through an ideological consensus, and such a consensus is not easily attainable, as the implications of industrialisation have been assimilated in different degrees by different people in the world. This differential absorption has already created explosive emotional divisions. When Gulf War II began, Alvin Toffler described it as a clash between two waves, thereby implying that it was a clash between the agrarian mindset of Iraq and the industrial mindset of America. We could differ slightly from Toffler and say that Saddam Hussain represented a mix of the mindset and munitions of the Agrarian Society, while George Bush Jr. represented a curious mix of the agrarian mind-set and munitions of the Industrial

Society. This latter mixture is far more calamitous and can spell the ultimate disaster.

The atavistic passions that lay dormant in the West have erupted in the second decade of the twenty-first century through nativism in culture and protectionism in economics. This new development shows that the outlook of the West is not much more advanced than that of the East. As one of the Chief Justices of the US Supreme Court, Earl Warren, said: 'The most tragic paradox of the time is to be found in the failure of nation-states to recognise the imperatives of internationalism' (Peter 1980: 354). This paradox is true not only of the United States, but also of all parts of the world. It can only be countered through focused education of the masses about the inescapable interconnectedness of our times. However, this is easier said than done. It is not easy to educate the erudite either, as they also labour under their load of learned prejudices. The diplomats and defence experts do not lack in knowledge or intelligence, but may be suffering from want of larger perspectives and, more importantly, wider sympathies. Nuclear scientists like J. Robert Oppenheimer and Andrei Sakharov did more to awaken the conscience for nuclear peace than many statesmen and strategists. The same is true in the case of ecological protection in that social activists have done more than development economists.

Cultural integration should march hand in hand with economic integration. Economic globalisation unaccompanied by emotional integration is bound to lead to tensions even in developed countries, as is evident from the political convulsions in America and Europe. Globalisation of the intellectual, cultural, and emotional kind seems to be an absolute necessity for enhancing economic globalisation. In other words, emotional globalism must accompany economic globalisation. In the process of deepening the outlook of globalism, new scientific discoveries establishing the original genetic oneness of our species should provide an indisputable intellectual foundation. Apart from this, the terror of a global apocalypse that can be caused either through nuclear war or through environmental degradation could be used to bring the peoples of the world together. Neither the light of scientific knowledge nor the fear of collective death is motivating people to decrease their differences. The nostalgic attachment of the people of various nations to their selective memories of the Agrarian Society is coming in the way of global integration. The passions of Agrarian Society have been so deeply ingrained in every fibre of our beings that we are gleefully using the technology of Industrial Society without giving up the psychology of Agrarian Society. Therein lies the unbridged gap between the thoughts of Agrarian Society and the tools of Industrial Society. It is the ultimate example of what is known as 'cognitive dissonance', which means that most people, when confronted with new and disturbing information, reject, explain away, or avoid the information by convincing themselves that no conflict really exists.

Despite the daunting psychological obstacles, unifying perspectives need to be drilled into both the masses and the leaders. While dealing with ten modern ideologies, we may note that nine out of ten deal with issues that concern all sections of humanity, and are global and modern in their character. The only exception is 'Nationalism', which deals with the emotions of particular peoples of the world. We have therefore treated it as a necessary intermediate phase, paving the way for international integration. As Spanish philosopher Jose Ortega y Gasset shrewdly observed, 'Nationalism is always an effort in a direction opposed to that of the principle which creates nations. The former is exclusive in tendency, the latter is inclusive' (1957: 183). Although nationalism has accomplished healthy tasks in most parts of the world, its continuing vehemence has begun to be counter-productive. Nationalism is prolonging its lifespan by becoming a strong peg on which many issues, such as religion, race, language, economic grievances, etc., can be hung. This protean capacity of nationalism is obscuring its ideological obsolescence. It is therefore still dominating not only the mass psyche, but also the agenda of political leaders, who generally seek power through exploitation rather than the elevation of baser emotions. Alas!

There is no Lincoln on the horizon today, who appealed to the 'better angels' of his people in the nineteenth century. Nor do we have Gandhiji, who brought about similar change in the social and moral ethic on a larger scale. It is instructive to note that both men met the fate of martyrs.

We could pray, like George Bernard Shaw in his play, *Saint Joan*: 'O God that madest this beautiful earth, when will it be ready to receive thy Saints? How long, O Lord, how long? (Shaw 2003: 164).

This lack of tolerance for different opinions, even if they be of saints, has been part of the problem of organised societies since their inception. This parochial narrow-mindedness stems substantially from a sense of insecurity; these societies are invariably ordered around their respective worldviews and cultures. Any perceived threat to their worldview or culture is met with resistance and violence. Various sections of people in the world are even now armed with their respective ways of life, to which they cling vigorously. This pressing urge to hang on to their systems of thought fundamentally arises from their agrarian past. In the current Industrial Society, most agrarian perspectives are antiquated, albeit by different degrees. We could live with this gigantic gap in the worldviews of the two Societies of two different eras if we were armed with the temper of tolerance or relieved of weapons of mass destruction. Building up the spirit of charity and effecting the intellectual bridging of different mindsets are the twin tasks confronting the world today. The need for tolerance was recognised by early modern philosophers such as John Locke and Immanuel Kant. Although the two philosophers differed in their theories of knowledge, they both eloquently pleaded for tolerance. Kant went a step further in his treatise on 'perpetual peace' (1795) and advocated a federation of free States, bound together by a covenant forbidding war. He further argues that reason condemns war, which only an international government can prevent.

As the European Enlightenment took place first in England and then in France and other countries of Western Europe, it was taken as the irreversible triumph of sceptical rationality against blind adoration, among other vitally important principles. Such triumphs do not last long, and are soon resisted by a strange assortment of forces. Edmund Burke, the great English champion of individual liberty, reacted so fiercely against the excesses of the French Revolution that he later became the de facto founder of modern conservatism. Even Rousseau, who made his distinctive contribution to the French Enlightenment and to the French Revolution through his radical egalitarianism, revolted against reason and said that 'a thinking man is a depraved animal'. It is relevant to recall that some of the great nineteenth-century philosophers pleaded for closed systems and promoted personality cults. For instance, Napoleon, even after his final defeat at Waterloo and despite his reprehensible record of power-hungry wars, became the greatest model of a strong man in the nineteenth century. Even such non-French thinkers as Nietzsche, Fichte, and Carlyle promoted the concept of strong leaders. It is important to note that none of these thinkers bothered about individual liberty or justice for the masses or the cause of general peace. Despite the French and the Industrial Revolutions, the scientific temper promoted in the seventeenth and eighteenth centuries could not be sustained in the nineteenth and twentieth centuries.

This huge intellectual regression shows that groundbreaking material changes do not automatically lead to major changes in mental outlook. This is further evident from the fact that the floodlight of liberalism that shone in the wake of World War II as part of a massive reaction against fascism and Nazism is now dimming. Liberal democracy is once again facing a formidable crisis, exemplified in events such as 'Brexit' in Great Britain (the oldest democracy in the world); and xenophobia in the United States (the richest democracy in the world). The shadow of illiberalism is looming large on the remaining parts of the democratic world. Major parts of the world that have never witnessed democratisation continue to be animated by revivalist or jingoistic fervour. This new situation should worry not only liberals, but all men and women of goodwill. In the meantime, technology is making inconceivable strides and opening new areas of threat to our species. For example,

Artificial Intelligence, which can give rise to such unimaginable automation that can dispense with human judgement, is also troubling many. Extensive cyber-attacks by private cyber pirates, witnessed in the second week of June 2017, is just a minor example of the devastation they can cause when aimed at international airports or even nuclear codes.

The technological development of Artificial Intelligence is opposed by Stephen Hawking, Elon Musk, Bill Gates, etc., on the plea that its dangers are both unknowable and unquantifiable. Such pre-eminent personalities are being ridiculed as neo-Luddites. It might be better to be a neo-Luddite than a nonchalant Nero. Elon Musk and Bill Gates have received inspiration from an Oxford philosopher, Nick Bostrom, who researched the relationship between language and reality while studying the analytic philosophy of W. V. Quine. He previously worked with Stephen Hawking and warns against the potential dangers of Artificial Intelligence. The discussion on Artificial Intelligence has recently acquired a sensational dimension with Mark Zuckerberg questioning Elon Musk's cautious approach. Musk shot back by saying that Zuckerberg's understanding of the question is limited, and continued to plead for stringent regulations. It may be too early to adjudicate on the merits. But we can safely say that humanity is marching with technology at a breathless pace. Such speed would need stringent regulation in hyper-sensitive matters. Stephen Hawking lost hope in the rationality of the powers-that-be, and therefore recommended the preparation for the mass migration of humans to other planets. According to him, this has been necessitated by an incurable malady in human nature—aggression. This aggression can be seen in the depredations on natural resources, corporate operations, and military preparations. We need to note that the spirit of aggression is the most important takeaway from all leading international institutions of management today. Aggression, which is intrinsic to human nature, is being reinforced rather than diluted by modern business education. The promotion of aggression was never a part of the curricula in agrarian civilisation, which implies that unwittingly, the better part of our agrarian legacy is being whittled down.

Against this backdrop, the impact of the Internet on forces of globalism must be recognised. With lowered costs of communication, the Internet has become the channel for the free flow of ideas that can lead to the development of the 'global civic culture' based on shared values of democracy, liberalism, and human rights, and eventually lead to a closer integration of societies. We now live in what sociologist and communications scholar Manuel Castells (author of the trilogy, *The Information Age: Economy, Society and Culture* [1996–98]) terms the Age of Informationalism.

Political opinion and behaviour are now crystallised on the basis of relevant messages captured from the vastly expanded communications space and processed and interpreted at the individual level. Castells says: 'We are not in an Orwellian universe, but in a world of diversified messages, recombining themselves in the electronic hypertext, and processed by minds with increasingly autonomous sources of information' (Castells 2006: 14). We now know the movement against genetically modified foods as an example of the immense power of the Internet to mobilise political protests. The Internet is a force-multiplier for ideas, and thus has the potential to challenge the sovereignty of the State. When non-State players employ digitised communication to further democratic agendas or, conversely, to spread jihadism, the State seeks to impose curbs on Internet Service Providers, citing security concerns. China famously monitors all international traffic; Vietnam practises Internet censorship; and the USA's Patriot Act infringes upon the privacy of netizens.

In economic terms, globalisation and the Internet are inextricably interlinked. Transnational markets and production processes rely on the Internet, which itself depends on them for the creation of the mechanisms and technology—software and hardware—necessary for its functioning and spread. But globalisation and the Internet serve different masters, and it would be tragic if the former were to be promoted while the freedoms of the latter are restricted.

We are used to thinking, under the impact of the Enlightenment, that humanity will move happily from the poverty of Agrarian Society to the plenty of Industrial Society. But as Castells rightly observes:

> Yet, even a superficial look at the historical record belies this fairy tale of human progress, as the Nazi or Stalinist Holocausts are witness to the destructive potential of the industrial age, and as the wonders of the information technology revolution coexist with the self-destructive processes of global warming or the resurgence of pandemics on a planetary scale. (Castells 2006: 5)

With regard to the dual use of the Internet, the international community needs to reach a binding consensus concerning its international use as part of its minimum multilateralism.

As mentioned earlier, the French Revolution heralded the three great modern political ideals—liberty, equality, and fraternity—for all people in the world, regardless of race, religion, or nation. But these ideals, in the past 200-odd years, have travelled on different roads and at different speeds. Liberty, for example, came to be championed by capitalists, to the neglect of the two other ideals. Likewise, equality was championed by communists, who neglected liberty and fraternity; social democrats tried to champion the ideals of both liberty and equality, but did not do enough to promote fraternity. We have consequently paid a colossal price through the two World Wars and revolutionary conflicts, and are now paying through the numerous conflicts in the world today. We need to return to the drawing board and revitalise the original revolutionary principle of fraternity. Owing to the invention of weapons of mass destruction since World War II, we can be bold enough to say that the principle of fraternity has become more urgent than those of liberty and equality, although the latter two principles remain just as important.

We are not contending that fraternity, as a principle, has been forgotten, but it has been relegated to the background in the heat of war between the champions of liberty and equality. The economic claims of liberty and equality, when pressed to their logical limit, have been found to be mutually antagonistic.

The problem has arisen because of the exclusive emphasis on these economic aspects; the noble ideals of liberty and equality have other essential non-economic aspects such as the political and intellectual freedoms of individuals, distributive justice for the toiling masses, etc. David Ricardo, the second great classical economist after Adam Smith, was so obsessed with economic production that he propounded the 'Iron Law of Wages' in the early nineteenth century, and contended that attempts to improve the real income of workers were futile as wages tended to stabilise at a subsistence level. His utter lack of concern for the welfare of labour is symptomatic of most of the later capitalist thinkers. We need to recollect that labour had to struggle through their trade unions or take advantage of revolutionary conflicts to have their conditions ameliorated. Even in the second decade of the twenty-first century, labour in America is still found to be struggling for a minimum wage of $15/hour. While the capitalists in America have been rolling in unprecedented profits for the past thirty-odd years, capitalist thinkers are even now contending that the American economy cannot accommodate this demand for minimum wages. While the exclusive champions of economic liberty have not changed much since the French Revolution, socialists such as Robert Owen, Saint-Simon, Charles Fourier, etc., had been opposing anti-labour theories right from the time of David Ricardo. In addition to opposing classical economics, the early socialists and others who came after them did not plead for violence as a technique of systemic change. From this perspective, it can be said that they tried to promote the cause of fraternity.

The champions of nationalism in Western Europe waged their wars in the second part of the nineteenth century. In this regard, the three wars waged by Bismarck can be cited as a major illustration. Colonial countries also persisted with their own imperialistic wars in various parts of the world, which eventually led to World War I. The victors of World War I characteristically proceeded to impose unbearable burdens on Germany through the Versailles Treaty. This burden, coupled with the effects of the Great Depression, led to the rise of Hitler and outbreak of World War II. In all these nationalist and imperialist conflicts, the ideal of fraternity was buried fathoms deep. The end of World War II unleashed a tidal wave of liberal ideas throughout the world. However, before the flames of World War II could even be extinguished, the new era of the Cold War had begun. Conflicts such as the Vietnam War and Soviet invasion of Afghanistan were cloaked in alluring ideological colours of capitalism and communism, respectively.

The Cold War lasted about forty-five years (1945–90), and its end brought no respite from international tensions. The Western powers regarded the end of the Cold War as an unqualified triumph of capitalist ideology; Francis Fukuyama's *The End of History and the Last Man* (1992) should be taken as the archetypal reaction of the West to the end of the Cold War. While Fukuyama soon changed his opinion and pleaded for a consensual policy in global affairs, the leaders of NATO proceeded with their triumphalist approach. Gulf War I and II were manifestations of this triumphalist mindset. We are in need of the same wisdom that T. S. Eliot was desperately looking for; such elevating wisdom is generated not by diplomatic geniuses as Kautilya (of ancient India) or Machiavelli, but only by apostles of fraternity such as St. Francis of Assisi or Gandhiji. We must hasten to add that the pearls of wisdom thrown up by Kautilya or Machiavelli are still of considerable use in domestic politics.

In view of the impending threat of environmental extinction, we may add one more principle and give it the same importance and urgency as liberty, equality, and fraternity. That should be *frugality*. This addition may be dismissed as intellectual insolence; however, while none of us may be a Voltaire or a Rousseau, we do have a Gandhiji of our times to lean on. Gandhiji stressed the importance of meeting the minimum needs of all people, while condemning the creed of greed. Frugality is a principle that needs to be practised urgently by the rich, who not only mock the poor through vulgar display of their pelf, but also contribute disproportionately to the depredations on natural resources.

This gulf between never-ending longing for luxury on the part of the world's elite and the fast approaching limits of nature can be narrowed only through a paradigmatic change in human culture (with 'culture' being used here in its most comprehensive sense). A. N. Whitehead rightly observed that a genuine change in culture takes a thousand years. We could afford such a leisurely pace of change in the Agrarian Society. In our Industrial Society, however, we should aim at accelerating the pace of change to an optimal degree. For that, we need a new kind of education, both for our masters and the masses.

H. G. Wells had said a century ago, anticipating this problem: 'Human history becomes more and more a race between education and catastrophe' (1920: Ch. 42, pt. 4).

While everybody agrees with Wells about the infinite importance of education, there is a problem with the direction and content of education. Apart from curricula, education is imparted through traditional literature and mythology. It is not so much the content of this informal education as the interpretations placed on it. Take, for instance, epics like the Mahabharata of Vyasa or the Iliad of Homer. The stories point unerringly to the utter waste that the wars in these epics end in. In Mahabharata, everybody on the side of the Kauravas dies in the war, except the blind king Dhritharashtra and his queen Gandhari. All 100 sons of Dhritharashtra and all their relatives perish. On the side of the Pandavas, all their relatives and children die, leaving everybody to wonder whether the Mahabharata can be characterised as a tragedy or a comedy. At any rate, the total dissipation of military prowess in the Mahabharata war may have, in all probability, exposed the northwestern borders of India to the raids of barbarian hordes. Keeping such terrible consequences in mind, Bhishma, the revered grandfather and mightiest hero of the family, advises strongly against the war. His sane advice is, however, not heeded. King Dhritharashtra goes by the advice of his jealous son, Duryodhana. There is yet another luminous figure (albeit a low-profile one), Vidura, who not only differs from the king, but also refuses to cooperate in the conduct of war as his prime minister. Vidura can thus be regarded as the first conscientious objector, be it in mythology or history. We need to draw inspiration from Vidura's example and see that his tribe thrives in our times.

In the Trojan war, which lasted for ten years, most of the Trojan soldiers, including the king and his family, die, leaving behind a gargantuan graveyard. This carnage includes Hector, the prince of Troy, who embodies a most beautiful blend of military prowess and righteousness. Hector shows utmost wisdom when he advises his father and younger brother against the war, advice which was not heeded. As a result of his brother's lust for Helen and his father's royal ambition, Hector loses his life and his future monarchy. Hector, like Bhishma, shares the same tragic trait of subordinating his voice of conscience to his traditional sense of duty. The wars do not discriminate between the meek and the mighty, nor do they discriminate between the righteous and the unrighteous. The mightiest Greek hero, Achilles, dies. Even their king of kings, Agamemnon (who concealed his imperialistic ambition under the pretext of righting the injustice done to his brother whose wife Helen is stolen away) is killed upon his victorial return to his kingdom by his wife, in collusion with her paramour.

Through the recorded history of both the East and the West, military exploits and intricate qualities of various heroes have been described in colourful language, but the ultimate sterility of wars has never been highlighted. How can such education help humanity, which is now so inebriated with petty sectarian wars as not to bother about its own possible holocaust? The teaching of history is even trickier than mythology, with its distortions based on race, religion, nation, etc. While we, no doubt, need more study of humanities, it is to be remembered that history is a slippery slope. History has never been based on a consensus between two contending parties; it has always been a version of victors. It is therefore difficult to learn objective lessons from history. Will Durant said: 'History is mostly guessing; the rest is prejudice.' A no-nonsense businessman like Henry Ford went a step further and said: 'History is bunk.'

To illustrate the point, we should note that Israel and Palestine cannot agree upon the history of the past seventy years of their two small countries, let alone the Jewish version of their long and ancient history. We can comprehend the complexity involved in writing history, in the context of the phenomenon of fake news under President Donald Trump in America. It is therefore less difficult to develop a new ethic based on science, charity, and, above all, the recognition of the need for the survival of the human species than it is to develop an agreed-upon version of past history. It would perhaps be a blessing if humanity could develop a collective amnesia. American political philosopher John Rawls developed the evocative analogy of a 'Veil of Ignorance'. He asserted that if people had to choose the principles of justice from behind a 'Veil of Ignorance', which restricted knowledge of their class or belief systems, they would not seek to maximise overall utility, but would instead both protect their liberty and safeguard themselves against the worst possible outcome. He further asserted that they would sanction only such inequalities that are strictly required for enhancing efficiency for the benefit of all, without harming the cause of the poorest. This thought experiment could be applied to people's opinion as part of the exploration of international principles. If people are asked to choose a set of principles without any knowledge of their race or nation, they would infinitely prefer peace to war; a clean environment to pollution; and a responsible technology to a reckless one. However, if wishes were horses, philosophers would be kings, as desired by Plato. To be more realistic, we cannot depend merely on world leaders to bring about such an ideal situation. We, as citizens of the world, must play our humble part in our respective walks of life in the process of effecting an international consensus on the need to prevent war and pollution.

A huge controversy broke out in the columns of *The Guardian* between philosopher John Gray and psychologist Steven Pinker. Pinker, in his 2011 book *The Better Angels of Our Nature*, argued that humanity, especially since the European Enlightenment, has become 'more civilized and less violent'. In his *Guardian* essay, John Gray asserts that Pinker is wrong about the history of violence and war, and particularly ridicules the underplaying of casualties in the period following World War II. Gray rightly accuses Pinker of discounting a host of modern horrors, including 'the proxy war between the US and Russia that is being waged in Ukraine'. Apart from disagreeing with the numbers of those killed in various periods of history, Gray faults Pinker's argument that peace has prevailed since World War II. He further argues that a single nuclear detonation could shatter what Pinker and others call the 'long peace'. While Gray's specific arguments against the optimistic Pinker can be supported in this context, his general propositions are too deterministic for us to accept. For example, Gray insists that 'peace and freedom alternate with war and tyranny, eras of increasing wealth with periods of economic collapse. Instead of becoming ever stronger and more widely spread, civilisation remains inherently fragile and regularly succumbs to barbarism.'

While Gray is dystopian, Pinker is certain (without rigorous reasoning) about the avoidance of war and increasing reduction in violence in the future. Pinker is, however, correct in asserting that humanity's condition has improved remarkably in terms of general wealth and public health since the Enlightenment. He is also right when he points out that the anti-Enlightenment trends seen during the same period cannot be invoked by Gray to play down the vast progress. But, as John Horgan says in his article (*The Guardian*, 1 April 2015),

> Pinker fails to acknowledge the enormous contributions of the US, especially since September 11 2001, to global violence. Far from eliminating Muslim extremism, US military actions in Afghanistan, Iraq and elsewhere arguably exacerbated it. The US spends almost as much in defence as all the nations combined, and it is the dominant innovator, manufacturer and exporter of arms in the world.

Horgan rightly states that continual peace activism can provide the solution to war. We may note that both Gray and Pinker are unduly deterministic about the future of humanity, either in a pessimistic or an optimistic manner. We may also recall that philosopher Karl Popper observed in *The Poverty of Historicism* (1957) that iron-cast predictions should not be made of the future, illustrating his point by describing how both Hegel and Marx went wrong in their historical prognostications. Both Gray and Pinker have gone against Popper's injunction with their historical prognoses. At any rate, we cannot underestimate the power of collective rationality, particularly in a world more enlightened than ever before, despite the seemingly incurable stupidity of world leaders and the continuing increase in the arms stockpile.

In modern political thought, theories justifying the choice of means to attain the so-called noble ends have gained huge currency. This is known as 'the end justifying the means'. These theories are not modern in any sense of the term. They are as old as political thought itself. The notable aspect of these theories is that they are championed by both the left and the right. On the right, they are supported by the Instrumentalists, led by John Dewey. On the left, they are supported by none other than Karl Marx. In pre-atomic times, the consequences of this policy were not fully appreciated. It is time that we attach paramount importance to the nobility of means and subordinate the ends, however urgent and important, to the humanistic consequences of the means. This would call for a radical revision in our political ethic. In the twentieth century, popular leaders like Gandhiji, Martin Luther King, and Nelson Mandela trod this new path of purity of means and attained spectacular success. It is therefore not as utopian a principle as it may sound. It is no longer just a pious platitude, but an ineluctable imperative.

Philosophers and scientists have been toying with the idea of a world government since the end of World War I. They have since become less optimistic and are now rightly emphasising the need for a consensual multilateralism, with regard to such issues as control of nuclear arms, steps against climate change, the permissible limits of technology (including Artificial Intelligence), legitimate use of the Internet, international trade, the basis of new education, etc. This is the least that the world currently requires before dreaming of such distant goals as world government. The global situation is currently so divisive that even this modest proposal for multilateralism seems embarrassingly idealistic. However, no constructive proposal can do without an element of idealism. The English poet Alexander Pope sings: 'Hope springs eternal in the human breast' (*Concise Oxford Dictionary of Quotations* 1964: 164). Let hope triumph over despair. Hope should not be based on such naiveté as to neglect negative assessments. Negativity can be countered by nobility. As the Rigveda prays: 'Let noble thoughts come to us from every side' (Rigveda, 1–89–i). All said and done, everything depends upon thought. Elevating thoughts can potentially eliminate all threats to humanity by building a bridge across the great asymmetry between the traditions of Agrarianism and transformations of Industrialism.

Bibliography

Aristotle. *Politics* (London: Penguin, 2000).

_____. *The Nicomachean Ethics* (London: Penguin, 2004).

Allen, Robert C. 'The Spread of Manufacturing'. In *The Cambridge History of Capitalism*, Vol. II, *The Spread of Capitalism: From 1848 to the Present* (Cambridge: Cambridge University Press, 2014).

Altman, Daniel. 'Managing Globalization: Q & A with Joseph Stiglitz'. *International Herald Tribune*, 11 October 2006. Available at https://web.archive.org/web/20090626040606/http://blogs.iht.com/tribtalk/business/globalization/?p=177 (accessed 18 February 2017).

Bacon, Sir Francis. *Novum Organum*, Joseph Devey (ed.) (CreateSpace, 2015).

Basham, A. L. *The Wonder that was India: A Survey of the History and Culture of the Indian Subcontinent before the Coming of the Muslims* (New York: Hawthorne Books, rev. edn 1963 [1954]).

Beard, Charles, A. *An Economic Interpretation of the Constitution of the United States* (New York: The Macmillan Company, 1925).

Beaud, Michel. *A History of Capitalism: 1500–2000* (New Delhi: Aakar, 2004).

Breuilly, John. *Introduction to* Nations and Nationalism *by Ernest Gellner* (London: Blackwell, 2006).

Brotton, Jerry. *The Renaissance Bazaar: From the Silk Road to Michaelangelo* (Oxford and New York: Oxford University Press, 2002).

Brown, Lester R. *Eco-economy: Building an Economy for the Earth* (New York: W. W. Norton and Co., 2001).

_____. *Plan B: Rescuing a Planet under Stress and a Civilization in Trouble* (New York: W. W. Norton and Co., 2006).

Carson, Rachel. *Silent Spring* (New York: Houghton Mifflin, 1962).

Castells, Manuel. *The Network Society: From Knowledge to Policy* (Washington, D.C.: John Hopkins Center for Translantic Relations, 2006).

Cole, G. D. H. *The Fabian Society: Past and Present* (London: Fabian Society, 1942). Available at https://digital.library.lse.ac.uk/objects/lse:veq776xay (accessed 18 March 2017).

The Concise Oxford Dictionary of Quotations (London: Oxford University Press, 1964).

The Concise Oxford Dictionary of Quotations (New York: Oxford University Press, 1977).

De Souza, Shaila. 'Mapping the Women's Movement in India'. In 'Organising Women for Empowerment: A Study of an Experiment in Goa', Unpublished Ph.D. thesis. (Mumbai: Tata Institute of Social Sciences, 2009). Available at http://shodhganga.inflibnet.ac.in/handle/10603/2722.

Dearden, James. *John Ruskin: A Life in Pictures* (Sheffield, 1999).

Dryden, John. *Essay of Dramatic Poesy* (London, 1668).

Durant, Will. *The Story of Philosophy* (New York: Simon & Schuster, 1991).

The Economist. 'A Less Dismal Science—If Economists Reformed Themselves', 16–22 July 2016. Available at www.worldif.economist.com/article/12134/less-dismal-science (accessed 27 February 2017).

Encyclopaedia Britannica, Vol. 4, 1967.

Ferguson, Niall. *Civilization: The West and the Rest* (London: Allen Lane, 2011).

Ferris, Timothy. *The Science of Liberty: Democracy, Reason and the Laws of Nature* (New York: Harper Collins, 2010).

Frank, Robert. *Richistan: A Journey through the American Wealth Boom and the Lives of the New Rich* (New York: Crown Business, 2007).

Fox, Justin. 'The Comeback Keynes', *Time*, 23 October 2008.

Fukuyama, Francis. *The Origins of Political Order* (London: Hachette, 2012).

Galbraith, J. K. *The Affluent Society* (USA: Houghton Mifflin Harcourt, 1958).

Gasset, Ortega J. *The Revolt of the Masses (1929): Chapter XIV, Who Rules in the World?* (New York: W.W. Norton & Company, 1957).

Gellner, Ernest. *Nations and Nationalism* (Ithaca: Cornell University Press, 1983).

Gibbon, Edward. *The History of the Decline and Fall of the Roman Empire*, Vol. I (London: Penguin, 1996).

Gould, Stephen Jay. 'Essays on Science and Society: The Great Asymetry', *Science* 279 (5352), 1998, 812–13.

Guha, Ramachandra. 'Mahatma Gandhi and the Environmental Movement'. In Mahesh Rangarajan (ed.), *Environmental Issues in India: A Reader* (New Delhi: Pearson, 2007).

Hasan, Zoya. 'Women in Retreat after Independence', *Infochange India* 25, 2012.

Heilbroner, Robert L. *The Worldly Philosophers: The Lives, Times and Ideas of the Great Economic Thinkers* (New York: Touchstone, 1999).

Henri, Ernst. *Hitler Over Europe* (New York: Simon and Schuster, 1934).

Hobbes, Thomas. *Leviathan* (London: Penguin, 2002).

Hobhouse, L. T. *Liberalism* (Oxford: Oxford University Press, 1963).

Kazancigil, Ali and Mattei Dogan. *The State in Global Perspective: Comparing Nations, Concepts, Strategies and Substance* (London: Blackwell, 1994).

Keynes, John Maynard. *The General Theory of Employment, Interest and Money* (New York: Harcourt, 1964 [1936]).

______. *A Tract on Monetary Reform* (New York: Prometheus, 2000 [1923]).

______. *The End of Laissez Faire: The Economic Consequences of Peace* (New York: Prometheus, 2004 [1926]).

Krasny, Ros. 'Nobel Economics Laureate Samuelson dies at 94'. *Reuters,* 13 December 2009. Available at http://www.reuters.com/article/us-samuelson-idUSTRE5BC15620091213 (accessed 18 March 2017).

Kries, Steven. 'Renaissance Humanism', in *The History Guide: Lectures on Modern European Intellectual History*, 2000. Available at http://www.historyguide.org/intellect/humanism.html (accessed 25 July 2017).

Kristol, Irving. 'Income inequality without class conflict'. *Wall Street Journal* 18 December 1997, 39.

Krugman, Paul. *The Conscience of a Liberal* (London: Norton, 2009).

Lewontin, Richard. "The Apportionment of Human Diversity', *Evolutionary Biology* 6, 1972, 381–98.

Lincoln, Abraham. *Gettysburg Address from Britannica Encyclopaedia—Vol. 14* (USA: William Benton, 1967).

Liu, Wu, et al. 'The earliest unequivocally modern humans in southern China', *Nature* 526, 2015, 696–99. Available at https://www.nature.com/articles/nature15696 (accessed 12 January 2018).

Oxford Dictionary of Modern Quotations (London: Oxford University Press, 1996).
Malthus, Thomas Robert. *An Essay on the Principle of Population as it Affects the Future Improvement of Society with Remarks on the Speculations of Mr. Godwin, M. Condorcet, and Other Writers* (England, 1798).
Marx, Karl. *The German Ideology* (Oxford, 1977).
_____. *Economic and Philosophical Manuscripts of 1844: The Power of Money*. Available at https://www.marxists.org/archive/marx/works/1844/manuscripts/power.htm (accessed 16 January 2017).
Mehta, Asoka. *Studies in Socialism* (Bombay: Bharatiya Vidya Bhavan, 1964).
Mill, John Stuart. 1869. *The Subjection of Women*. Available at http://www.earlymoderntexts.com/assets/pdfs/mill1869.pdf.
Milton, John. *Areopagitica and other Writings* (London: Penguin, 2016).
Nasar, Sylvia. *Grand Pursuit: The Story of Economic Genius* (London: HarperCollins, 2011).
Nozick, Robert. *Anarchy, State and Utopia* (New York: Basic Books, 1974).
Oxford Dictionary of Modern Quotations (New York: Oxford University Press, 1991).
Peter, Laurence J. 'Earl Warren—Nationalism'. In *Peter's Quotations: Ideas for Our Time* (New York: Bantam Books, 1980).
Popper, Karl. *The Poverty of Historicism* (London: Routledge, 1957).
Prize Committee of the Royal Swedish Academy of Sciences. 'Trade and Geography—Economies of Scale, Differentiated Products and Transport Costs'. Scientific background on the Sveriges Riksbank Prize in Economic Sciences in Memory of Alfred Nobel, 13 October 2008.
Radcliffe, Susan (ed.). *Oxford Treasury of Sayings and Quotations* (Oxford: Oxford University Press, 2011).
Radhakrishnan, S. *Indian Philosophy*, Vol. I (New Delhi: Oxford University Press, 2008).
Rangarajan, Mahesh (ed.). *Environmental Issues in India: A Reader* (New Delhi: Pearson, 2007).
Rawls, John. *A Theory of Justice* (Boston: Harvard University Press, rev. edn 1999 [1971]).
_____. *Political Liberalism* (New York, Columbia University Press, 1993).

———. *Lectures on the History of Political Philosophy* (Harvard University Press, 2008).

Russell, Bertrand. *Freedom Versus Organization 1814–1914* (New York: W. W. Norton & Company, 1934).

———. *New Hopes for a Changing World* (New York: Simon and Schuster, 1951).

———. *Wisdom of the West* (London: Fawcett, 1959).

———. 'Heraclitus'. In *History of Western Philosophy* (London: Routledge, 1996).

Sabine, George H. *A History of Political Theory* (New Delhi: Oxford University Press and IBH, 1973).

Sabine, George H. and T. L. Thorson. *A History of Political Theory*, 4E (New Delhi: Oxford and IBH, 1993).

Sapp, Jan. 'Race Finished', Book Review of *Race? Debunking a Scientific Myth*, by Ian Tattersall and Rob DeSalle. *American Scientist* 100 (2), March–April 2012.

Samuelson, Paul. *Economics* (New Delhi: McGraw Hill, 2000).

Sen, Amartya. *On Ethics and Economics: Economic Behaviour and Moral Sentiments* (New Delhi: Oxford University Press, 1987).

———. *Identity and Violence: The Illusion of Destiny* (London: Penguin, 2006).

Sen, Samita. 'Toward a Feminist Politics: The Indian Women's Movement in Historical Perspective'. Policy Research Report on Gender and Development, Working Paper Series No. 9. Washington, D.C.: The World Bank, 2000.

Shaw, George Bernard. *Saint Joan* (New York: Penguin Classics, 2003).

Skidelsky, Robert. *Keynes: The Return of the Master* (London: Penguin Books, 2009).

Smith, Adam. *The Wealth of Nations* (New York: Bantam, 2003).

Smith, Anthony D. *Nationalism and Modernism: A Critical Survey of Recent Theories of Nations and Nationalism* (London: Routledge, 1998).

Stiglitz, Joseph E. 'John Kenneth Galbraith understood Capitalism as lived—not as theorized'. *The Christian Science Monitor*, 28 December 2006.

———. *The Great Divide* (London: Allen Lane, 2015).

Swaminathan, M. S. 'Agriculture on Spaceship Earth'. In Mahesh Rangarajan (ed.), *Environmental Issues in India: A Reader* (New Delhi: Pearson, 2007).

Tagore, Rabindranath. *Nationalism: Nationalism in the West* (New Delhi: Niyogi Books, 2012a).

_____. *Nationalism: Nationalism in Japan* (New Delhi: Niyogi Books, 2012b).

_____. *Nationalism: Sunset of the Century* (New Delhi: Niyogi Books, 2012c).

Tamang, Rakesh, Lalji Singh, and KumaraswamyThangaraj. 'Complex genetic origins of Indian populations and its implications', *J. Biosci*, 37 (5), November 2012, 911–19. Available at https://www.nebi.nlm.nih.gov/pubmed/23107926 (accessed 12 January 2018).

Tattersall, Ian and Rob DeSalle. *Race? Debunking a Scientific Myth*, Texas A&M University Anthropology Series (Texas: A&M University Press, 2011).

Tawney, R. H. *Religion and the Rise of Capitalism: A Historical Study* (New Brunswick, NJ: Transaction Publishers, 1998 [1926]).

Thapar, Romila. *The Penguin History of Early India: From the Origins of AD 1300* (New Delhi: Penguin, 2002).

Thucydides. 'Pericles' Funeral Oration', in *Thucydides' History of the Peloponnesian War*.

Toynbee, Arnold J. *A Study of History*, Vols VII–X, abridged by D. C. Somervell (New York: Oxford University Press, 1987).

Tse-Tung, Mao. 'A Single Spark Can Start a Prairie Fire', 5 January 1930. Available at https://www.marxists.org/reference/archive/mao/selected-works/volume-1/mswv1_6.htm (accessed 16 January 2017).

Wallace, Alfred Russel. *The Wonderful Century: Its Successes and its Failures* (New York: Cosimo Classics, 2007 [1898]).

Webb, Sidney, Sydney Haldane Olivier, Annie Besant, and Graham Wallas. *Fabian Essays in Socialism* (London: The Fabian Society, 1889).

Weber, Max. *The Protestant Ethic and the Spirit of Capitalism* (London and Boston: Unwin Hyman 1930 [1905]).

Wells, H. G. *The Outline of History*, Vol. II (New York: The Macmillan Company, 1920).

_____. *The Outline of History: Being a Plain History of Life and Mankind* (New York: The Macmillan Company, 1921).

Whitman, Walt. *The Complete Poems* (London: Penguin, 2004).

Wilson, Ben. *Heyday: Britain and the Birth of the Modern World* (London: Orion Publishing Group, 2016).

Wollstonecraft, Mary. *A Vindication of the Rights of Woman* (New York: Dover Publications, 1996).

Wordsworth, William. *Guide to the Lakes* (London: Henry Frowde, 1906). Available at https://ia902607.us.archive.org/21/items/

guidetolakesfif00slgoog/guidetolakesfif00slgoog.pdf (accessed 10 November 2016).

Yuval-Davis, Nira. *Gender and Nation* (London: Sage Publications, 1997).

Zakaria, Fareed. *The Future of Freedom: Illiberal Democracy at Home and Abroad* (New York: W. W. Norton and Company, 2003).

INDEX